JFK

This book presented
by the
Wingate College Student Body, 1963-64
in memory of

John Fitzgerald Kennedy
35th President of the United States

JOHN F. KENNEDY:
A sense of purpose

CHARLES LAM MARKMANN and MARK SHERWIN

ST MARTIN'S PRESS
NEW YORK

For MARY and DIANE

Contents

23390

CONTENTS

JFK

1. The Man

The United States has not often elected Presidents whose personalities have dominated their administrations, whose individualities have remained as immediately recognizable symbols, whose official records can be weighed for success and failure only in constant and direct reference to the intellect and character of the single man who was the head of both state and government. Washington was one of these few dynamic Presidents; Jackson was another; and there were Lincoln, the two Roosevelts, Wilson and Truman. The name of John F. Kennedy must be added to the roster of those American Chief Executives marked by a complete rejection of Olympian detachment and a compelling passion for constant involvement in all the business of government.

Kennedy takes himself seriously—more seriously, perhaps, than many men who have occupied the Presidency: and on balance this can be only beneficial. For, as a corollary, he takes others as seriously as he takes himself. This is evident in the simple directness of his behavior—it is the President, not a flunkey, who, when a conference has run into the time allotted to another appointment, opens the door between the Oval Room and his secretary's office to say to two strangers whom he has agreed to see, "I'm sorry to have had to delay you; I'll be with you in a few minutes"; and who quite naturally takes it upon himself to conduct his callers into his office and find them the most comfortable circumstances for the conduct of their business. It is evident in the automatic courtesy of the sureness and firmness with which he guides and corrects an assistant, seeking to focus his attention on a specific item in a cumbersome document, while visitors interrupt their discussion with him. It is evident in the almost instantaneous perception with which he seizes upon the most sensitive question of a typewritten list of a dozen handed to him by the authors and proceeds at once to marshal arguments in reply while anticipating further challenges.

Kennedy's is a restless mind; it is not always satisfied to learn from reports and cloistered analysis alone. From the beginning of his term as President he astounded White House personnel with his inquiring visits to quarters of the building that few other Presidents had ever thought of looking into, such as the mail room, or to other government buildings where he could observe first-hand how the work was planned, organized and carried out. If he heard a telephone near him ring, he answered it himself; if he wanted to confer with a Congressman or a staff assistant in an agency, he made the telephone call without an intermediary.

His methods in larger matters are analogous. From the first he has used the Cabinet not as a semi-autonomous arm of the executive but as a group of men who have jobs to do that have been assigned by the President and must be passed by him. If he has seemed to follow Franklin Roosevelt's implied principle of *Divide et impera* in his frequent selection of advisers who were ostensibly antagonists, it has been because, as Kennedy himself has put it, "I simply cannot afford to have only one set of advisers." Unlike his predecessor, Kennedy reads every document prepared for him; he goes farther: he frequently consults the source, whether it be cables from embassies, unedited intelligence reports or complex technical surveys. In addition, he reads voraciously a wide variety of books and periodicals. By radically reducing, where he has not wiped them out, the great complex of committees erected in the preceding eight years to serve as a series of shock absorbers between the White House and the outside world, Kennedy has again personalized government leadership as Franklin Roosevelt did.

That there is danger as well as advantage in such personalized leadership is a platitude. If it provides the undoubted value of dramatic stimulus to emulation and effort, it introduces as well the possibility of the adoption of policies that have not benefited by contrasting analyses, and the irreducible element of the influence of one man's unconscious on his decisions, however determined and disciplined his intellectual self-policing. Whether the sharpening of Kennedy's long-noted predilection for taking all the reins in one hand was such an unconscious defense reaction to the very narrowness of his victory in the popular vote, whether his acceptance and implementation of Eisenhower's illegal and immoral plan for American intervention in Cuba's internal affairs was unconsciously furthered by the anti-Communist obsession that has ridden the Catholic Church in America since Kennedy's childhood, it is impossible to say with certainty. And the continuing danger that always lies dormant in such concentrated leadership is not obviated by Kennedy's unquestionably high-minded insistence on allowing no one but himself to bear the blame for the Cuban debacle.

This moral imperative is very much a part of the man. Perhaps the strongest impression made by his personality, whether in his official acts or in the most formal of encounters, is that of an intellectual integrity that has always been rare in American public life and that is doubly surprising when it survives political success. One is immediately aware that John F. Kennedy is always, with the utmost critical detachment, observing himself quantitatively and qualitatively. Like Franklin Roosevelt, he has a sense of history and, probably, a great ambition to be a major element in it; he has in addition an overwhelming sense of moral and intellectual responsibility.

Kennedy views the Presidency as a mission. His own task, as he conceives it, has two aspects that are interdependent. One is the elaboration and expansion and strengthening of the New Deal begun by Roosevelt; the other is the extension of the American concept of freedom and opportunity to the entire world. The American example, in Kennedy's thinking, must be purged of flaws if it is to be held up to other nations as a goal; as it is brought closer to the ideal it must by its own merit ultimately become the goal of all who have the freedom to choose. Therefore he considers it part of his mission to do everything possible to make that freedom available to those to whom it is denied. He counts on the good sense of self-preservation of the American people to help him carry forward his social planning; he counts on the traditional idealism of the American people to help him overcome poverty and bondage in other countries.

It is in these intangibles, rather than in a hairline electoral victory, that he sees the source of the mandate that he believes to be his. But his conviction of a mandate does not allow him to minimize his equally strong conviction of responsibility. "I bear the responsibility of the Presidency of the United States," he said in his report to the nation after his first meeting with Khrushchev, "and it is my duty to make decisions that no adviser and no ally can make for me."

His conviction of the place of the intellect and the arts in the community led directly to a Presidential impetus toward an elevation of television standards when, one Sunday afternoon, Kennedy appeared with Robert Frost in a friendly, conversational program that brought warm satisfaction to millions and evoked mild criticism because the President of the United States and its unofficial poet laureate were interrupted frequently by commercials. Nevertheless, it went off quite well. The President explained his presence on the program by telling a story. "Some years ago," he said, "an interested mother wrote to the principal of a school: 'Don't teach my boy poetry, he's going to run for Congress.' I've never taken the view that the world of poetry and the world of politics are so far apart. I think politicians and poets share at least one thing, and that is that their greatness depends upon the courage with which they face the challenges of life. I asked Robert Frost to come and speak at the inauguration not merely because I was desirous of according a recognition to his trade but also because I felt that he had something important to say to those of us who were occupied with the business of government; that he would remind us that we were dealing with life, the hopes and fears of millions of people, and also tell us that our own deep convictions must be the ultimate guide to all of our actions."

The 86-year-old Frost's comment on the New Frontier was made in lyrical prose: "We've decided to go the length, decided to go the length and lead from our strength. We're going to go the length and lead from our strength, not from our timidity or weakness, but lead like fighting, you know, lead from our strength. Sum it all up in saying: an Augustan age of poetry and power. That belongs to my poetry, and it belongs to politics all the time."

It was entirely logical that Kennedy should seek to surround himself as much as possible with men whose intellectual powers and integrity he respected, particularly in those areas he considered most influential. Occasionally his judgment seemed to err, as in the unfortunate selection of Earl E. T. Smith, former Ambassador to Cuba, to head the Embassy in Switzerland; opposition in Berne was so strong and so open that ultimately Smith's name had to be withdrawn.

Very often Kennedy's choice was stimulated by an individual's publications. Raymond Moley observed that in his four years as a close associate of Roosevelt he had never seen him read a serious book, or any book. If Roosevelt heard that someone had written an important book bearing on government problems, he reacted as Al Smith had done: he sent for the author, preferring to learn by ear rather than by eye. Kennedy, on the other hand, was a voracious reader; it was only when he had digested the book that he knew whether he wanted to send for the author.

It was the books of such scholars as Professors John Kenneth Galbraith and Arthur Schlesinger Jr. of Harvard that first roused Kennedy's interest in them as potentially valuable public servants. The designation of Galbraith as Ambassador to India, of the distinguished Japanese scholar, Professor Edwin Reischauer, as Ambassador to Japan, of George Kennan as Ambassador to Yugoslavia was exciting to those who respected the world of the intellect. On the other hand, the announcement of Schlesinger's appointment as a Presidential adviser irritated the New York *Daily News*, a militantly anti-intellectual tabloid with the largest circulation in the country, to observe in an editorial titled HOT TIP: PUT NOT THY TRUST IN ANY EGG-HEAD:

He has been named as a special assistant to the President, mainly, it seems, to help write speeches; and we're both sighing and chortling over that.

Junior is an egghead to end all eggheads, so we shudder to

think of the dangerous tripe he may sneak into Kennedy's speeches unless the President watches him like a hawk.

On the other hand, Junior is a cartoonist's dream and a natural figure of fun for columnists and editorial writers. For that reason, we're glad he landed this job; and we can hardly wait, folks, we can hardly wait . . .

On the major policy level few Kennedy appointments were open to serious criticism from thinking observers. He chose one of television's most responsible news experts, Edward R. Murrow, to head the United States Information Agency (only to be unexpectedly embarrassed when Murrow tried to prevent the British Broadcasting Corp. from showing a documentary, which Murrow himself had made for the Columbia Broadcasting System, because he feared its rigorous truthfulness about migratory labor might embarrass this country abroad). William Lucius Cary, a Columbia law professor respected in Wall Street as well as in Government and in Academe, was made chairman of the Securities and Exchange Commission. Diplomatic appointments, when they were not offered to non-Foreign Service men of eminence, were in the main admirably assigned to the best qualified career diplomats, such as G. Frederick Reinhardt, Ambassador to Italy, and Livingston T. Merchant, Ambassador to Canada. By no means all fell into the stereotyped category of "liberal"; many were known to hold, at least in some fields, positions to the right of the President's. As his appointments reached down into less important echelons he strove to maintain the same standards as far as this was feasible in a system that had made patronage without regard to qualification almost a sacred institution, leavening wherever possible the payment of political obligations with the selection of men of ability and integrity.

The question of integrity was an important one to Kennedy. Both the Truman and the Eisenhower Administrations had produced too many sordid scandals of venality at many levels and on many scales; it had become a tradition to exploit Government service for private gain, sometimes even while men were still on the public payroll. Before taking office Kennedy had re-arranged his private fortune to prevent the slightest likelihood of any conflict of interest or loyalty in his own affairs; the members of his Cabinet had emulated him. Soon after his accession, he had ordered that anyone in full-time Government service who accepted fees for writing or speaking must turn them over to recognized charities. But he had long been preoccupied with a more official and effective means of minimizing, if not eliminating, the kind of "within the law" activity that had nevertheless too often toed, if not crossed, the threshold of corruption.

On April 27 he sent to Congress a message requesting specific legislation to govern the conduct of officials and employes of independent agencies. The present laws covering the judiciary required no emendation, he found, adding: "The adequacy and effectiveness of laws regulating the conduct of members of Congress and Congressional employes should be left to strictly Congressional determination." This was thought by some to be a rather naively optimistic view; but Kennedy's proposals for deportment in the executive branch were admirable. Exempting from the current laws those part-time consultants and advisers who gave the Government less than one-third of their time in any one year, he implied clearly that, in seeking to improve the moral climate of government, he was aware —and much concerned—that it reflected that of a society flawed "by fixed athletic contests or television quiz shows —by widespread business conspiracies to fix prices—by the collusion of business men and unions with organized crime —by cheating on expense accounts, by the ignoring of traffic laws or by petty tax evasion."

Under Kennedy's code of ethics, lawyers leaving Government service would be permanently barred from handling any matter in which they had participated officially. On the other hand, the President would end the existing bar on their handling, during the first two years after they left the Government, all matters that might have been pending in any Government department during their employment.

He attacked the vagueness and inconsistency of statutes under which, by their wording, it would be a penal offense "for a postal clerk to assist his mother in filing a routine claim for a tax refund, but it would be permissible for a Cabinet officer to seek to influence an independent agency to award a license for a valuable TV station to a business associate in a venture where he shared the profits." Kennedy sought to prohibit the use of official position, influence or information to aid private individuals or organizations "in Government proceedings which involve no claims for money or property"—that is, in applications for franchises or similar aid.

Because of the delicacy of informal contacts between an agency official and persons interested in matters under his jurisdiction, Kennedy asked that each agency be required to publish its own code on such problems. He asked that all informal, undisclosed contacts of this kind be prohibited absolutely in situations where the agency's decision must depend solely on the record of a formal hearing; yet at the same time he recognized the legitimacy of other situations in which informal communication was necessary for the collection of required information.

In addition, the President proposed to issue an executive order that would prohibit anyone in Government from accepting a gift "whenever (a) the employe has reason to believe that the gift would not have been made except for his official position; or (b) whenever a regular Government employe has reason to believe that the donor's private interests are likely to be affected by actions of this employe or his agency. When it is impossible or inappropriate to refuse the gift, it will be turned over to an appropriate public or charitable institution." Kennedy also planned an order prohibiting Government employes from using for private gain any official information not available publicly. For his own appointees he would forbid any outside activity incompatible with the proper discharge of their duties, outside compensation for any activity normally part of their official duties, and the acceptance of fees for lectures or writings devoted to the work of their departments or based on official matters not generally disclosed. Throughout the Government he proposed to apply the standards on property ownership by executive appointees. Each Cabinet officer and agency head would be asked to frame rules for his own group and to establish a committee to consider problems or violations arising from them. Finally, Kennedy announced, he would appoint an executive assistant to supervise, coordinate and study all Government activity in the field of ethics.

Whether all these eminently desirable reforms would be enacted into law, and whether such a law would be enforced with the rigor that Kennedy himself applied to his own conduct and that of his appointees, was open to question. But, for the first time since the Administration of Woodrow Wilson, there was a reasonable prospect that a genuine effort would be made to elevate the standards of Government.

2. The Hundred Days of Franklin Roosevelt

Franklin Roosevelt began his "Hundred Days" with three clear advantages lacking to John F. Kennedy twenty-eight years later. The nation's long-drawn-out crisis was manifest in every home; and the new President had not only an unquestionable electoral mandate but also an unquestioning Congressional commitment.

The crisis of 1929-1933 affected every American's day-to-day living. He could not pretend it did not exist; he could not minimize it or rationalize it into a theoretical or academic issue. It was real; it was urgent; it required solutions not for some problematic future but for today and tomorrow, not for some remote area whose people were only names but for himself and his neighbor. After more than a decade of complacency, America was floundering in leaderless despair: it turned to Roosevelt because he promised not only leadership but action.

On Inauguration Day, March 4, 1933, 26 per cent of the

nation's employables were without jobs, dependent on the most rudimentary arrangements for their survival; big businesses were frequently operating at a deficit and small businesses were failing in frightening numbers; agriculture was virtually bankrupt; a nation-wide banking collapse threatened to destroy the entire financial structure; stupidity, manipulation, and outright dishonesty not only had wiped out millions of dollars of investments but were eroding the country's confidence. The need for action was urgent.

And action began even before the stage settings of the inauguration had been dismantled. Roosevelt was sworn in at noon on a Saturday; within thirty hours the President, a more successful Canute, dramatically dammed the seemingly ungovernable tide by a proclamation based on the Trading with the Enemy Act left over from the First World War. He ordered the closing of all banks until further notice, an immediate embargo on gold exports, and the surrender of all privately held gold and gold certificates.

The first seven of the hundred days were dominated by the banking crisis. Congress was summoned into special session for the following Thursday, March 9. By that time Roosevelt and his Secretary of the Treasury, William H. Woodin, had worked out with their advisers the draft of the regulations under which they proposed to reopen the banks. Democratic Congressional leaders had joined in drawing an emergency banking act that would retroactively ratify the President's proclamation closing the banks and grant him new powers over currency and banking. The bill was introduced by unanimous consent and exactly forty minutes were allowed for debate on it; but Congressmen themselves were so eager to act, to demonstrate their solidarity behind Roosevelt, that cries of "Vote!" frequently drowned out such scanty debate as was offered. The bill passed by voice vote; the Senate also approved it and by 9 P.M. it was law, signed by Roosevelt.

A few hours later the dichotomy of Roosevelt's political

character was made manifest. He had of course, in his campaign, stressed the need for federal economy and a balanced
budget, but this was taken as routine campaign oratory eight
years before Wendell Willkie made the words a catch
phrase. On March 10 the President sent to Congress a message it had not expected: a demand for executive power to
effect broad economies before the government went bankrupt. Roosevelt foresaw a budget-year deficit of more than
a billion dollars—in those days a staggering figure. "Too
often," he warned, "in recent history liberal governments
have been wrecked on the rocks of loose fiscal policy." The
first outcry of pain came from a lobby never brevetted liberal: the American Legion, anguished at the thought of reductions in veterans' pensions.

In the thirteen years of its life the Legion, like other veterans' organizations, had become a Congressional bogy. No
one, Republican or Democrat, had ever dreamed of defying
this powerful and vocal group, and the avalanche of telegrams that poured in on Washington frightened the new
Congressmen as much as their more sophisticated seniors.
In the House the Democratic ranks broke; the lawgivers
refused point-blank to go along with the President and for
a while their leaders could not manage them, until they fell
back on the magic of Roosevelt's name. They warned that
Roosevelt would read—and remember—the roll-call vote on
the bill; and in the end they were able almost to rally their
panicked forces. Ninety Democrats, however, including
seven leaders of the party, stood firm and voted against the
bill, which would not have passed the House if sixty-nine
Republicans had not temporarily abandoned party loyalty
to support it. But in those weeks party allegiance was in
abeyance. Nonetheless, the Senate was known to be sharply
divided on the economy bill and there was some anxiety in
the White House.

But Roosevelt and the men around him knew intuitively
that the key to everything at this time was the reaction of

the public. Exactly eight days after the inauguration, therefore, Roosevelt went directly to the people with the first of his Fireside Chats, a tool that all his successors have eagerly used. The President knew and utilized to the full his overwhelming personal charm: he exploited, then and often afterward, his own magnetism to use popular sentiment as a club with which to coerce the legislative branch. In effect, he created a fourth branch of the government at the outset of his hundred days: public opinion. For twenty minutes he explained the nation's economic crisis to the people, without talking down and without mystifying; on his way to bed afterward, he told his secretary, Louis McHenry Howe: "I think it's time for beer." Idealist though he may have been, he was enough of a calculating stage manager to know when and how to divert the attention of public and Congress alike with the implied promise of a boon in return for the fulfillment of a distasteful chore.

His platform had promised the end of Prohibition, which could be accomplished only by the slow means of Constitutional amendment, and indeed the machinery for this had been started in the closing days of Herbert Hoover's administration. But on March 13, while the Senate was marshaling itself for battle on the economy bill, Roosevelt sent Congress a new, laconic message: a seventy-two-word demand for the immediate modification of the Volstead Act to legalize light wines and beers and to impose substantial taxes on them. The effect that the President wanted was realized: on March 15 the Senate passed the economy act and the next day light wines and beer became legal.

In these first twelve days of his administration Roosevelt had become a national hero. Ten thousand adulatory telegrams poured in on the White House in one week. An Iowa Congressman wrote: "I will do anything you ask. You are my leader." And this was representative of the quasi-religious devotion of the overwhelming majority of Americans. Only a small core of arch-conservatives—and another, much smaller, of arch-revolutionaries—dissented. He was the virtually undisputed leader, so regarded by wide-eyed unquestioning followers. Two decades later it was possible for dispassionate students to argue that Roosevelt was not a creative leader: that he merely mirrored American society of his time and took rôles that, in the last analysis, plainly indicated a lack of leadership. Within his first few days of power he had demonstrated, with his interjection of the beer bill, an opportunism that was to recur often, it is true; but opportunism is hardly the hallmark of the non-leader. "The democratic leader," as Mario Einaudi pointed out in *The Roosevelt Revolution*, "is the man who is able to express the urge of his society to achieve common and deeply felt needs. The failure of democratic leadership is the failure of the leader to identify those needs and realize them."

American society at this time certainly wished no radical revisions: it urgently desired the rectification of many existing conditions but it did not want to change its character. Roosevelt's intuitive recognition of the fact was evidenced not only in his choice of a Cabinet composed almost exclusively of successful middle-class businessmen and professionals, but also in the more varied composition of his corps of unofficial and subordinate advisers: Adolf A. Berle Jr. and Rexford G. Tugwell were outspoken collectivists but against them stood that champion of individualism and competition and economic decentralization, the then Professor Felix Frankfurter, and the spokesman for conservative economy, Lewis W. Douglas. While Secretary of State Hull never yielded in his insistence on international economic co-operation as the touchstone of a healthy domestic economy, there were many others who were even more obstinate in their stand that recovery at home came first, if indeed international economics mattered at all. Roosevelt at this time was innocent of Keynesian philosophy (that was to come much later); he was primarily a pragmatist seeking whatever means might succeed in maintaining the established order. And it was his pragmatism that enabled him to demonstrate the theorem formulated much later in a series of articles in that weekly Bible of Wall Street, *Barron's:* that, as a free capitalist society becomes increasingly complex in its ramifications, it must turn more and more toward Socialist techniques and tools in order to preserve its fundamental capitalism, as, conversely, the growing complexities of a Socialist economy must force it to approach closer to capitalism in order to maintain its Socialist base. Roosevelt was a conservative, in essence, who found radical means very often the best suited to his conservative purpose.

"Our last frontier has long since been reached," he had declared during his campaign in 1932; what occupied his attention now was the consolidation of everything within the frontiers. In the same speech he contended that private economic power was a public trust, the fulfillment of which must be the condition of continued enjoyment of that power by any individual or group. As a political administrator, equally—and to attempt any further exploration of motivations would be fatuous—he was primarily concerned with power. From the first he took a firm grip on it and this was never relinquished. He had sought and gained it in order to restore the national strength in those areas in which it was most sorely sapped. Having taken the first exigent steps—the rescue of the financial structure—he had planned to let Congress go home until permanent legislation was ready to be submitted to it. But, in the atmosphere of hero worship in which he was now working, his personal and political power could be far more effective than any influence he might be able to exercise after an interval of letdown.

To Roosevelt the agricultural crisis was next in gravity to the financial. He turned to the radical of his Cabinet, Secretary of Agriculture Henry A. Wallace, for a bill that would raise the farmer's purchasing power, relieve him of the pressure of mortgages, and expand the value of the loans he could get from the banks. On March 16 the first Agricultural Adjustment Act, hastily drawn by Wallace and his advisers, was presented to Congress, and six days later the House approved it by a vote of 315 to 98. But it was four more weeks before it passed the Senate, and it was mid-May before the President signed it. The Act frightened and enraged the conservatives, for it was putting government squarely into the functioning of the economic machinery. Its object was to restore "farm parity"—the relationship between the prices of farm products and those of nonagricultural goods and services that had existed between 1909 and 1914. The means chosen was the imposition of processing taxes that equaled the difference between actual prices and parity; the proceeds of these taxes were earmarked for payments to farmers in return for their limiting their production, either by taking land out of use or by reducing production and destroying any surplus above their quotas. Whatever their private doubts of such unorthodoxies, Representatives and Senators gave Roosevelt what he wanted. After the first aborted spat over the veterans, the honeymoon had been resumed.

The President's restless mind was still wrestling with other basic problems, of which one of the most disturbing was unemployment and the hardships it entailed. Five days after sending the AAA to Congress, Roosevelt asked for the creation of the Civilian Conservation Corps, arguing that it would serve a double purpose: it would provide thousands of young men with healthful outdoor work and it would contribute to the preservation and growth of the nation's forest resources. The men were to receive army pay and to live in army-style barracks while they built dams, drained marshes, planted trees, and battled forest fires. Ignoring the howls from the far Left that Roosevelt was building a Fascist army and the roars from the far Right that he was putting a premium on loafing, Congress enacted the CCC bill within ten days without a roll-call vote.

While this legislation took care of a small number of the

jobless, it offered no aid to the vast majority who were not eligible for the CCC. With it, Roosevelt sent to Congress a proposal for direct federal relief for the unemployed, a measure that Herbert Hoover had steadfastly refused to countenance. Unemployment relief had thus far been the province of the states, which, for the most part, provided no cash to the recipients and only some of the necessities. Most generally, the jobless man's rent, gas, and electricity were paid for directly by a local relief agency, and he received food orders that were not supposed to be redeemable in cash. He had no means of providing clothes for himself or his family, buying a newspaper to look through the *Help Wanted* columns, or paying his fare to apply for a job in another part of town. Roosevelt's bill to give the states federal funds for the payment of cash allowances to the unemployed, at first by a Reconstruction Finance Corporation loan of $500 million to the new Federal Emergency Relief Administration, was rushed through both Houses by overwhelming majorities.

Roosevelt was still concerned with what he considered the fundamentals essential to starting the economy back on an upswing, as well as with correcting abuses that had contributed, in his view, to the depression and that, if ignored, might well bring on another crisis. He boasted that he was following no systematic plan but was playing by ear, and he likened himself to a football quarterback who called a new play when he saw the results of the previous one. "Snap judgments have to be made," he told Colonel E.M. House, President Wilson's adviser and intimate. His snap judgments were now to be made in the complicated field of banking and investment.

The memory of the 1929 stock-market collapse was still vivid. Presumably the President knew that nothing can long deter those who are determined to destroy themselves and that neither greed nor stupidity can be legislated out of existence, but he was resolved to do whatever was feasible toward protecting fools from their own folly. Unquestionably many stock issues of the nineteen-twenties had been tainted; dishonest manipulation was not unknown. Neither was undisciplined speculation by individuals who lacked the cash, the knowledge, and the intelligence for it. The New Deal's first measure to regulate the sales of securities, sent to Congress on March 29, was a primitive affair in comparison to what was to follow. While offering no dissent to the old maxim, *Caveat emptor*, Roosevelt added a phrase: *Caveat venditor*. The new bill, passed early in May, was intended to prescribe full publicity for all the facts surrounding any securities offered in interstate commerce; heavy penalties were provided for failure to file complete and authentic information with the new Securities and Exchange Commission. As a corollary, based on the National City Bank scandals in New York that were being laid before the public even as the hundred days began, Roosevelt demanded—and got—legislation implementing the divorce between banks and their securities-dealing affiliates that had been ordered by legislation enacted much earlier in the century and then ignored.

Perhaps the most radical and the most paradoxical phenomenon of the hundred days occurred on April 10, when the President proposed that Congress establish a Tennessee Valley Authority to organize the "proper use, conservation and development of the Tennessee River drainage basin and adjoining territory." Behind these generalizations lay the unremitting battle of the progressives, led by Senator George Norris of Nebraska, to prevent the sale of the government-built dam and power plant at Muscle Shoals to a private company. Roosevelt had remained more or less loyal to private ownership: "I do not hold," he said during his campaign, "with those who advocate government ownership or government operation of all utilities. I state to you categorically that as a broad general rule the development of utilities should remain, with certain exceptions, a function for private initiative and private capital." Yet now he proposed to make Muscle Shoals part of a network of publicly owned and operated power stations; at the same time he envisaged wide ramifications for the whole project in the form of flood control, curbing erosion, reforesting, and the development of new industrial areas. The enemies of the TVA were accurate in denouncing it as Socialism; but Congress created it with despatch.

With his talent for diverting public attention from a major controversy on a broad scale to a subject that touched thousands or millions of individuals, Roosevelt followed his TVA proposal within three days by asking federal legislative safeguards against the mounting foreclosures of mortgages on small homes. The President rightly viewed the wholesale destruction of homes and family entities as a mortal threat to social and economic stability; he proposed—and obtained —the creation of a Home Owners' Loan Corporation, which was to refinance existing mortgages at lower interest rates, sometimes for longer periods, and which had the power, for those in extreme need, to postpone payments on interest, principal or both. The measure became law within a month of its proposal.

There was some opposition to such measures, of course; but it was vocal rather than numerical and, after lengthy debate in some cases, Congress uniformly gave Roosevelt his way, whether for private mortgages or for public power. Early in May he turned his attention to the railroads, whose power was still great. Untroubled by the threat of over-the-road trucking to their monopoly on long-distance hauls, and oblivious to the prospect of aerial competion for freight, the carriers were often guilty of duplications of service, waste in many forms and corporate milking, frequently through holding companies. Roosevelt easily obtained the legislation he sought in this field and moved on to the climax of his hundred days, the National Industrial Recovery Act.

On May 17 he asked Congress to establish the machinery

for "a great cooperative movement throughout all industry in order to obtain wide re-employment, to shorten the working week, to pay a decent wage for the shorter week and to prevent unfair competition and disastrous overproduction." At the same time he requested the power to launch a vast program of direct government employment on public works, asking for $3.3 billion for a Public Works Administration that would build public structures and improvements where needed and thus not only put thousands to work directly but further stimulate employment by reason of its need for materials.

It was the NIRA, more than anything else, that drove the first wedge between the Administration and Congress, if not between the Administration and a considerable segment of the public. Two years earlier Huey Long had said: "When Fascism comes to America, it will call itself democracy"; and the proposed National Recovery Administration, in the eyes of many, showed decidedly Italian ancestry. Code authorities for all industries were proposed in the legislation: in each industry the code authority would—while expressly forbidding cartel or monopoly practices—stop wasteful competition (which was not defined), establish pricing and selling policies, enforce higher wages, shorter hours, and improved conditions of work, and, under the famous Section 7(a), protect the right of labor to organize. Within each industry, compliance with the rules formulated by the code authority—composed of representatives of government, industry, labor, and that indefinable group called *the public*— was to be purely voluntary; the adherents would have the right to display in their places of business the Blue Eagle, insigne of their enlistment in the war on depression. Rigid government licensing power was available to force the rest into line. What was unstated—and what negated the whole *façade* of a voluntary co-operation—was the pressure that would be brought on the nation to boycott any entrepreneur who did not display the Blue Eagle.

It was the left wing of the Senate that offered the greatest opposition to the National Industrial Recovery Act; but Roosevelt got what he wanted nonetheless just before Congress adjourned in mid-June. The foundations of the entire New Deal had thus been laid in those famous hundred days.

It was obvious that the real crisis, as Roosevelt viewed it then, was domestic. He was aware of European economic problems, of course, and of the inescapable tie between the vexatious question of war debts, on the one hand, and monetary stabilization, on the other. In April and May he was visited successively by Laborite Prime Minister Ramsay MacDonald of Britain's coalition Government and Premier Edouard Herriot, but the President emphasized that these talks were merely "exploratory"; he was unhappy at the prospect of the unavoidable World Economic Conference to be held in London in the summer. Throughout his campaign he had neglected foreign affairs; he shared the isolationist nationalism of all his fellow-citizens and, in his zeal to protect his own inflationary program, he procured from Congress, in direct contradiction of traditional Democratic thinking, the power to raise protective tariffs even higher than they then were.

During the weekend of his inauguration the Japanese were striking deep into Manchuria, and at his second Cabinet meeting Roosevelt did discuss, with some gravity, the future likelihood of a war with Japan. But from then on he in effect refused to think of international affairs, except to attack in private conversations the international financiers who, he thought, were damaging the dollar. But then, in mid-May, when the disarmament conference in Geneva was nearing the end of its year-long death agony, he pleaded directly and skillfully with the heads of the world's major states to join in a "solemn and definite pact of non-aggression." But he had clearly repudiated the League of Nations in his election campaign and he could do no more. To

Roosevelt at this time, the United States was world enough and more.

James MacGregor Burns, in *Roosevelt: The Lion and the Fox*, has skillfully summed up the hundred days as a jumble of orderly continuities with the past (Wilsonian economic reform, Theodore Roosevelt's conservation policies, American Socialism, Hooverian budget-balancing and economy) and a host of new inconsistencies (cuts in veterans' pensions, economic nationalism, reduction of government salaries, the use of government as an instrument for social betterment). The outstanding characteristic was *action;* it was rivaled by *experimentation;* and both were implemented by a skillful use of *power* not lately seen in American government. Roosevelt, Burns observes, resembled Stalin in that he was a political administrator whose first concern was power—though for far different purposes—and who followed the old Roman injunction, *Divide et impera,* by putting into the same function men who differed widely in character and thinking, often with overlapping functions. Roosevelt, Burns observes, "disliked being completely committed to any one person. He enjoyed being at the center of attention and action, and the system made him the focus through which the main lines of action radiated . . . The main reason for Roosevelt's methods, however, involved a tenacious effort to keep control of the executive branch in the face of the centrifugal forces of the American political system. By establishing in an agency one power center that counteracted another, he made each official more dependent on White House support; the President in effect became the necessary ally and partner of each. He lessened bureaucratic tendencies toward self-aggrandizement; he curbed any attempt to gang up on him."

3. The Eight Years of Eisenhower

The administration of Dwight David Eisenhower can best be described as one of excitement cushioned in complacency. For eight years great historic events at home and abroad moved within the periphery of the White House but rarely gained entrance or the attention of its occupant. For the most part they were treated with a philosophy of calculated postponement and the unuttered prayer that perhaps in time the problems they created would fade from view.

This attitude was deplored by the small voice of the opposition and the even smaller voice of the opposition press, but nothing could diminish the adoration the people had for the man; for never in the history of the United States had a President been cradled in the safety of popularity and good will as had Eisenhower.

The man had come upon the scene at a time of great superficial contentment. The Second World War was over. The immediate postwar years had been saturated with shortages, labor strife, and irritating scandals. The nation-wide intellectual, moral, and physical exhaustion had been aggravated by the Korean War, which heightened the desperate need for a period of lassitude and recuperation. Eisenhower, the great general, had pledged himself during his election campaign to go to Korea and speed the end of the fighting. No father figure could have promised a bigger and better lollipop.

It required no exceptional political acumen to appreciate that the record popular vote that swept him into office was for Eisenhower and not for the Republican Party. He delighted most people when he subtly contrasted himself with the peppery Harry Truman by pointing out that he was not "the desk-pounding type that likes to stick out his jaw and look like he's bossing the show," but preferred to "try to persuade a man to go along." He laid the basis for all his activities when he stated that he was opposed to the concept of a strong Presidency, stressing that Congress was an equal and independent branch of the government. It was characteristic of his Administration that the powers he had so casually renounced were swiftly seized by Congress, and it was ironic that most of his legislation would have failed to pass without the active support of the Democrats.

Eisenhower's attitude toward the Presidency was refreshing. To him it was a "fascinating business. It's the kind of thing that would engage the interest of any man alive." By contrast, Harry Truman described the White House as "the finest prison in the world"; George Washington likened himself to "a culprit who is going to his place of execution," and Thomas Jefferson called the office a "splendid misery."

When Eisenhower entered the White House he could not shake the habits of a lifetime in the army. He earnestly felt that the best way to conduct the Presidency was under the traditional army system of administration by report: delegate all authority and assume as little responsibility as possible. Patience and discreet silence, he had learned, can make most problems disappear. In peacetime this had been the accepted pattern for the commanding officer, giving him the maximum time for such garrison amusements as golf, bridge, and horseback riding. He announced early in his term that he would refuse to be distracted by secondary matters; that his prime purpose would be peace, and a relaxation of the domestic and international tensions, and that he would strive to give the country a chance to "draw its breath" and regain its energy.

What he failed to realize was that the President has little opportunity to "draw his breath." The day after he took office he was hurled into a series of organization meetings that left him breathless. On the third day he had his first official meeting with his Cabinet, and, surrounded by secretaries, aides, Cabinet members, politicians, and advisers, he remarked wryly and ruefully: "When does a man get a chance to think around here?"

As he looked at the members of his Cabinet, perhaps the idea came to him that here was a group of highly capable men who could do a great deal of thinking. These were: Ezra Taft Benson, Agriculture; Herbert Brownell Jr., Attorney General; John Foster Dulles, State; Martin P. Durkin, Labor; Oveta Culp Hobby, Health, Education and Welfare; George M. Humphrey, Treasury; Douglas McKay, Interior; Arthur E. Summerfield, Postmaster General; Sinclair Weeks, Commerce; and Charles E. Wilson, Defense.

Whether these men's thoughts ran in the same pattern as Eisenhower's is subject to speculation, but Dulles gave the country brinkmanship; Benson earned the distrust of the small farmers; Mrs. Hobby blundered on the distribution of the Salk vaccine against infantile paralysis; Wilson become notorious for saying the wrong thing at the wrong time ("What's good for General Motors is good for the country"); Summerfield was hated by the postal workers; Durkin failed to gain the confidence of labor; McKay helped mastermind the giveaway of the tidelands oil, and Humphrey gave the erroneous (if unintentional) impression that he was the all-powerful moving force behind Eisenhower's thinking. As the years went by and Eisenhower was stricken by three serious illnesses, other men were mentioned as the power behind the Oval Room, including Wilson, Brownell, and James Hagerty, the press secretary, and the unfortunate Sherman Adams, who came closest to being what he was accused of being. Richard Nixon, touted by the right wing of the party, was never more than the eager young Vice-President who was encouraged by Eisenhower to remain eager—at a distance.

Surrounded by a Cabinet composed largely of successful corporation executives (good staff officers), Eisenhower proceeded to confront the immediate crises he had inherited from Truman. These were: a $10,000,000,000 deficit in the budget, the increased stockpiling of atomic bombs by Russia, troubles in Iran and Southeast Asia, and dissension among America's allies in Europe. There was the Korean war, which was going to vanish in a few months after the magic visit by the General, and there was also the political tragicomedy starring, directed, and produced by Joseph McCarthy, the senator from Wisconsin. Eisenhower said he would approach all these with the dignity and decorum so lacking in Truman's Administration.

The conflict in Korea ended in the summer of 1953 after thirty-seven months. It cost the United States more than 142,000 dead, wounded, and missing—23,345 were killed in action; 7,537 died of other causes, and 105,768 were wounded. Prime Minister Winston Churchill commended "the President's decisive guidance in paving the way for the end of the fighting." Eisenhower's popularity rose to a new high.

Keeping certain promises made during his first campaign, Eisenhower took calculated risks on his popularity and managed to survive. His tendency to trust "men who had met a payroll" caused him to reduce corporation taxes while opposing any reduction in personal income taxes. He encouraged legislation that gave away the immensely valuable offshore oil lands to the states despite the fact that the Supreme Court had ruled that these were the property of the entire nation. The value of these tidelands rights ran into incalculable billions. It was the biggest giveaway the country had ever experienced, and the most remarkable because, after it was accomplished, the people and most of the press appeared to have forgotten it.

Even some of his most enthusiastic followers were dismayed when Eisenhower gave tacit aid and comfort in the campaign to Senator McCarthy, who, among other brutalities, had denounced General George C. Marshall as a traitor. It was felt that the least amount of loyalty would have prompted Eisenhower to come to the proper defense of the man who had selected and backed him in his rise from lieutenant colonel to Supreme Allied Commander in the Second World War.

But Eisenhower maintained his silence and aloofness from the gutter extravaganza that McCarthy was staging as chairman of the Senate Permanent Subcommittee on Investigations. In one press conference after another the President brushed aside direct questions on the McCarthy issue. When the questions became too persistent to be ignored, Eisenhower finally gave official cognizance to McCarthy by officially ignoring him. The President said he stood for positive thinking and did not indulge in personal vituperation or quarrels of any kind. However, in words unmistakably aimed at McCarthy, the President declared that he was against "disregard of fair play." When McCarthy finally made the unforgivable error of attacking Eisenhower's beloved Army, the President moved in his subtle but effective manner. At the height of the tumultous McCarthy-Army hearings, replete with television cameras and the atmosphere of an American Inquisition, Eisenhower privately indicated his displeasure with the Wisconsin Senator. He wrote a note to Senator Ralph Flanders of Vermont that commended him for an address he had made assailing McCarthy. Later Eisenhower told Senator Arthur Watkins of Utah that he had done "a very splendid job" as chairman of a committee that had recommended Senate censure of McCarthy.

It was the first time that Eisenhower had moved so boldly —even bravely—because McCarthy was master of the devilish device of intimidating all his critics by equating them with Communism. With broad sarcasm he "apologized" for having told the voters in 1952 that the election of Eisenhower would spell a vigorous fight against Communism, and he lumped the President with the "starry-eyed" liberals who did not flail at the Red Menace. "I was mistaken about Eisenhower," he declared with a righteousness that was meant to banish the President forever from the popular scene. But Eisenhower delivered the final blow by crossing McCarthy off the White House social invitation list. Eisenhower remained on the popular scene, but McCarthy faded and died unrepentant in the spring of 1957.

Organized labor and Eisenhower were never on friendly terms. Although, as opposed to Senator Taft, Eisenhower was regarded as a liberal Republican, he listened more to the business groups that sought new controls in the old Taft-Hartley Law that would end union racketeering and "other abuses." Leaders in the AFL-CIO battled the proposals, charging that some of the provisions would hamstring labor's legitimate functions while admitting that the proposals would truly curb the activities of some corrupt unions. They argued that honest unions were being penalized for a few dishonest ones. The battle in Congress was deadlocked when Eisenhower gave his support to the restrictions. It was regarded as one of his biggest legislative victories. He again acted firmly and affirmatively when he invoked the eighty-day "cooling-off" period during the longest steel strike in history. He stopped it after 116 days with a back-to-work injunction on the ground that the strike had caused almost 350,000 layoffs in allied industries, that the strikers had lost about $1,160,000,000 in wages, and that industry had lost about $5,000,000,000 in production.

The labor leaders never forgave Eisenhower but the rank and file forgot the "episode" in the midst of a prosperity and a desire for fun that surpassed anything this country had ever seen. Building was booming, modern new shopping centers with unlimited parking facilities and sensational displays of consumer goods were attracting millions, automobiles were becoming more luxurious with bigger windshields and giant fins, men's and women's fashions were changing rapidly, creating an exciting race for comformity, and the cost of living was steadily going up. For the first time in history the service industries showed a larger national income than manufacturing. If there were crises, they were not apparent. Other than rock and roll and the beatniks there was nothing zany about the eight years, but in the people's attitude toward government there was a great similarity to the twenties. Even better, Eisenhower was a much more charming man than the dour Calvin Coolidge and most citizens seemed not to mind when, reading glaring headlines in their newspapers about serious developments at home or abroad, they learned at the same time that their President was spending a day at golf. It seemed to fit into a national philosophy to resent the intrusion of serious matters during a weekend of hunting, fishing, boating, golf, or bridge.

Despite Eisenhower's fundamental distrust of a powerful federal government, some important social reforms were effected, mainly through the efforts of Democrats and liberal Republicans in Congress. The minimum wage was raised from seventy-five cents to one dollar an hour, and the Social Security system was liberalized and extended to include 10,000,000 more workers. It was amended also to permit women to retire at sixty-two and disabled workers at fifty. Despite strong opposition from his own party, Eisenhower supported the Democratic program of economic foreign aid. Congress passed a bill for a 41,000-mile network of interstate superhighways costing $27,000,000,000, the Federal Government paying 90 per cent. In the field of public power, Eisenhower denounced Roosevelt's Tennessee Valley Authority as "creeping socialism" and declared that the "primary responsibility for developing power rests with the people locally."

The Administration's shiny and sanctimonious attitude toward the scandals under Truman was considerably tarnished by several unsavory disturbances of its own. There was the Dixon-Yates scandal, which resulted from Eisenhower's order to the Atomic Energy Commission to negotiate a contract with a private utility group to build a steam-power plant in West Memphis, Arkansas, to supply the TVA system with power. This was to replace the power that TVA was furnishing to atomic-energy plants. A Congressional investigation into the machinations of the deal made matters so unpleasant for the Administration that the contract was canceled.

No administration is immune to petty and grand thievery, and Eisenhower's was no exception. Despite his strongly publicized "crusade against corruption in government," he was dismayed to discover that there were many who enjoyed certain advantages because of their connections within the Administration. By 1958 charges involving conflict of interest had forced eight important officials to resign under fire. Finally the scandals reached the second most important man in the White House—Sherman Adams, the President's chief assistant. Adams, a lean, thrifty, and forbidding New Englander, was accused of accepting gifts from industrialist Bernard Goldfine. Adams, who had labored loyally, assuming some of the heaviest burdens for the President, was charged with making telephone calls to regulatory agencies about cases in which Goldfine was involved. Vicuña coats, expensive carpets, and other sundries were mentioned, and in September, 1958, Adams resigned.

Only a few intellectuals and the politically alert were aware of the smarting contrast when on October 4, 1957, America introduced a new car, the Edsel, with a fancier grill and more lights, while the Russians hurled their first satellite into orbit.

Eisenhower swiftly called a press conference to explain that the United States could have put a satellite into orbit earlier, but that this would have been to the detriment of other scientific goals and military progress in the long-range missile. Several American scientists said this country could have beaten Russia by as much as a year if there had been more awareness in the White House. While Americans were reading about the mild recriminations over our space program, the Russians waited a month and sent a second "moon" into orbit—much larger and containing a live dog. It was typical for America to adopt a sentimental attitude toward Laika, the space dog, and there was genuine sadness when it was announced that she had perished as a martyr to science. Finally, on January 31, 1958, the United States Army launched a Jupiter-C satellite at Cape Canaveral, Florida. But our prestige was short-lived when the Russians lofted a 3,000-pound monster, Sputnik III. This made ours "look like an orange," according to the taunt flung by Nikita Khrushchev on a day when Eisenhower was on the golf course. Commentators pointed out that this was mere coincidence and a President had not only a right but a duty to relax, but the coincidence occurred too often at moments of crisis to be ignored by American or foreign papers. Many news editors, including those on Republican newspapers, made it a practice to display a story that Eisenhower was "at golf" next to important national or international stories.

The space race was on and there was no turning back. The United States achieved escape velocity when it hurled a thirteen-pound rocket payload into outer space. The Russians launched a space probe of 3,000 pounds that went past the moon and swung around the sun. After a time inner space and outer space were becoming quite crowded, and there were those who felt that, as long as the two mighty rivals expended their ammunition outward toward the stars, there was less likelihood of nuclear war.

Golf, bridge, and good companions notwithstanding, the pressures must have made themselves felt on the physical and emotional structure of the President. On September 24, 1955, the nation had been stunned when it learned that Eisenhower had suffered a coronary thrombosis while vacationing in Colorado. He was stricken in his sleep about 2 A.M. in the Denver home of his mother-in-law, Mrs. John S. Doud. The President spent seven weeks in the Fitzsimmons Army Hospital. When he returned, he confessed ruefully that "the doctors have given me at least a parole, if not a pardon." There was a good deal of speculation whether Eisenhower was fit for the tasks ahead of him, but he went about his business so cheerfully and casually that talk of his illness was regarded as a partisan affair.

His second illness also came on suddenly. Early on the morning of June 8, 1956, the President suffered severe abdominal pains and was rushed to Walter Reed hospital, where twenty-four hours later he underwent emergency surgery. Major General Leonard D. Heaton, who performed the operation after twelve hours of medical treatment had failed to relieve the condition, described the illness as an inflammation of the ileum, "which is much more common than is diagnosed." He said there was no connection between this illness and the heart attack.

The Democrats made much of the health question, sometimes openly, more frequently in whispering campaigns, but the popularity of Eisenhower was such that he decisively defeated Adlai Stevenson in the 1956 election. He carefully followed his physicians' orders for ease, relaxation, and limited exercise, but on November 25, 1957, he suffered a blockage of a blood vessel leading to the brain, a condition generally described as a mild stroke. For a time this caused a slight impairment of his speech. The country was deeply concerned, but the President made a remarkable recovery, returning to work with renewed verve and vigor that astonished even his critics.

For those who sought an explanation for the amazing stamina of Eisenhower, a clue was provided by Major General Howard Snyder, his personal physician. "He watches his weight carefully," Dr. Snyder said. "When he reaches 180 he automatically cuts his eating. I remember the exact hour he stopped smoking. It was 3 P.M., March 21, 1949. He had an upset stomach. I had convinced him that he had to give up cigarettes for a while, and then I added: 'As long as you have to give them up temporarily, why don't you make it permanent?' He had just reached for a cigarette: He stopped midway and put it back. That was his last smoke to date. Truly, he was the ideal patient."

In some quarters there was the question whether he was the ideal President. Skeptics cited the matter of integration.

The United States Supreme Court, by a unanimous 9-0 decision, had ruled that no state has the right to separate Negro and white pupils into different public schools. Holding that such segregation was unconstitutional, the court struck out the long-standing doctrine of "separate but equal" facilities laid down by the Supreme Court in 1896, when it decided that segregation was legal if equal facilities were made available to Negroes and whites. Later the court ruled that nonsegregation applied not only to elementary and secondary schools, but also to tax-supported colleges and universities. The liberals were delighted; the reactionaries were appalled. Both sides looked to the President for comment or implementation.

Eisenhower withdrew to what appeared to be an unprepared position. He indicated that it was up to the states to obey the court ruling. As time dragged and token integration began to develop slowly in the border states with small Negro populations, the President was besieged with pleas to use his persuasive powers, to place the obligation on a moral plane. He abstained from action, and critics accused him of being a "Southerner at heart." The seventeen Southern states with two-thirds of the nation's Negro population simply refused to "act in deliberate haste" as the Supreme Court had urged. Five years after the ruling, the Deep South remained obdurate and was prepared to retain complete segregation as long as possible. Only an incident was needed to dramatize the situation, and it occurred in the pleasant city of Little Rock.

When the first of that city's schools started integration in 1957, Arkansas Governor Orval Faubus ordered the National Guard to keep nine Negroes from entering Central High School, which was attended by 2,000 white children. A Federal District Court immediately ordered the Guardsmen removed. Parents from the city and "outside elements" rioted, and the nation became aware of the challenge. Editorials in the North shouted for positive action by the federal government. Heeding close advisers, Eisenhower ordered United States troops into the city, the first time since Reconstruction days that the government, by executive order, had used soldiers to force equal treatment of Negroes in the South. The President federalized ten thousand National Guardsmen and sent one thousand seasoned regulars of the 101st Airborne Division into Little Rock. The school was surrounded by steel-helmeted soldiers with bayonets at the ready. The paratroopers, in rigid obedience to the orders of their Commander-in-Chief, escorted the six girls and three boys to and from school for several weeks. They led them inside the buildings, guarded the classrooms and corridors, and led them home. After the tension eased, the paratroopers were gradually replaced by federalized Guardsmen. Even these were withdrawn after sixty-four days. At the conclusion of the school year in May, 1958, the

President withdrew all the troops. The tensions were visibly eased, and the entire nation was genuinely heartened by Eisenhower's action and his declaration of hope that local officials would "assume their full responsibilities and duty for seeing that the orders of the Federal Court were not obstructed."

The President's action aroused bitterness among many Southerners, even after he explained that he had ordered the troops into Little Rock because "mob rule cannot be allowed to override the decisions of the courts. In other nations our enemies are gloating over this incident and seeking to undermine the nation's prestige and influence around the globe." He declared he had no choice but to dispatch the troops—"unless the President did so, anarchy would result." It was a noble sentiment, worthy of the President's fundamental decency, but a year later it was revealed that the mayor of Little Rock had pleaded with the federal government for such action long before the first of the riots.

The problem of integration did not end in Little Rock or Alabama, or Virginia or New Orleans. It was one of the several, including the civil-rights issue, that Eisenhower left to his successor. Congress, in 1957, had enacted the first civil-rights measure since the Reconstruction days. It was created mainly to protect the voting rights of Negroes through federal powers of enforcement, but it also dealt with discrimination against Negroes and all minorities in other fields. It encouraged the National Association for the Advancement of Colored People to test these rights in interstate buses, in voting booths, in restaurants, and at lunch counters. The Eisenhower era saw the rise of the Negro as an active fighter for his own rights, and the conflict was expected to continue through the Kennedy administration and longer. Both sides agreed it was a matter of time and education.

Eisenhower expressed his optimism toward the eventual solution of what he liked to describe as "irritating problems." He told one group of visitors to the White House that "there is nothing wrong with America that the faith, love of freedom, intelligence and energy of her citizens cannot cure. The rights that we have today we may consider as natural rights, but they were won by blood, sweat, sacrifice and death."

There were bright peaks in the day-to-day existence of the Chief Executive, filled with momentous events of a non-controversial nature. America acquired two new states, Alaska and Hawaii; men traveled under atomic power for the first time with the commissioning of the 3,000-ton submarine *Nautilus*; the submarine *Triton* circumnavigated the world entirely under water, voyaging 41,500 miles in 83 days (better than even Jules Verne dreamed); and the St. Lawrence Seaway was completed.

It is noteworthy that the major part of President Kennedy's inaugural address was devoted to foreign problems, because it was in the field of international affairs that Eisenhower faced his greatest criticism. Whether the fault lay in simple ineptitude, complacency, or a tendency to place too much responsibility on Secretary of State Dulles, the inevitable conclusion remained that the United States had lost the initiative in foreign affairs to the Soviet Union. There was evidence to prove that we had lost ground physically in Asia, Eastern Europe, the Levant, and Africa. And, strangely, even more comprehensible to most Americans was our evident loss of prestige.

Eisenhower inherited the cold war from Truman and proceeded with the hope that in a spirit of Rotarian friendliness he could conduct business with the Russians. In 1953, he went before the United Nations and proposed an "atoms-for-peace" plan, under which atomic powers would pool at least part of their resources for peaceful purposes. Three years later this became a reality when eighty-two nations voted unanimously to establish the International Atomic Energy Agency. Eisenhower allocated $1,700,000,-

ooo—half to be used for peaceful atomic energy in the United States and the other half to be used by friendly foreign nations for the same purposes.

He went to Geneva in July, 1955, with genuine hope for positive accomplishments. Meeting Premier Bulganin of Russia, Premier Faure of France, and Prime Minister Eden of Great Britain, Eisenhower took the initiative with a proposal whose sincerity could not fail to impress the world. He told this first summit meeting that he would pinpoint American military establishments and let them come under the eyes of Russian aerial reconnaissance teams—if the Russians would do the same. At the time of the conference Nikita Khrushchev held no official government post, although he was the leader of the Soviet Communist Party. He rejected Eisenhower's "open skies" proposal a few months later. Eisenhower, grim but grinning, felt this rebuff keenly, but encouraged subsequent conferences on a lower diplomatic level to explore other methods of a mutually satisfactory control and inspection system. These faded into quiet failure and were completely overshadowed by the bloody revolt of Hungarians against Soviet domination in 1956.

Eisenhower appealed to the Soviet Union to pull its soldiers out of Hungary and agree to political independence for that country. The Russians refused and sent in more troops to crush the outbreak. The President ordered the admission of more than 38,000 refugees to the United States. Later that year, at a Human Rights Day ceremony, he called upon free people to take fresh note of Russian ruthlessness and never forget "what tyranny has done to our fellow-man in Hungary. The brutal purge of liberty which followed their heroic struggle will be long and sorrowfully remembered."

In the same year the Soviets seized the initiative once more in an attempt to penetrate the oil-rich Middle East after Gamal Abdel Nasser became president of Egypt and leader of the Arab bloc dedicated to the destruction of Israel. Khrushchev moved to increase Nasser's strength by furnishing him with arms in exchange for a mortgage on Egyptian cotton. After Nasser became openly and violently anti-Western, Dulles withdrew an offer to help finance the Aswan Dam development on the Nile. Nasser's swift reply was to nationalize the Suez Canal, through which all oil to Europe was shipped.

Israel moved suddenly and resolutely in a spectacular seven-day campaign against Egypt, routing Nasser's army and occupying the Sinai Peninsula. At the same time, France and Britain bombed Egyptian airfields and began occupying the canal area. Nasser sank enough shipping to block the waterway. Russia threatened to "crush the aggressors" and the world held its breath, for here were all the ingredients of a major conflict. President Eisenhower called the invasion an error. He sponsored a United Nations resolution for a cease-fire. The three nations, reluctant, angry, and frustrated, withdrew to make way for a United Nations police force. Vice-President Nixon declaimed later that "the United Nations has been saved."

Nasser also was saved. The episode cost Eden his job. Soviet influence in the Arab states was greater than ever before, and relations between United States and Britain and France were at their lowest point. Eisenhower made a face-saving gesture with a Congressional resolution warning that the United States was "prepared to use armed force in response to an appeal from any victim of armed aggression in the Near East."

Eisenhower hoped for an interlude of relaxation, but the Soviet had other plans. Within a short time, pro-Communist, pro-Egyptian Jordanians threatened King Hussein. The President gave the King $10,000,000 in emergency aid and rushed the Sixth Fleet to the rescue. The King won the struggle, but there was no respite from crises in that area of the world. In 1958 the pro-Western government of Iraq was overthrown by the army in a short revolt in which King Faisal and his chief ministers were slain. At the request of President Chamoun of Lebanon, Eisenhower rushed several thousand Marines and soldiers in to that country, where pro-Nasser rebels were fighting the government. The British airlifted troops into Jordan, the world was on the brink once more, but the "incident" ended quietly.

Matters had barely simmered down in the Middle East when Communist China began a massive bombardment of Quemoy and Matsu. The President interrupted his vacation at Newport, R.I., for a nation-wide radio-television address in which he said America must fight if necessary to prevent the conquest of the two islands. However, he urged negotiations, and the shooting abated, to be resumed from time to time as an irritating reminder that Communist China wanted admission to the United Nations. Eisenhower remarked promptly that no nation should be allowed to shoot its way into the United Nations.

In crisis after crisis the United States had lost prestige as a nation, but in 1958, while Eisenhower and Dulles were fighting defensive diplomatic wars against the Communists, the degradation assumed a personal nature. Vice-President Nixon embarked on a nineteen-day good-will tour of Latin America that year. In Lima, Peru, he was spat upon and stoned; Venezuelan students in Caracas rioted and attacked his car. Nixon comported himself bravely against these obviously inspired assaults, but the President, taking no risks, rushed 1,000 paratroopers and Marines to Cuban and Puerto Rican bases. The incidents ceased and the troops did not have to leave their bases, but Americans were startled into awareness that the good-neighbor policy of Franklin Roosevelt had been allowed to deteriorate and that once friendly and safe Latin America had again become a problem area.

When Dulles died in 1959, Eisenhower began to take a much greater part in foreign affairs. It was no secret that he did not have the same confidence in Christian Herter that he had had in Dulles. On a 22,000-mile, eleven-nation trip, which he called a "mission of peace and good will," Eisenhower scored one of the greatest personal triumphs ever enjoyed by a head of state. Immense crowds cheered him in Asia, Africa, and Europe. On his return he called upon the non-Communist world to join him in a long-range program of aid to "peoples who desperately need help in their struggle for a better life."

Relations between the Soviet Union and the United States reached another low in November, 1958, when the Russians sought to maneuver the Western powers out of Berlin. The West stood firm and the battle went through the usual routine of notes, threats, speeches, warnings, and accusations. The crisis vanished quickly when plans were announced for visits by Khrushchev to America and by Eisenhower to Russia. These were the most promising gestures toward harmony in many years, and the President expressed the hope "by the exchange of visits to melt a little of the ice that seems to freeze our relationships."

Khrushchev arrived in the United States with "open heart and good intentions." He declared that "the Soviet people want to live in friendship with the American people. There are no obstacles to having the relations between our two countries develop as relations between good neighbors." Eisenhower replied that his goal was a "just, universal and enduring peace." Never had the two great powers been closer and never had there been greater hope on both sides of the Iron Curtain. The whole world, except Communist China's leaders, glowed with friendship and good will, looking forward to Eisenhower's return visit to Russia.

Then came the U-2 incident. Francis Gary Powers, pilot of a United States jet, was downed 1,200 miles inside Russia and the Soviets decided to make the most of it, charging espionage and demanding an apology from President Eisenhower. The official fumbling that followed the news of the

U-2 incident caused dismay and embarrassment in the United States and among her allies. Eisenhower finally admitted that the flight had taken place and tried unsuccessfully to explain that American espionage was a "distasteful but vital necessity . . . and no one wants another Pearl Harbor." Khrushchev, evidently under pressure from his own party, exploited the incident to the limit. He not only broke up the summit meeting scheduled for Paris but also canceled the invitation to Eisenhower to visit Russia, saying the Russians would not be able to receive the President with "proper cordiality." Eisenhower, in one of his rare displays of genuine wrath, accused the Soviet leader of insulting the United States and charged that Khrushchev had "brushed aside all arguments of reason."

As low as America's prestige had sunk, it was to go even lower. The planned trip to Russia was part of Eisenhower's final extended good-will tour and was to take him to the Far East, including Japan. That visit, too, had to be canceled after prolonged and violent Communist-led riots and demonstrations against Premier Kishi and the new security treaty with the United States. The treaty was eventually signed, but Kishi was ousted.

Somehow, Eisenhower managed to grasp victory out of defeat. Because of the open and crude insults inflicted upon him by Khrushchev, he returned to this country a hero. In a nation-wide broadcast, he portrayed his trip as so successful that "I would not hesitate a second to venture abroad again in quest of world peace." He declared that the ratification of the security treaty with Japan, "which the rioters sought to thwart," was a "signal defeat of international Communism that far outweighs" the frustrated visit to Tokyo.

There seemed to be some hope that Eisenhower would finish his days in the White House with some tranquility. On October 3, 1960, eleven days short of his seventieth birthday, he set a record as the oldest occupant of 1600

Pennsylvania Avenue, enjoying the respect and good will of most Americans.

But there were two pieces of unfinished business upon which he acted so swiftly and decisively that some critics remarked that it had taken Eisenhower eight years to learn his trade. The first was the gold crisis in mid-November. To offset a serious drain on United States gold, largely attributed to the nation's generosity to its allies, the President ordered a $1,000,000,000 cut in foreign spending and the return of dependents of members of the armed forces at overseas bases. The second was the severance of relations with Cuba after Eisenhower had "lost patience with Fidel Castro." The incidents leading to the break were many and irritating, beginning in June, when the Castro Government instituted a long list of seizures of foreign assets by taking over American-owned oil refineries, sugar mills, rubber factories, and utilities valued in excess of $1,000,000,000. Eisenhower suspended most sugar purchases from Cuba. Khrushchev immediately offered to buy Cuba's sugar, paying with goods, not cash, and threatened the United States with rockets. The President told Khrushchev to stay out of the Western Hemisphere. Communist China declared its solidarity with Cuba, and Khrushchev, hedging slightly, asked Castro to tone down his attacks on the United States.

There was one more burning crisis, which reached apparent anticlimax six days after Kennedy took office. This was the case of Laos, a country of 2,000,000 that, in the words of the cliché-mongers, seemed about to become the "tinderbox" of Southeast Asia. Laos emerged as an autonomous state under the Geneva agreement of 1954 that stopped the struggle in Indochina. The Laotians never appeared to indicate any yearning for involvement in the world power conflict, but it was their misfortune to occupy strategic ground as a corridor to Communist China. To play it safe, the United States supported a rightist group under

Prince Boun Oum. In the autumn of 1960 he charged that North Vietnam forces had invaded Laos, and a major problem was tossed into the final days of Eisenhower's regime. Senator Mike Mansfield of Montana decried the chaos of American policy in Laos and demanded to know whether United States policy had been dictated by the State Department, the Pentagon, or the Central Intelligence Agency. As the reports of fighting and fresh invasion forces grew, the West began to look fearfully toward its position in the Far East despite several dispatches from the area quoting observers of the highest competence and repute as declaring that there was not then and never had been any sign of an invasion. But Prince Boun Oum made strong appeals for international assistance. Eisenhower was visibly concerned when his term ended.

Then, on January 26, 1961, Boun Oum called a press conference and confessed that the government of Laos had cried "wolf." He revealed that his requests for help had been intended only to serve as internal propaganda—to assure the people of Laos that their government had friends abroad.

"If the Southeast Asia Treaty Organization really came in there would be international war and this country would be the battleground. Nobody really wants that," he said.

By the time he was ready to leave the White House, Eisenhower had regained his popularity to the point where there was well-founded belief that he could have won over Kennedy. He also seemed to be enjoying those final days, indicating an understandable reluctance to leave. On seeing the stands going up for the inaugural parade, he remarked: "I feel like the fellow in jail who is watching his scaffold being built." When Kennedy called on him on the day before the inauguration, Eisenhower could not resist a little demonstration of the power of the Presidency. He told the younger man that helicopters were available to the President on quick notice. To prove it, he sent word that he wanted a helicopter at the White House. Five minutes later it was there.

The editorial farewells to Eisenhower were mostly partisan. *Life* entitled its piece "From the Heart of America," and said in part:

If Ike's speeches assay high in cliché (and tortured syntax), you always know what he means and never doubt that he means it. He is innocent of techniques for manipulating crowds; instead he warms (and is warmed by) them. Grace and magnanimity marked the gesture at Chicago after his nomination in '52, when he walked across the street from the Blackstone to the Hilton to salute the defeated Bob Taft. He is at his best ad-libbing directly to small groups—mailmen, Boy Scouts, Republican women, whatever—with the right sentiment always, the right word often . . . he has been . . . the superb embodiment of what this pluralistic, semi-articulate country stands for and is trying to say. Dwight Eisenhower has convinced millions of non-Americans that even a nuclear superpower can be decent, non-predatory and morally responsible. . . . Thank you, Mr. President.

William V. Shannon, Washington correspondent of *The New York Post*, was not agreeably impressed with Eisenhower's televised farewell to the nation. He called it "woolly and sentimental in its thought, undistinguished in its language, pretentious and in bad taste." *The Atlanta Constitution* said: "There was dismay in his speech, and there was hope. Both were justified." *The Dallas Morning News* said: "Eisenhower leaves office with the affection, respect and confidence of the nation and much of the world." *The Los Angeles Times* described the President as a "man of ripened wisdom. His adversaries have nourished his good will and sharpened his perception. Surely the people are proud of this man and proud of themselves for electing him while he was available." *The Kansas City Star* did not feel that the retiring President "deserved accolades as one of the most brilliant or imaginative of Presidents," but admitted his charm. "Few men in the decades of the republic have so captured the trust, the hearts and the faith of the people."

Two newspapers representing the most consistently divergent views were the *New York Herald Tribune* and *The New York Post.* On January 15, 1961, under the title "Mr. Eisenhower's Magnificent Record," the *Herald Tribune* said:

The Commander-in-Chief has held his last review. The President has given his last message to Congress, held his last Cabinet meeting and will soon make his last address to the people. And on Friday Dwight D. Eisenhower will become a private citizen.

This is not the end, of course, of a remarkable career. The reservoirs of good will that Mr. Eisenhower has accumulated, here and abroad, no less than his wealth of experience, are American assets that must be used. His cheerful and co-operative attitude in paving the way for his successor insures that neither partisan nor personal bitterness will stand in the way of such use.

There are some who profess great astonishment at the way in which President Eisenhower has retained the affection and respect of his own countrymen, as well as of millions of plain people in other lands, despite the clouds that hover over the international horizon as his second term draws to a close. Extreme liberals (who mistrust the electorate quite as strongly as the most reactionary conservative when the electorate fails to indorse liberal tenets) have found solace in speaking of Mr. Eisenhower as the "father image," or, when that palled, as "the symbol of the paternal unifier."

But those liberals—who are chiefly annoyed because the President failed to model himself on the image they had created of him—never explained how this symbol was able to project itself into the minds of millions around the world; into Indian villagers, for example, who came from miles around New Delhi to cheer for "Ike."

* * *

President Eisenhower did unify a nation in which the frustrations of Korea, violent debates and assorted witch-hunts had gouged deep divisions. Nothing could testify to that fact better than the patience and good humor displayed as the recent vote for the Presidency was being counted to its razor-edged finish. Even the dispute over civil rights, with all the sordid and ugly clashes that still persist, is less of a threat to national unity and Federal sovereignty than in the days of Little Rock, when the President ordered troops into the city and demonstrated that the law and the courts would be upheld.

President Eisenhower could and did act with vigor when he believed the situation demanded it, whether in Little Rock or Lebanon. But he abstained from action when he thought that best, and not all the clamor of press or Congress could pressure him to change.

His technique of leadership has been disdainfully referred to as that of the chairman of the board; to the extent that he preferred persuasion to command and consensus to coercion, the term is accurate. But to charge with indecisiveness the commander who, in the stark loneliness of supreme responsibility, launched the world's greatest armada on stormy seas toward Fortress Europe, is simply silly. General Eisenhower could never have commanded the huge, polyglot army that freed Western Europe had he not been sensitive to the emotions and thoughts of others; he would not have won had he not been able to make the crucial decisions alone.

* * *

It was this mixture of sensitivity and authority that made Dwight Eisenhower the general and the President he was; that was communicated by his manner and bearing; that, coupled with patent sincerity and intergrity, won the loyal allegiance of whole peoples—including, but not confined to, his own. If to have that is to be a father image, so be it; the world could use more men of such qualities.

* * *

A day later, under the heading "History Rewritten," *The Post* said:

The last days of the Eisenhower era have brought forth some astonishing sermons from Republican typewriters. In yesterday's Herald Tribune a tribute to Ike's "Magnificent Record" was mingled with an angry denunciation of those who have questioned the luster of his performance. All across the land similar recitals are being issued or prepared in the GOP press.

We are reluctant to mar the farewell addresses, or to deny Mr. Eisenhower the illusory comfort of such rhetoric. Yet we cannot avoid a few wry words about the uncritical adulation. For what most of these salutes seem to say is hail to the chief because things could be a lot worse.

And they could be. We are not at war; we have 4,500,000, not 10,000,000 unemployed; we still have some allies; Cuba has not attacked us; we have avoided civil war; we haven't quit the United Nations; we have not had a major conflict-of-interest scandal in recent months; the Bill of Rights has not been repealed.

In short, there can be no question that the republic is still alive and even prospering in some areas as Mr. Eisenhower prepares to leave office. It is only against the glowing early hopes, the large promises and the great potential for leadership that the actualities of record seem so small. Indeed, given the measure of popular affection he has so widely retained, it is an affront to Ike to say this is the best he could have done if he had really believed that the business of government is to govern.

We respect him as a man of good will. But to depict these eight years of sluggish stalemate as a great national adventure is a banal falsification of history. In these fading hours of his regime there must be moments when Mr. Eisenhower himself ponders the squandered opportunities of The Great Crusade.

There was always an aura of good will about Eisenhower. His faults were glossed over and his accomplishments were extravagantly praised. It is worth noting how often the phrase "good will" occurred in commentaries on Eisenhower. The most revealing comment came from Herbert Block, the *Washington Post* editorial cartoonist who draws under the name of Herblock. His final devastating cartoon on the Eisenhower Administration shows an aide looking at a newspaper carrying the old President's last message, and saying to Kennedy: "Briefly, it's up to you to clean up the success in Washington."

4. The Interregnum

John Fitzgerald Kennedy, the youngest man ever elected President of the United States, awoke on the morning after Election Day in the midst of doubt whether he or Richard Nixon had been chosen. The vote was so close—and it was getting closer—that Thruston Morton, the Republican National Chairman, within a week called for a re-examination of the states in which Kennedy had a questionable margin: Texas, Illinois, Delaware, Michigan, Minnesota, Missouri, Nevada, New Mexico, New Jersey, Pennsylvania, and South Carolina. Nixon wisely disassociated himself from partisan shouts of "recount," but Democratic leaders and the millions who had voted for Kennedy spent several agonizing days, alternately damning and blessing the Electoral College system, until the results indicated that, while Kennedy was due to win by an uncomfortably low popular vote, he was certain to get 303 electoral votes.

Post-election analysis, which many realists believe is a

polite phrase for second-guessing, pointed out that Kennedy had won by a much smaller margin than expected. According to voter registration, the United States is about 47 per cent Democratic, 30 per cent Republican. The Democrats had majorities in both Houses of Congress and dominated most state legislatures. Kennedy benefited by his party's traditional appeal to labor, Jews, and Negroes. He was considered strong with the millions of Catholics, and there were enough frightening headlines about poor business, increasing unemployment, and Eisenhower's fumbling in foreign affairs to create a favorable position for the Democrats.

In addition, Kennedy had made gratifying headway in the television debates. He became better known to those voters who maintained reservations about his youth and experience. His jutting jaw, his confident calm, his impressive command of facts and knowledge of history were making intellectual and emotional inroads on Nixon's following. There seemed, at times, a powerful surge toward the New Frontier that indicated a landslide.

When the tight returns were finally in, the analysts who sought a quick and easy explanation were faced with a number of imponderables that refused to fall into a pattern of predictable hindsight. Indiana, Nebraska, and North Dakota went for Nixon but elected Democratic governors. With unbridled ticket-splitting, Massachusetts, Minnesota, and New Mexico went for Kennedy and elected Republican governors. The recession issue failed to support Democratic predictions when hard-hit areas like San Diego County, California, and Oregon's slumping lumber areas wound up in the Nixon column. Despite an unyielding contempt and hatred for Secretary of Agriculture Benson, most farm areas maintained their Republican tradition.

One episode that was believed to have swung a telling number of Negro votes to Kennedy was the capricious arrest of the Reverend Martin Luther King in Georgia on an old traffic charge. While Eisenhower had prepared a sympa-

thetic statement, and some Republicans were all for pressing the issue, Nixon, playing safe, uttered only a "no comment." Kennedy issued a personal message of support to the
Reverend King's wife; his brother, Robert, made a fateful
phone call; King was released and Nixon had missed his big
chance.

Perhaps it was Adlai Stevenson who gave the best summa-
tion of the Democratic candidate when, trying to describe
the difference between himself and Kennedy, he told an
East Los Angeles meeting: "Do you remember that in class-
ical times, when Cicero had finished speaking, the people
said: 'How well he spoke,' but, when Demosthenes had
finished speaking, the people said: 'Let us march'?"

Despite the uncertainty felt by many Democrats, Kennedy proceeded immediately to act as President-elect. The
problem of taking over the Government with 2,380,500
federal employees, a continuing cold war, a $77-billion bud-
get, a business recession, unemployment, and a restless population was not to be approached casually. There is no
constitutional machinery for transferring power from one
administration to another. Clark Clifford, who had been
counsel to Harry Truman, had been working with the
Brookings Institution for several weeks on the change and
gave his report to Kennedy. It suggested that Kennedy place
observers in the State Department and the Budget Bureau;
that he be prepared to offer a revised budget soon after the
inauguration, and that he appoint his Cabinet by mid-
December "so that they can be informed and ready to make
decisions."

Kennedy's first appointments were three: Clifford to be
special liaison man to the White House during the transition; Ted Sorensen to be Kennedy's special counsel and
Pierre Salinger to be press secretary.

Theodore Chaikin Sorensen, called Ted, was at thirty-two
one of the youngest men in the Kennedy organization. Born
in Nebraska, he was the son of a Republican lawyer who was

both stern and fair. A follower of Senator Norris and once State Attorney General, the elder Sorensen offered Ted a silver dollar if he reached his twenty-first birthday without smoking or drinking. Joseph Kennedy offered his son, John, $1,000 on identical terms. Sorensen collected but Kennedy sampled beer during his minority. Sorensen was graduated from the University of Nebraska Law School with highest honors. He went to Washington for the Federal Security Agency, then worked for Senator Paul Douglas of Illinois, finally becoming researcher and speech writer for the freshman Senator Kennedy. They were at once drawn together by their love of books and politics. Sorensen compiled the material for Kennedy's Pulitzer Prize-winning book, *Profiles in Courage,* while Kennedy was convalescing in Florida from a serious illness. Drew Pearson, the Washington columnist, charged that Sorensen had ghosted the book, but later retracted when the contrary was proved by Sorensen's notes, Kennedy's handwritten drafts, and some stern legal action by Clark Clifford. Sorensen assisted Kennedy in planning his drive for the 1956 vice-presidential nomination and spent the next three years preparing for the 1960 battle. A Unitarian, Sorensen prepared Kennedy's principal speeches on the "religious issue."

Salinger was born in San Francisco. His German father was a mining engineer and a musician. His mother, a Frenchwoman, was a journalist in Indochina. At the age of six, Salinger was a prodigy at the piano. He was graduated from high school at fifteen and spent two years at San Francisco State College before enlisting in the Navy. He commanded a Navy sub-chaser in the Pacific when he was nineteen years old, and when the war was over went to work as a copy boy, rising to reporter on *The San Francisco Chronicle.* At twenty-five he was night city editor. He took a leave of absence to manage Richard P. Graves in his unsuccessful attempt to become governor of California. Salinger became a regional editor for the now-defunct *Colliers' Magazine.*

After investigating the Teamsters' Union for a magazine article, he became the chief investigator for Robert Kennedy, then chief counsel of the Senate Rackets Committee. John Kennedy immediately liked the portly, energetic young man who manifested a charming, subdued kind of helpless humor that hid an incisive intellect and a boundless verve. Salinger, a cigar chain-smoker, easily captured the affection and respect of the press corps.

Before Kennedy went to his first press conference at the Hyannis National Guard Armory, he made two telephone calls that got his Administration off to a popular beginning. He asked Allen Dulles, Director of the Central Intelligence Agency, to remain on the job. Dulles agreed. Kennedy then asked J. Edgar Hoover to remain as chief of the Federal Bureau of Investigation. Hoover accepted.

The press conference in the crowded armory was Kennedy's coming-out party. He indicated that, since the phrase, "Mr. President-elect," was awkward, he would like to be called "Senator—a mighty good title." Nevertheless, the conference ended with the traditional: "Thank you, Mr. President."

He told the assembled reporters and the national television audience: "I didn't think it was going to be quite that close." Nonetheless he felt in no way inhibited from pressing forward with his program. While some Republicans had made the point that the close election clearly represented the absence of a mandate, Kennedy quickly brushed that aside, and then generously declared that "an alternative course, an alternative group, an alternative philosophy and an alternative party was selected, but . . . I certainly would not use the word *repudiation* of the Republicans."

Kennedy announced that he had asked James M. Landis, sixty-one, former dean of the Harvard Law School and a veteran member of the Roosevelt Administration, to provide him with a report on federal regulatory agencies, a sore spot in the Eisenhower Administration. He said he had no knowledge of any future rôles that his brothers, "Bobby and Ted," might have in his Administration. He also announced his grateful acceptance of an invitation from Eisenhower for a meeting in the White House to discuss transition problems.

As the days went on and the election of Kennedy seemed to become more certain, Americans settled down with a quiet satisfaction that once again they had selected the proper man. The European press seemed cautious but hopeful. It was recalled that the late Aneurin Bevan had once remarked that it seemed "unfair that Europeans are not allowed to participate in the election of the United States President since their fate is in so many ways in the hands of men chosen by Americans alone." Kennedy's youth was to Europeans the most amazing aspect of the man. At forty-three, he was young enough to be the son of any of the aging leaders. He was twenty-three years younger than Khrushchev, Mao Tse-tung, and Harold Macmillan, twenty-six years younger than Charles de Gaulle, and forty-one years younger than Konrad Adenauer.

"The American people have chosen adventure," said the conservative London *Daily Telegraph*. "Such a choice from such a people could well mark a turning point in history towards an era of full peril but also of great promise." Castro's official newspaper, *Revolución*, said: "Four years of a rich illiterate," but in the rest of Latin America the victory was hailed as a return to the policies of Roosevelt. Khrushchev, whose inspired writers had scoffed at the election as the battle between "Tweedledum and Tweedledee," cabled the following message: "Esteemed Mr. Kennedy, allow me to congratulate you. We hope that while you are at this post the relations between our countries would again follow the line along which they were developing in Franklin Roosevelt's time." *Izvestia* described the results as a "terrible defeat" for the Eisenhower-Nixon policies. Communist China warned that, while both candidates were slaves to the ruling

The Interregnum   **57**

circles, Kennedy would "greatly increase military spending and extend war preparations."

Some Britons were concerned over the ending of the close relationship between Macmillan and Eisenhower, but Ian Gilmour in *The Spectator* declared that "America, under a Kennedy administration, is going to be an exciting place. Europe will need monkey glands to keep up." The French privately expressed concern over the men around Kennedy who "seemed overexcited about Africa and Asia," but de Gaulle promptly sent off a cable that began: "Welcome, dear partner." Adenauer had been the most open supporter of Nixon, fearing "Democratic flexibility" over the Berlin issue, but *der Alte*, experienced in the ways of diplomatic acrobatics, somersaulted neatly with this statement: "We need have no worries. A steady continuation of American policy will be maintained."

From Hyannis, Kennedy flew to his father's Palm Beach mansion, where he was planning a series of conferences, but the people were not prepared for the grand gesture that was to follow. Without any prior notice to the press, Kennedy paid a visit to Nixon, who was staying at a villa in Key Biscayne. The former rivals greeted each other warmly, then went behind Nixon's screened sun porch and talked for more than an hour. They discussed foreign policy, transition, and the Republicans who might be useful in the Kennedy Administration.

Then they posed for the newsreel and television cameras. "The fact that I am here," Kennedy said, "indicates, I think, what my desire is for our relationship." Nixon said it was a very gracious act. "I, of course, would have been very glad to have called upon him, and the fact that he wanted to come here, I think, is an excellent example of how our American system works." Nixon then explained that he and Kennedy agreed on the "proper rôle of an opposition party and of an opposition leader." This was correctly interpreted to mean that Nixon would not accept a post with Kennedy and that he intended to remain the leader of the Republican Party.

Kennedy's visit to Lyndon Johnson's ranch in Texas two days later was taken up with talks on NATO and the reorganization of Congress. "It is my belief," Kennedy said, "that Senator Johnson's great talents and experience equip him to be the most effective Vice-President in the history of our country." Perhaps this was the first step Kennedy was taking to obtain a more sympathetic Rules Committee in the House and some form of curb on the filibuster in the Senate.

While the Republicans were still hoping for a miracle that would swing the election to Nixon, sending investigators into eight marginal states—Texas, Illinois, Missouri, Nevada, New Mexico, South Carolina, New Jersey, and Pennsylvania—some Southern Democrats also cherished an impossible dream. R. Lea Harris, a Montgomery, Alabama, lawyer, suggested a conference of Southern electors to force Kennedy to agree "to restoration of states' rights," an all-embracing condition. If Kennedy refused, Harris said, the 128 Southern electors should seek a coalition with Republican electors for a more congenial ticket such as Richard Russell of Georgia and Barry Goldwater of Arizona.

Other, more practical Southern politicians hoped that Nixon and Kennedy would fall short of an electoral majority and the election would have to be decided by the new Congress. There were many other schemes and plans, which faded as Kennedy's margin became more certain. But the situation created a massive criticism of the Electoral College system, with solutions ranging from total abolition to intricate and impossible mazes of regional and popular voting. Kennedy declared he favored only one major change: that electors be forced to vote for the ticket that had received a clear majority in their states.

Meanwhile, Kennedy was the center of a raging speculation on the appointment of a Secretary of State. Adlai Stev-

enson and Chester Bowles had been mentioned prominently and enthusiastically during the campaign by the
liberals in the party. Truman's Secretary of State, Dean
Acheson, declared: "That would be disastrous." Kennedy
held a long talk with Robert Lovett, sixty-five, a banker, and
at one time Truman's Secretary of Defense, who had also
worked closely with Henry Stimson and General Marshall.
It was reported that Lovett was being considered for Treasury, Defense or State, but he discouraged any consideration
for a Cabinet post because of poor health. Senator Fulbright of Arkansas was mentioned as Kennedy's favorite for
the State job, but he was furiously opposed by Negroes because of his pusillanimous silence during the Little Rock
outrages, and by Jews because of his friendliness toward the
countries of the Arab League. There was studied silence
when the name of Dean Rusk was offered.

In the middle of all this, Kennedy was distracted by an
event that delighted the entire world. He had spent Thanksgiving Day with his wife, Jacqueline, and his three-year-old
daughter, Caroline, and was on his way to Palm Beach,
when he was informed that his wife had been rushed to the
hospital for a Caesarean section. Kennedy was astonished
because the child was not due for another month. He flew
back and was told by his airplane radio that he was the
father of a boy and that both mother and child were doing
well. No father ever had a greater number of well-wishers,
and a new image of the young President of the United
States was created around the world. As is typical of most
fathers, especially Americans, Kennedy had to "sit" with
Caroline during the first few days after the birth of her
brother. Photographs appeared in all papers, here and
abroad, showing the young father strolling with his
daughter, assisting her with her doll's carriage, and generally
displaying the kind of paternal patience that earned him the
envy, admiration, and sympathy of the sentimentalists of
the world. There were satisfied cluckings from millions of

ladies over a photograph showing the handsome President-elect walking bareheaded behind his bright daughter and carrying a rag doll in his hand.

Now, while the controversy over the new Secretary of State was filling the news columns, Kennedy, with a planned single-mindedness, proceeded in his own way. He named David E. Bell, a Harvard economist, as Budget Director, and Governor G. Mennen Williams of Michigan as Assistant Secretary of State for African Affairs. Bell, forty-one, a Presbyterian, was graduated from California's highly respected Pomona College, taught briefly in Harvard's economics department, and then became an analyst in the Budget Bureau. After three years as a Marine combat tactics instructor, Bell became an examiner in the Budget Bureau, where he attracted the attention of Clark Clifford and was promoted to assistant to the chief of the bureau's fiscal division. Later he served for three years as a speech writer and administrative aide in Truman's "kitchen" or backstairs cabinet. He went back to Harvard, where he became assistant dean in the Graduate School of Public Administration and did extra work as an economic adviser to Pakistan. His public position on his new post is that the Budget Bureau is an instrument of Presidential policy rather than a watchdog for the taxpayer.

Williams completed six terms as governor of Michigan, and told Kennedy that "I would like to work for the cause of peace in some public office where I could be effective." In his twelve years as governor, Williams, forty-nine, a Princeton graduate and heir to a shaving-soap fortune, was a highly competent administrator who dedicated himself to his state's welfare needs. He actively promoted the cause of the Negro in Michigan and was a member of the N.A.A.C.P. and the Urban League.

When Kennedy was finally forced to discard Fulbright, his favorite for the State Department, he surprised the liberals by offering Stevenson the post of Ambassador to the

United Nations. This pleased many who felt this was the perfect platform for the highly literate, idealistic, and articulate leader of what had once been known as the "intellectual wing of the party." Stevenson hesitated until he was informed that Rusk would be the Secretary of State. Kennedy, giving a demonstration of practical intellect, had loosened a sticky situation in his party.

Kennedy managed to combine decorum with a personal independence that gained him much favor with those who prefer to base their judgment of a man not only on his practical achievements but also on his personality. As a fierce young campaigner, he had leaped over automobile tops to get to a platform and had to be cautioned by his escorts not to drive too fast. As a golfer, the story is told, he almost got a hole in one. It was during the campaign, and, as the ball rolled toward the cup, his companions shouted: "In . . . in . . . get in." But Kennedy stood dismayed, shouting: "No . . . no . . . no . . ." The ball did not make it, and, as Kennedy putted out for a respectable birdie, he was asked why he had shouted: "No." "Because, he explained, "I don't want to be known as another famous golfer."

During the campaign, jokes on his wealth and religion were part of the repartee in living rooms throughout the nation. Kennedy and Nixon took no notice of them, but, after the battle was over, Kennedy managed to laugh when he heard them. This was best demonstrated when he paid an unexpected visit to *The Best Man*, an election-year play about heroes and villains in a convention fight. Kennedy roared with the audience when an "ex-President" told a young candidate: "And, for another thing, you're a millionaire. People trust you rich boys. They figure you have so much money of your own you won't go stealin' theirs." Or when a "senator" remarked: "I suppose we ought to try for a Catholic—that seems to be the thing this year—for second place, that is."

If the jokes during the campaign could be construed as

vicious, these same jokes got good-natured receptions after the election. Some examples: Kennedy will have fireside chats, just like F.D.R., but he will call them "Coast to Coast with the Holy Ghost." . . . How to make a Kennedy cocktail—three parts Old Fitzgerald, one part holy water, one part sacramental wine, and a twist of Norman Vincent Peale . . . How to get to the White House—go to Harvard and turn left . . . Kennedy would like to erect a cross on the White House lawn but he is afraid Johnson will burn it.

After a while the jokes and the jokesters got tired. But sociologists agreed that they had to come out and they had to run their course.

As he approached the halfway mark between election and inauguration, Kennedy had a close look at the Defense Department, which consumes more than half the federal budget. He had commissioned Senator Stuart Symington of Missouri and a five-man group of civilian experts to study ways and means to modernize the ant hill called the Pentagon. Symington called for the most thorough housecleaning ever suggested for the military. The group recommended that:

The separate departments of Army, Navy, and Air Force, with their secretaries, undersecretaries, and assistant secretaries, be abolished. All defense funds be appropriated directly to the Secretary of Defense, who would have authority to spend them as he decided. The Joint Chiefs of Staff be replaced by a Military Advisory Council made up of senior officers who would be permanently separated from their respective services. The council be headed by a Joint Staff Chairman who would be principal military adviser to the President and the Secretary of Defense. The three services maintain their identity but be subordinate to three separate commands: a Strategic Command, responsible for the missions of an all-out nuclear war; a Tactical Command, responsible for a limited war operation, and a Defense Command, responsible for all continental defense missions. A Civil Defense Command, somewhat lower in the scale of importance than the first three, be composed of the National Guard and the Reserve of the three services and be responsible for civil defense.

Symington estimated this plan would save $8,000,000,000. The plan received a cool reception from Kennedy, who described it as "interesting and constructive . . . I know [it] will be carefully analyzed by the Congress and the incoming Administration."

Kennedy made his long-heralded visit to Eisenhower in December, driving from his Georgetown home in a cream-colored Lincoln. There had been some bad feeling between the men. Eisenhower had resented some of the attacks on his Administration, while Kennedy's ego was still bruised over Eisenhower's scornful campaign reference to him as "this young genius." But the older man greeted the young genius with a cordial smile and an outstretched hand. The oldest President and the youngest President-elect talked for an hour and forty-five minutes, each sometimes referring to notes on the major problems. The talk was on disarmament, the gold deficit, the recession and unemployment. Kennedy asked and Eisenhower told him of his personal impressions of Khrushchev, de Gaulle, Adenauer, and Macmillan. Kennedy admired Eisenhower's clean desk in contrast to his own, cluttered with papers and books. At this point, it is said, Eisenhower said something to Kennedy that made the younger man laugh. When their personal meeting was ended, Eisenhower took Kennedy into the Cabinet room, where he met Herter, Defense Secretary Thomas Gates, and Treasury Secretary Robert Anderson. Kennedy plied them with questions for an hour and fifteen minutes.

After the meeting, Kennedy said: "The President was extremely helpful. I want to express my thanks to him." Eisenhower later told some friends that he had always considered Kennedy a "young whippersnapper" but he had been tremendously impressed by his knowledge and personality at the White House meeting.

By mid-December Kennedy had completed the roster of his Cabinet. In some cases the appointees were men whom he had never met, whose names had been submitted to him after meticulous screening and study and exploratory conversations. In some cases, too, the appointees were not his first choices but compromise selections, chosen because of violent bloc opposition to the original candidate, as in the case of Senator Fulbright. Other compromises were based on purely political considerations. In at least one case Kennedy refused to compromise despite the violent protests of many leading Democrats inside and outside Congress.

His Secretary of State was Dean Rusk, at the time of the appointment president of the Rockefeller Foundation. Now fifty-one, Rusk, a former college professor, had previously held high posts in the State Department; he was Assistant Secretary for Far Eastern Affairs when the Korean war began. During the Second World War he campaigned in China with General Stilwell and rose to a colonelcy.

C. Douglas Dillon, Eisenhower's Under Secretary of State (he had previously been Ambassador to France), was chosen as Secretary of the Treasury without regard to the protests of Kennedy's own party leaders. Kennedy considered Dillon, a respected Wall Street banker before he took on his Ambassadorship, the right man for the job and refused to be swayed. Dillon himself accepted the appointment against the wishes and the urgings of both Eisenhower and Nixon, who did not want to see the outgoing Administration linked in any way with its successor.

Some Democratic protests had also greeted Kennedy's selection of the forty-four-year-old president of the Ford Motor Company, Robert S. McNamara, as Secretary of Defense. Noted at once for the scholarly methods by which he reached decisions and the vigor with which he executed them, McNamara was at least a nominal Republican who had migrated rather suddenly from the academic cloister to the power and the fleshpots of Detroit without losing his sense of proportion or of values.

By far the most controversial Cabinet appointee was the Attorney General-designate, the President-elect's thirty-five-year-old brother, Robert, who had managed his election campaign. Robert Kennedy had served in the Justice Department just after his graduation from Harvard Law School and had proved his abilities as counsel to the Senate committee investigating labor racketeering; but his opponents argued that the scope of the post for which he had been chosen was far wider than anything for which his experience had qualified him. Even men who had worked for John Kennedy's election deplored the choice of his brother: one of the principal functions of the Attorney General, they pointed out, is to aid and advise the President in selecting new federal judges at all levels and it was obvious that Robert Kennedy could not pretend to the knowledge or the experience for such a rôle. The question of nepotism was never seriously raised since, from the economic point of view, none of the Kennedys needed a government salary.

J. Edward Day, vice-president of the Prudential Insurance Company and a lawyer, was appointed Postmaster General after the position had been offered to and refused by Representative William Dawson, a Chicago Negro, in what was said to have been a pre-arranged "deal," the rumors of which Dawson refused to answer. Day had served as state insurance director in Illinois when Adlai Stevenson was governor.

An outspoken critic of Ezra Benson, Eisenhower's Secretary of Agriculture, was chosen to succeed him. Orville L. Freeman had served three terms as Governor of Minnesota, losing his fourth bid for the office in the election that made Kennedy President.

Arthur J. Goldberg, one of the most articulate of labor's

top strategists, was chosen to be Secretary of Labor. General counsel to the United Steel Workers of America since 1948, and special counsel to the AFL-CIO, he immediately severed all his connections with the labor movement and with his law partnerships. To balance him as Secretary of Commerce, Kennedy nominated Governor Luther Hodges of North Carolina, who worked his way through college, started his business life as a textile-mill worker and became general manager of twenty-nine mills and then vice-president of Marshall Field & Company.

The new Secretary of the Interior, Representative Stewart L. Udall of Arizona, was a lawyer before he entered Congress. It was he who, delighted by Robert Frost's wit when the poet was consultant to the Library of Congress, became his friend and introduced him to Kennedy.

The appointment of Governor Abraham Ribicoff of Connecticut as Secretary of Health, Education, and Welfare was a shrewd selection: it put at the head of a government department dispensing vast sums of federal money a man noted for his fiscal soundness as well as for his broad social sympathies. And there were those who complained: "Why Ribicoff? He's opposed to speeding, floods, and unbalanced budgets."

Several aspects of the proposed Cabinet were noteworthy. Its average age was forty-seven; the youngest member was thirty-five, the oldest was sixty-two. All were college graduates—four from Harvard; one had graduated *summa cum laude* and three were members of Phi Beta Kappa; six also held law degrees. Eight were veterans of the Second World War, and most of them saw combat; none rose higher than a colonelcy. Two clues to Kennedy's thinking were revealed in sidelights on his selections. "For God's sake, Orville," he urged Governor Freeman, "find yourself an Under Secretary who can carry on a civilized conversation." And, when Professor James Tobin of Yale, whom Kennedy was determined to have for his Council of Economic Advisers, balked, tell-

ing Kennedy he would not tailor his economic views to fit
the Administration's political exigencies "because, Mr. President, I am what you might call an ivory-tower economist,"
Kennedy reassured him quickly: "That's all right, Professor,
I am what you might call an ivory-tower President."

But it was also evident that he would be a President who
could cope with the world outside the ivory tower. He had
often spoken plainly of his belief that the President should
exercise his tremendous power; his selection of Rusk, generally considered primarily an administrator, gave rise to the
belief that Kennedy, like Roosevelt, would be in effect his
own Secretary of State; he never really discouraged it.
Arthur Krock of *The New York Times* did not hesitate to
say that the new Cabinet would be "a disciplined lot with
a clear insight into who is boss and no patience with mav-
ericks."

Kennedy turned his attention next to the legislative
branch and called to a conference Vice-President-elect
Johnson, Senator Mansfield of Montana, the probable
Senate majority leader, and House Speaker Rayburn. They
spent two days with Kennedy in Palm Beach, concerting
their plans to deal, in Kennedy's words, with "some of the
problems involved in the orderly transition of responsibility,
and also some of the matters which will come before the
Administration and the Congress in the winter of 1961."
Out of this meeting came evidence that Johnson, as Vice-
President, would be no figurehead: he was appointed to
head the President's advisory council on space and, in addition, the Government Contract Compliance Committee. In
this latter capacity Johnson was specifically charged with a
directive to end racial, religious, and other discrimination in
employment by holders of contracts to furnish products and
services to the government.

Unemployment, which stood then at 4.5 million, or
about 6.3 per cent of the total work force of 71.1 million
(a figure that excluded the 2.5 million in the armed forces),

and what Kennedy called "the lack of vigor in the economy at this time" were major matters of concern in the meeting. Plans were laid to introduce as early as possible legislation relating to medical care for the aged, aid to education, public housing, an increase in the $1-an-hour minimum wage, and federal aid to depressed areas. Kennedy took the occasion, too, to halt the rumors that he planned to visit one or more chiefs of government in Europe during the spring.

The day after Christmas, Johnson returned to Palm Beach for another conference called by Kennedy. This meeting was attended also by Dillon, Senator Kerr of Oklahoma, and Representative John J. Rooney of Brooklyn. Kerr was there principally because he was slated to succeed Johnson as chairman of the Senate Committee on Aeronautics and Space Science, and the expansion of American efforts in this field was a major item on the agenda. Rooney's presence resulted from the fact that he was a powerful member of the House Appropriations Committee and had long been instrumental in cutting appropriations for the State Department at home and abroad. Kennedy wanted to end Rooney's opposition in order to be able to appoint to key ambassadorial posts men whose private means were insufficient to permit them to serve unless federal allowances were liberalized. Kennedy's reliance on the close friendship between Johnson and Rooney was vindicated when the latter yielded.

In addition to the usual fixed ambassadors, Kennedy appointed a roving envoy to perform special missions for the President and the Secretary of State. His choice was W. Averell Harriman, once Roosevelt's Ambassador to Russia. But Harriman, he made it clear, would serve as a representative without the unusual powers that President Wilson had given to Colonel House or President Roosevelt had conferred on Harry Hopkins. An equally important, if less spectacular, appointment was that of Robert V. Roosa as Under Secretary of the Treasury for Monetary Affairs. An official of the Federal Reserve Bank in New York, a member of Phi Beta Kappa and a Rhodes scholar with a doctorate in economics, Roosa was to be charged with the management of the public debt, amounting to some $290 billion, and with the direction of the Treasury's relations with the Federal Reserve Board.

A few days earlier Kennedy had received from James M. Landis the first of the studies he had commissioned after his election. Landis, assigned to analyze the Government's administrative and regulatory agencies, had been sharply critical of the management of these under both Truman and Eisenhower. He emphasized deterioration in the quality of personnel both at the top and in the staffs, and he urged the President-elect to press for five immediate remedial steps:

1. A Congressional grant of power to the President to reorganize any of the agencies, subject only to a veto by a concurrent resolution of both Houses of Congress.
2. Presidential designation of the chairmen of all agencies (some bodies elected their own chiefs) and greater authority for the chairmen in hiring and in handling budgets.
3. A reorganization plan to enable any agency to delegate decisions to single members, panels or staff examiners, to be reviewed by the agency's head only at his discretion.
4. The creation, in the President's Executive Office, of an arm for the co-ordination and development of transportation, communications and energy policies (Landis' study was especially critical of the work of the agencies in those fields).
5. The establishment of a Presidential office to oversee the regulatory agencies.

Kennedy's reaction was prompt: he appointed Landis a temporary special assistant to the President, assigned to drafting the reorganizational plans he had recommended. As former chairman of the Securities and Exchange Commission and of the Civil Aeronautics Board, as well as former dean of Harvard Law School, Landis could claim a thorough background in administration and organization.

The President-elect crossed party lines to designate Mc-George Bundy as special assistant for national security affairs. Dean of the Faculty of Arts and Sciences at Harvard, Bundy was a scholar in the field of foreign affairs. He was to become the factotum of the National Security Council, one of the most secret of all Government bodies, whose basic task is the co-ordination of domestic, military, and foreign policies relating to national security and the drafting of long-range plans in the defense and foreign spheres. The appointment of Bundy was bitterly opposed by Massachusetts' Democratic Governor, Foster Furcolo, who denounced it publicly and threatened a personal *démarche* to Kennedy; but the President-elect ignored him.

Plans for a quiet New Year's weekend had been made but they were pushed aside, first by preparation for a meeting early in January to discuss farm problems and then by a succession of conferences. Early on New Year's morning a greeting arrived in Palm Beach from Premier Khrushchev and Chairman Leonid Brezhnev of the Soviet Presidium, containing the conventional wishes for the season and the suggestion that, under the new Administration, relations between the United States and Russia "will develop on a new and reasonable basis—on the basis of the joint desire of the peoples of our countries for peace and friendship." The President-elect replied formally and correctly, entirely ignoring the latter part of the Russian message and thus tacitly rejecting any Soviet criticism of Eisenhower's conduct of Russian-American relations. Nor would Kennedy comment on Khrushchev's declaration the preceding evening that he might be willing, in view of the change of government here, to forget about the unfortunate U-2 incident.

It was on New Year's Day that Kennedy pledged top priority after his inauguration to the relief of distressed areas. He had just received the report of another of his task forces, that assigned, under Senator Paul Douglas of Illinois, to study the problems of these areas and recommend solutions. The task force, made up of representatives of labor, business, and government, offered four primary recommendations:

1. An executive order doubling the Government's distribution of surplus foods in distressed areas.
2. The passage of the redevelopment bill twice vetoed by Eisenhower, which would provide almost $370 million, mostly in low-interest loans, to help economically crippled areas to attract new industry or expand existing plants.
3. Federal grants to the states, as opposed to the loans made in the 1958 recession, for the extension and liberalization of unemployment benefits.
4. Special public-works programs for depressed areas.

Pointing out that such areas accounted for 20 to 25 million of the population, Douglas' group also urged that Government contracts be channeled to such regions and that their labor forces be trained or retrained in new skills. Other recommendations presented to the President-elect included measures for soil conservation, the development of natural resources, accelerated research to find new uses for coal and other minerals, and the creation of a youth conservation corps. Kennedy's warm reaction to the report of the task force indicated a probable early trend in his Administration.

Meanwhile he was still striving to fill all the key posts in the Government before Inauguration Day. In line with his plans for an early major test of Russian intentions and attitudes, he appointed John J. McCloy, a New York banker who had been Assistant Secretary of War and then United States High Commissioner in West Germany, as his principal adviser and negotiator on disarmament. At the same time, Kennedy gave himself a powerful weapon for the inescapable struggle between the President and Congress by choosing Lawrence F. O'Brien, one of his oldest Massachusetts political associates, to be special assistant to the President for personnel and Congressional relations: in other words, boss of patronage, which was obviously to be used as a lever to expedite Kennedy's legislative program. In Congress itself, Speaker Rayburn was preparing vital assistance for the President by planning to purge from the powerful House Rules Committee an outspoken Kennedy opponent, Representative William M. Colmer of Mississippi, and to replace him with a "safe" party regular—Colmer was one of the Southern Democrats whose coalition with Republicans had so often stalemated the liberals. But this project was finally abandoned for the smoother one of simply enlarging the committee and appointing the right men to the new seats. The Senate was girding for the perennial fight on the filibuster, though both Kennedy and Mansfield had indicated rather clearly that they would prefer to defer this procedural battle rather than jeopardize the Administration's program at the very start.

Day by day the President-elect was filling the gaps in his staff. Roger Jones, appointed chairman of the United States Civil Service Committee by Eisenhower, was selected as Deputy Under Secretary of State for Administration. From New York, where he was now working in order to be able to maintain closer contact with key aides, Kennedy chose John W. Macy, a university vice-president, to succeed Jones. He then telephoned to Governor S. Ernest Vandiver of Georgia to ask whether the Governor would become Secretary of War. But so much resentment was manifested by Negro leaders at the thought of a militant segregationist at the head of the desegregated army that within a few days Vandiver politely declined because of the pressure of duties at home.

Meanwhile more task-force reports were arriving on the President-elect's desk as new crises gathered beyond the borders. Kennedy's task force studying the needs of the country's schools proposed a $9.4-billion program for the next four and a half years, embracing loans and grants to improve public schools and both public and private universities and colleges by increasing plant, raising teachers' salaries, and reducing bonded indebtedness. The $1.4 billion in grants proposed for the private institutions would have to be matched by them; in addition, they would be eligible for loans totaling $2.15 billion. Aid to segregationist schools was not specifically advocated or condemned; that question was left for future settlement. But both Kennedy and Ribicoff, under whose department its implementation would fall, considered the study extremely valuable, though Kennedy was dubious whether the nation's resources would enable it to take on the whole program immediately.

The Eisenhower Administration was keeping Kennedy and Rusk constantly informed of mounting tension abroad, especially in Cuba and Laos. Before the official rupture with Cuba, the State Department advised Rusk what was planned and offered to defer the move if Kennedy wished. Rusk telephoned Kennedy to give him the news and receive his views; but, with what political experts called outstanding sagacity, Kennedy refused to express any opinion whatever on the proposal: he could accept no responsibility until after his inauguration. Similarly, every change in the Laotian picture was reported to Kennedy and Rusk and they maintained their aloofness.

A minor domestic storm was blowing up, however, as a result of the report on aid to education. Francis Cardinal Spellman denounced the exclusion of parochial and other religious schools from the proposed federal program; he declared that the parents of students in such schools would be unjustly taxed and the students would be deprived of educational necessaries "because their parents choose for them a God-centered education." But the President-elect, who had always emphasized his opposition to federal help for private and religious schools, refused to reply.

His attention—and the nation's—were soon drawn to other things. Kennedy's economic task force, headed by Professor Paul A. Samuelson of the Massachusetts Institute of Technology, completed its work with the warning that, unless the economy reversed its downward course, a temporary reduction in income taxes might be required in order to increase purchasing power. The experts dashed the hopes of those who had expected that, in the manner of Roosevelt's advisers, they would advocate a vast pump-priming program of public works; they relied instead on the flexible taxation system that they envisaged, asking for legislation to vest the President with power to alter tax rates fixed by Congress when circumstances warranted. Anticipating a deficit rather than the surplus forecast by the Eisenhower Administration for the current fiscal year, the report looked nevertheless to a long-range period of successive budgetary surpluses; meanwhile it urged such steps as the reduction of mortgage interest to stimulate expansion in the construction industry. The AFL-CIO simultaneously announced its own recovery program, which went to Rooseveltian lengths in its advocacy of heavy federal spending.

On the same day, barely two weeks before the inauguration, Kennedy, Johnson, and Freeman conferred with leaders of fourteen farm organizations, who agreed unanimously to co-operate with the new Administration in drafting new farm legislation. At the agricultural right stood the American Farm Bureau Federation, which had generally supported the Eisenhower Administration's flexible price supports; at the other end was the National Farmers' Union, backing the 90 per cent parity price supports pledged in Kennedy's platform. Both groups, as well as all those between the two extremes, agreed that compromises would have to be made, and they set a date in the post-inauguration week for the start of work.

The task forces were speeding their reports as the inauguration neared. A group headed by Dr. Max Millikan, director of the Center for International Studies at M.I.T., had examined and amended Kennedy's campaign proposal for an international "peace corps" of young Americans who would assist under-developed nations. Kennedy had suggested that volunteers for the corps be exempted from the draft; Millikan and his colleagues opposed this, contending there would be a wealth of volunteers without any such bait. He suggested an immediate pilot program of some hundreds of such young people, to serve as a proving ground for the program, which had already won enthusiastic acclaim abroad.

Kennedy also received a report from his housing study group. This force urged a new Cabinet department to supervise all housing and urban-development activities; a new subsidy program for low-income housing; increased assistance to nonprofit corporations building housing for the elderly; changes and expansion in the Federal Housing Administration, aiding the building of single-family dwelling units; grants for urban renewal and mass transportation facilities; help for orderly suburban development, and the expansion of the farm housing program.

As this report was made public, Kennedy announced the appointment of W. Willard Wirtz, law partner of Adlai Stevenson, as Under Secretary of Labor. People who professed to know Kennedy's plans for other unfilled posts were debating whether he was making the greater inroads on Harvard's faculty or Stevenson's law firm. At the same time, Senator Mansfield disclosed that he was marshaling Senate support for the quickest possible confirmation of the new Cabinet, preferably within twenty-four hours of the inauguration.

Kennedy himself stated the philosophy underlying his appointments and his program on January 9, when, departing briefly from the business of preparing to take up the Presidency, he went to Boston to attend a meeting of the Board of Overseers of Harvard University, of which he remained a member, and then addressed the Massachusetts Legislature. "History," he said, "will not judge our efforts—and a government cannot be selected—merely on the basis of color or even party affiliation. Neither will competence and loyalty and stature, while essential to the utmost, suffice in times such as these. For, of those to whom much is given, much is required. . . . Our success or failure, in whatever office we may hold, will be measured by the answers to four questions:

"First, were we truly men of courage—with the courage to stand up to one's enemies—and the courage to stand up, when necessary, to one's own associates—the courage to resist public pressure as well as private greed?

"Secondly, were we truly men of judgment . . . of our own mistakes as well as the mistakes of others—with enough wisdom to know what we did not know, and enough candor to admit it?

"Third, were we truly men of integrity . . . ?

"Finally, were we truly men of dedication—with an honor mortgaged to no single individual or group, and compromised by no private obligation or aim, but devoted solely to serving the public good and the national interest?"

Kennedy waited hardly long enough to hear the cheers of his audience before he was on his way back to New York to close his pre-inaugural headquarters there and go on to Washington and his Palm Beach home. In New York he received still another task-force report, on medical care for the aged; a greatly broadened program to cover 14.5 million people was advocated, tied directly to the Social Security system and financed by an increase in the payroll taxes on employers and employees alike. In Washington the President-elect conferred with outgoing Secretary of the Treasury Anderson on various problems, including the vexing one of the balance of payments and the fiscal aspects of the space program. To be informed on the latter, Johnson and Kerr also attended. Kennedy then spent some time with An-

derson's successor, Dillon, and Under Secretary-designate
Henry H. Fowler. Other conferences were conducted in
transit and between appointments.

The President-elect reached Palm Beach a few hours
ahead of the report of his task force on space problems.
Headed by Dr. Jerome B. Wiesner of M.I.T., whom Kennedy immediately appointed as his special assistant for science and technology, the group declared that Russia would
probably put a man in space before the United States could
do so, adding that more money alone would not enable us
to catch up. Wiesner, long an expert in radar and the development of weapons systems, was critcial of past and present
organization and management of the nation's space program, citing lack of planning and direction as well as dupli-
cation of effort by the various branches of the armed forces.
He urged greater co-ordination, unified responsibility within
the military establishments, a review and redefinition of
aims, both military and civilian, and industry-Government
administration of the civilian space program.

An equally sober note was sounded by the task force investigating disarmament. Wiesner was a member of this
group, as were Paul H. Nitze, Assistant Secretary-designate
of Defense for International Security Affairs, and Professor
Richard E. Neustadt of Columbia, special consultant on
government organization. Though the United States, Britain and Russia had been observing an unofficial moratorium on nuclear-weapons tests since October 31, 1958, the
task force urged a lengthy postponement of the talks on
such tests that were scheduled to be resumed in Geneva in
February. "A hiatus which resulted in the production of
sound positions would be time gained rather than lost," the
report observed . . . "Real accomplishments can be expected only if basic policy decisions are made. Since the
United States has never developed such basic policies in
the past, the policy-planning process could well be an extended one." Meanwhile, the President-elect was urged to

refrain from any specific statements in his own person; the Eisenhower Administration was praised for its caution in arms negotiations with Russia but criticized for its own lack of concrete policy. The document as a whole was a disappointment to all those who, like Stevenson a year earlier, had been calling for immediate permanent cessation of all nuclear testing, unilaterally if necessary.

Kennedy continued his methodical filling of top-level posts. He had asked all the members of the President's Science Advisory Committee, except its chairman, to continue in their posts; but he chose a new chairman for the Atomic Energy Commission: Dr. Glenn T. Seaborg, who had won the Nobel Prize for chemistry in 1951. Chancellor of the University of California in Berkeley, Seaborg was enough of a skeptical realist to wonder whether nuclear disarmament could be achieved with adequate safeguards against treachery, enough of a practical idealist to believe it "vital that we maintain a continuing evaluation of every possible approach." An outstanding research scholar, he was also a first-class administrator.

Though Kennedy, absorbed in his tasks and his plans, ignored personal attacks, they were still being made, especially in those quarters that suddenly discovered after Roosevelt's death how dangerously ill he had been when he when he headed the Grand Alliance (the same quarters had, however, never feared any impairment of Eisenhower's fitness regardless of his illnesses). Certain mass-circulation newspapers in New York and Chicago questioned editorially the wisdom of having elected to the Presidency a man whose lingering diseases were such that he was compelled to carry at all times large dosages of medicines whose side effects might well lead him to rash decisions on the spur of the moment and even to "shooting from the hip" in a moment of grave crisis. *Today's Health*, published by the American Medical Association (which, as a group, firmly opposed all Kennedy's thinking on medical subjects), disposed finally of the contention that he suffered from Addison's disease. "His barb-wire toughness," it added, had kept him "singularly free of health problems." He had indeed once suffered from an adrenal insufficiency, and he medicated orally against any possible aftermath. On the record and after exhaustive examination, his own physicians "find you fully capable of meeting any obligation of the Presidency without need for special medical treatment, unusual rest periods, or other limitations."

As the time neared for the President-elect's second meeting with the man he was to succeed, there was increasing evidence of the broad base of co-operation between the outgoing and the incoming Administrations. David Bell of Harvard, whom Kennedy had chosen to be Director of the Budget, was working closely with incumbent officials in the preparation of revisions of the final Eisenhower budget for Kennedy to recommend to Congress. There were frequent meetings between the old and new men in the other Government departments. Five days before the inauguration, outgoing Attorney General Rogers set a precedent by holding a luncheon for his successor, the aides of both, and the entire Supreme Court.

The next day, as Kennedy was preparing to leave Palm Beach again, he received a lengthy report on natural resources. While there was little that was novel in the document, it emphasized again such dangers as reckless depletion and stream pollution. There was a reminiscence of 1933 in its recommendation for the establishment of a youth corps to expedite such tasks as conservation and reforestation.

The President-elect's own economic resources were taken out of the field of controversy when he announced that he had liquidated all his holdings and created a trust limited to investment in Government bonds. Secretary-designate of Defense McNamara, no doubt remembering the furor over Secretary Wilson when the president of General Motors tried to retain his stock in that and other corporations after his appointment, had already liquidated his Ford holdings and set up an investment trust, but the Senate Armed Services Committee, which had to approve his nomination, was not satisfied. McNamara therefore offered to amend his arrangement to suit the committee and to publish his income-tax returns; but he insisted on retaining the right to choose his own investment counselor. Though committee members had indicated privately that McNamara would be confirmed, he was instructed to draw a new trust agreement that would preclude the purchase of stocks of any company doing or likely to do business with the Defense Department.

Despite this minor clash, McNamara was faring better with the Senators than with the AFL-CIO. Joseph D. Keenan, a vice-president of the AFL-CIO, had been suggested as Assistant Secretary of Defense for Manpower, but McNamara refused to have him, giving no reason. George Meany, AFL-CIO president, recalling that Keenan had been vice-chairman of the War Production Board during the Second World War, voiced his suspicion that McNamara had acted solely on the basis of Keenan's union position. Keenan himself, not having asked for the job, merely shrugged off the whole incident.

Kennedy, meanwhile, was conferring in New York with Governor Luis Muñoz Marin of Puerto Rico in addition to lunching with Harriman and Hugh Gaitskell, leader of the British Labor Party, and seeing his tailor and his dentist in preparation for the inauguration. Out of the talks with Muñoz Marin came a promise to make Puerto Rico "a meeting place and workshop" for the United States and the countries of Latin America. The President-elect then left for Washington, where he was to meet Eisenhower at nine the next morning. As he left he made it plain to his White House staff that he expected everyone on the job at nine the morning after inauguration, though it was a Saturday. He himself was punctual for his appointment with Eisenhower, and for two hours the President and the President-elect discussed the world situation, first alone and then with their respective Secretaries of State, Defense, and the Treasury. All the outgoing officials promised their help whenever needed, and Eisenhower pledged that he would not be second-guessing his successor from the side lines; he added, however, that he would not hesitate to speak publicly in opposition if the Kennedy Administration sought to change American policy toward Communist China. As he left the White House, Kennedy said of the men whom he and his associates were to succeed: "I don't think we've asked for anything that they haven't done."

He came out to the portico, where a reporter asked: "Are you excited?" The city was vibrating with memories of 1933 and its flood tide of fervent hopes; of 1953 and its anxious tension, as of a conquered city; the nation's newspapers were black with predictions that the new President would be a radical, a cautious moderate, a shrewd manipulator. As if he himself were fascinated by all the prophecies and wondered which would be proved true, Kennedy turned to his questioner and answered reflectively: "Interested."

5. The Inauguration

For the first time in forty years, power was transferred from one party to the other in an atmosphere of cordiality and co-operation. When Herbert Hoover yielded his place to Franklin Roosevelt in 1933, the outgoing President was depressed and bitter, impervious to the amicable overtures of his successor as they rode down Pennsylvania Avenue together in an open car. Twenty years later, Harry Truman sat beside Dwight Eisenhower in an armor of hostility matched by Eisenhower's.

But, contrary to all custom, which dictates that the President-elect merely stop at the White House to be joined in his car by his predecessor, Eisenhower suggested to Senator and Mrs. Kennedy that they might wish to arrive earlier than the official time in order to have coffee with the Eisenhowers and fortify themselves for the abnormal cold weather. The gesture was characteristic of a man who

wanted friends, not enemies; who had the grace to acknowledge publicly, after his first conference with his successor,
that he had mistakenly underestimated the younger man.

The Kennedys, after the President-elect had attended
Mass, drove to the White House in the official Presidential
automobile, which Eisenhower had sent to pick them up;
he came bareheaded from the Executive Mansion to receive
them, just after 11 A.M. Some minutes later, the old and
new Vice-Presidents arrived with their wives, followed by a
few Congressional leaders. A half-hour later the whole
party emerged, led by Eisenhower and Kennedy. The new
President had requested that top hats be worn and Eisenhower, who had forced Truman to wear a black Homburg,
had acceded. Eisenhower and Kennedy posed for pictures,
chatting and smiling; observers noted that the older man
was also the more relaxed. Then they entered the first car,
accompanied by Sam Rayburn, Speaker of the House, and
Senator John Sparkman, chairman of the Inaugural Committee. As the men left the portico of the White House,
Mrs. Eisenhower and Mrs. Kennedy came out together, and
Mrs. Kennedy stepped back to allow Mrs. Eisenhower to
precede her into their car.

The route had been cleared of the eight-inch snow that
had fallen the day before, and the sun was glaring, But the
wind was sharp and the crowd, smaller than had been expected, had relatively little breath for cheering. During the
trip to the Capitol the stream of conversation between
President and President-elect was uninterrupted; their faces
were animated, they smiled frequently; later, as they sat side
by side in the Capitol Rotunda, waiting for the ceremony to
begin, Kennedy became more taciturn and listened as Eisenhower gestured to emphasize his points. From time to time
the President turned to Mrs. Kennedy, at his right, to include her in the conversation. Almost a half-hour late,
Sparkman finally began the proceedings, introducing Rich-

ard Cardinal Cushing of Boston to deliver the invocation after Marian Anderson had sung "The Star-Spangled Banner."

As the tall, gray-haired prelate shot his clearly articulated syllables into the microphones in a voice harsh with reminiscences of one preaching a crusade, smoke began to curl round his feet from the lectern before him. Within the lectern was an electric heater, placed there to keep the speakers' feet warm; there was fear of a short-circuit and perhaps a fire, and, as unobtrusively as possible, men brought water and fire extinguishers while the Cardinal spoke on as if he did not notice the commotion. As if everyone concerned were mindful of the political capital that had been made of Kennedy's Roman Catholicism, the Cardinal was followed at once by Archbishop Iakavos of New York, who heads the Greek Orthodox Archdiocese of North and South America. The Archbishop was brief and rather eloquent; at the conclusion of the prayer, Kennedy made the sign of the cross as he had done when the Cardinal finished. Further prayer was offered by the Rev. Dr. John Barclay, of the Central Christian Church of the Disciples of Christ in Austin, Texas, which Vice-President Johnson attends; again Kennedy, as if automatically, began to cross himself at the end and then converted the movement into one of brushing the hair from his forehead.

Sparkman introduced Robert Frost as a distinguished American poet "who will recite an original composition," and the hatless old man, especially invited by Kennedy to grace the inauguration with his poem, "The Gift Outright," stepped to the lectern, his white hair blowing in the strong wind. He began to read a prefatory poem he had composed for the occasion, but the combination of wind and glare was too much and he broke off abruptly: "I am not having good light here at all." Johnson rose and tried to break the glare with his hat, but Frost waved him aside. "This," he said, "was to have been a preface to a poem that I can say

to you without reading it." His head and shoulders went
back and his voice rang clear in the iambic pentameter of
the poem Kennedy had requested.

Speaker Rayburn administered the oath of office to Johnson, who showed one of his rare occasions of nerves and
had difficulty repeating the phrases of the oath, one of
which he altered slightly. Then the Chief Justice of the
United States, Earl Warren, stepped forward, and John
Kennedy rose, slipping swiftly out of his overcoat. The
Kennedy family's old Douay Bible, containing the geneal-
ogy down to the President-elect's newly born son, was before him, and he laid his right hand upon it, standing
straight and solemn. In a clear, grave voice he pledged himself to the duties of his office and then, without resuming his
coat, he began his inaugural address—the second shortest in
history, it was of fewer than 1,400 words, elegantly austere
in its rhetoric, simple, direct and forceful in its content.

Vice President Johnson, Mr. Speaker, Mr. Chief Justice, President Eisenhower, Vice President Nixon, President Truman,
Reverend Clergy, fellow citizens:

We observe today not a victory of party but a celebration of
freedom—symbolizing an end as well as a beginning—signifying
renewal as well as change. For I have sworn before you and Almighty God the same solemn oath our forebears prescribed
nearly a century and three-quarters ago.

The world is very different now. For man holds in his mortal
hands the power to abolish all forms of human poverty and all
forms of human life. And yet the same revolutionary beliefs for
which our forebears fought are still at issue around the globe—
the belief that the rights of man come not from the generosity
of the state but from the hand of God.

We dare not forget today that we are the heirs of that first
revolution. Let the word go forth from this time and place to
friend and foe alike, that the torch has been passed to a new
generation of Americans—born in this century, tempered by
war, disciplined by a hard and bitter peace, proud of our ancient
heritage—and unwilling to witness or permit the slow undoing

of those human rights to which this nation has always been committed, and to which we are committed today at home and around the world.

Let every nation know, whether it wishes us well or ill, that we shall pay any price, bear any burden, meet any hardship, support any friend, oppose any foe to assure the survival and the success of liberty.

This much we pledge—and more.

To those old allies whose cultural and spiritual origins we share, we pledge the loyalty of faithful friends. United, there is little we cannot do in a host of new cooperative ventures. Divided, there is little we can do—for we dare not meet a powerful challenge at odds and split asunder.

To those new states whom we welcome to the ranks of the free, we pledge our word that one form of colonial control shall not have passed away merely to be replaced by a far more iron tyranny. We shall not always expect to find them supporting our view. But we shall always hope to find them strongly supporting their own freedom—and to remember that, in the past, those who foolishly sought power by riding the back of the tiger ended up inside.

To those peoples in the huts and villages of half the globe struggling to break the bonds of mass misery, we pledge our best efforts to help them help themselves, for whatever period is required—not because the Communists may be doing it, not because we seek their votes, but because it is right. If a free society cannot help the many who are poor, it can not save the few who are rich.

To our sister republics south of our border, we offer a special pledge—to convert our good words into good deeds—in a new alliance for progress—to assist free men and free governments in casting off the chains of poverty. But this peaceful revolution of hope cannot become the prey of hostile powers. Let all our neighbors know that we shall join with them to oppose aggression or subversion anywhere in the Americas. And let every other power know that this hemisphere intends to remain the master of its own house.

To that world assembly of sovereign states, the United Nations, our last best hope in an age where the instruments of war have far outpaced the instruments of peace, we renew our pledge of support—to prevent it from becoming merely a forum for invective—to strengthen its shield of the new and the weak—and to enlarge the area in which its writ may run.

Finally, to those nations who would make themselves our adversary, we offer not a pledge but a request: that both sides begin anew the quest for peace, before the dark powers of destruction unleashed by science engulf all humanity in planned or accidental self-destruction.

We dare not tempt them with weakness. For only when our arms are sufficient beyond doubt can we be certain beyond doubt that they will never be employed.

But neither can two great and powerful groups of nations take comfort from our present course—both sides overburdened by the cost of modern weapons, both rightly alarmed by the steady spread of the deadly atom, yet both racing to alter that uncertain balance of terror that stays the hand of mankind's final war.

So let us begin anew—remembering on both sides that civility is not a sign of weakness, and sincerity is always subject to proof. Let us never negotiate out of fear. But let us never fear to negotiate.

Let both sides explore what problems unite us instead of belaboring those problems which divide us.

Let both sides, for the first time, formulate serious and precise proposals for the inspection and control of arms—and bring the absolute power to destroy other nations under the absolute control of all nations.

Let both sides seek to invoke the wonders of science instead of its terrors. Together let us explore the stars, conquer the deserts, eradicate disease, tap the ocean depths and encourage the arts and commerce.

Let both sides unite to heed in all corners of the earth the command of Isaiah—to "undo the heavy burdens . . . [and] let the oppressed go free."

And if a beachhead of cooperation may push back the jungles of suspicion, let both sides join in creating a new endeavor—not a new balance of power, but a new world of law, where the strong are just and the weak secure and the peace preserved.

All this will not be finished in the first 100 days. Nor will it be finished in the first 1,000 days, nor in the life of this Administration, nor even perhaps in our lifetime on this planet. But let us begin.

In your hands, my fellow citizens, more than mine, will rest the final success or failure of our course. Since this country was founded, each generation of Americans has been summoned to give testimony to its national loyalty. The graves of young Americans who answered the call to service surround the globe.

Now the trumpet summons us again—not as a call to bear arms, though arms we need—not as a call to battle, though embattled we are—but a call to bear the burden of a long twilight struggle year in and year out, "rejoicing in hope, patient in tribulation"—a struggle against the common enemies of man: tyranny, poverty, disease and war itself.

Can we forge against these enemies a grand and global alliance, north and south, east and west, that can assure a more fruitful life for all mankind? Will you join in that historic effort?

In the long history of the world, only a few generations have been granted the rôle of defending freedom in its hour of maximum danger. I do not shrink from this responsibility—I welcome it. I do not believe that any of us would exchange places with any other people or any other generation. The energy, the faith, the devotion which we bring to this endeavor will light our country and all who serve it—and the glow from that fire can truly light the world.

And so, my fellow-Americans: ask not what your country can do for you—ask what you can do for your country.

My fellow-citizens of the world: ask not what America will do for you, but what together we can do for the freedom of man.

Finally, whether you are citizens of America or citizens of the world, ask of us here the same high standards of strength and sacrifice which we ask of you. With a good conscience our only sure reward, with history the final judge of our deeds, let us go forth to lead the land we love, asking His blessing and His help, but knowing that here on earth God's work must truly be our own.

There were fourteen interruptions, created by the applause of the crowd, in which even Eisenhower frequently joined. Obviously the basic aspirations of America at home and abroad had not altered; and at home and abroad the response was surprisingly uniform in its approval; only the Communist bloc remained silent. "It was," *The Guardian* commented, its Manchester voice virtually the spokesman for all in the free world, "the word of a courageous man speaking to a courageous people." Those who had dismissed the new President a few months earlier as "Mickey Rooney with a Harvard diploma" sat silent, balancing their regret for the slur with a new respect for the man.

When the last applause had quieted, the benediction was pronounced by Rabbi Nelson Glueck, president of the Hebrew Union College of Cincinnati. The Marine Band played *Hail to the Chief* and President Kennedy, having shaken hands with the Chief Justice, Mr. Eisenhower, and Mr. Nixon, introduced his predecessor to Frost. Then, pressed for time, the Kennedys left for the inaugural luncheon. But, characteristically, President Kennedy put business first: before he began to eat, he performed his first Presidential duty, signing the official nominating papers for his Cabinet and for Adlai Stevenson, the new American Ambassador to the United Nations. And, before the luncheon was over, he had again pointedly reminded his staff that, though the first business day of his Administration was a Saturday, he would expect them to be ready for a conference at 9 A.M.

6. The United States in World Affairs

Probably no President of the United States took office in so confused an atmosphere of international crisis as that awaiting Kennedy. The tensions between the United States and Russia were more acute than at any time since the end of the Second World War; the new nations of Africa were playing East against West with a skill that in many instances would have done credit to a Metternich; the Eisenhower Administration's blunders had put the United States in the wrong on some points and on the defensive on almost all, and the initiative lay clearly with Russia whether in Berlin or in Southeast Asia.

The North Atlantic Treaty Organization was overtly impatient with American leadership. France, her economy virile again and her government, under President de Gaulle, more stable than a French regime could be expected to be, was claiming her old stature in the Western configuration. Communist China, fighting her way to industrialization and military strength, was no longer content to be led by Russia. Latin America, so long tacitly accepted as a pro-consulate of the United States, was playing both sides in what appeared to be a long-range effort to emerge completely independent of either at the expense of both.

The tone as well as the matter of Kennedy's inaugural address led a good part of the world to look, even if cautiously, for some relaxation of the manifold strains. The Soviet press and radio made no comment on the speech—in itself a not unhopeful sign. Perhaps the greatest enthusiasm came from Germany, fearful though she was that West Berlin might yet be lost to Russia, and from Britain's Liberal and Labor wings. The French were rather more reserved, remembering Kennedy's 1957 Senate speech urging independence for Algeria and resenting his present emphasis on the United Nations. Even Fidel Castro expressed the willingness of Cuba to accept the President's invitation to "begin anew the quest for peace"; Castro added that the danger of "Yankee invasion" seemed to have vanished with the Eisenhower Administration, which he, like everyone else, knew was helping his exiled enemies to organize an assault force in Florida and Guatemala.

The inaugural festivities were still in progress in Washington when Premier Khrushchev broke the icy silence he had maintained since the U-2 incident of May, 1960, to send Kennedy a warmly congratulatory cable, to which the President replied with the assurance that his Administration was "ready and anxious to cooperate" in any genuine move for peace. The next day Khrushchev summoned Ambassador Llewellyn E. Thompson Jr. to the Kremlin for the first time since September, and for several hours they explored the major problems between their two countries. It was not any sudden enthusiasm for Kennedy that had moved Khrushchev: Moscow did not yet know what direction the new President would take; but at least his advent marked the end of the previous phase and warranted risking what Khrushchev's cable to Kennedy had called a "step-by-step" approach to the sources of mutual distrust. At the same time, Khrushchev made it clear to Thompson that Soviet support for the Algerian rebels and the Cuban government were unshaken, and, in the Kremlin's view, exiled Prince Souvanna Phouma, former Premier of Laos, was still the legitimate head of that country's government. However, Khrushchev indicated he sought no crises on any issue; nor did he press for an early meeting with the President.

Four days later Kennedy dramatically opened his first press conference with the announcement that the Russians had released two American fliers held prisoner since their unarmed RB-47 reconnaissance plane had been shot down on July 1, 1960, over the Barents Sea, north of the Arctic Circle and Lapland. An hour later the same news was announced from Moscow as Captains John R. McKone and Freeman B. Olmstead left for home and a Presidential welcome. No conditions had been made by the Russians for the fliers' release, Kennedy emphasized; at the same time he pointed out that he was continuing the ban on flights over Soviet territory that Eisenhower had imposed after the U-2 controversy.

The news of the fliers' release tended to overshadow a number of more important, if less spectacular, developments. Kennedy also disclosed that he had asked that the resumption of the Geneva talks looking toward a ban on nuclear testing, scheduled for February, be delayed at least a month to enable this country to clarify its own position. In consonance with his campaign declarations concerning the new African nations, he had ordered a considerable increase in American food contributions to the famine-ridden Congo. But no such aid was under consideration for Communist China for two reasons: the probability that Peiping would refuse, and the fact that China, despite her own needs, was systematically supplying foodstuffs to Cuba and African nations. As for Cuba, Kennedy had no intention of restoring the diplomatic relations that Eisenhower had ruptured; and the new President explained that it was impossible for him to recognize a movement that had been "seized by external forces and directed not to improving the welfare of the people involved but towards imposing an ideology which is alien to this hemisphere."

It was this reference to "an ideology which is alien" that was to explain virtually all that followed in the shaping of the foreign policy of the Kennedy Administration. It was not only the Catholic obsession with Communism that had so much to do with Kennedy's views and actions; it was the Communist phobia that had been endemic in the American culture longer than his lifetime. The whole problem of Communism had always been so enveloped in violent emotions that its intellectual merits and the philosophic question whether any nation had a right to enforce its way of life on another had been totally buried under a kind of chronic panic that alone could explain the readiness of otherwise upright men of intellectual stature to adopt against this enemy the very methods and values for which they condemned it. The possibility of military aggression, the more real threat of economic competition, the indisputable fact of pure imperialism and colonialism were far less often invoked, let alone rationally discussed, than the verbal bogey, *Communism*. It cannot be overlooked that no sign ever came forth during this period that the new Administration, dedicated to the principle of self-determination of peoples that stemmed from the days of Wilson, opposed *all* dictatorship or totalitarianism. One was to see, instead, the paradox of Truman's Administration in the immediate post-war years, when the United States, with its Puritanical sense of mission, was bidding the Yugoslavs on the left and the Argentines on the right to break out of chains that these peoples themselves had chosen to wear.

The crisis that the United States faced was indeed grave, but it should not have been disguised in quasi-mystical labels. It was simply what historians had predicted for at least two generations: a new imperialism of the East—only incidentally concerned with political and economic systems —that sought to engulf the West by whatever means were required. And in this sense Kennedy moved at once to equal its resolution with a combination of vigor, restraint and intellectual discipline that inspired new hope in more than half the world, not only among the traditional Western allies of the United States but in many of the uncommitted smaller nations as well.

He had anticipated that foreign affairs would require— if one could reduce the question to the absurdity of statistics—more than half his attention. The second day after his inauguration was a Sunday: he devoted it to a meeting with Secretary of State Rusk and Under-Secretary Chester Bowles on the report submitted by Thompson after his unexpected meeting with Khrushchev, as well as to the nagging problems of Cuba, the divided former Belgian Congo, Laos and the disarmament question. Both Kennedy and Rusk proposed to adhere to traditional diplomatic methods —to employ normal channels of communication and to operate with the customary privacy. Kennedy had implied rather plainly since his nomination that he expected to be to a large degree his own Secretary of State; and very often when Rusk spoke—as when he declared that Kennedy's present disinclination to a summit meeting did not represent an irrevocable policy—the thought was obviously the President's.

The preoccupation of his first ten days in office with questions of diplomacy, international economic problems and the military was reflected in his State of the Union message on January 30, which was predominantly concerned with the position of the country in the world: in Latin America, where he called for a "new alliance for progress" and immediate United States economic aid at the same time that he insisted, "Communist dominance in this hemisphere can never be negotiated"; in the United Nations, which he saw as the best avenue toward an end of the cold war; in Asia, where civil war dragged desultorily on in Laos and Communist China threatened other countries; in Africa, where disorders were crippling the Congo; in Europe, where alliances were frayed. He had already, he revealed, ordered acceleration in the construction of Polaris submarines, in missile development and in military airlift capacity. He promised to prepare the nation to resist all attempts to dominate the world by aggression or subversion; at the same time he emphasized his willingness to cooperate in any peaceful international scientific venture and to negotiate enforceable agreements for the control of armaments. Time had not been on the side of the United States, he said; he would soon call for specific new tools to enable the nation to redress the balance. Not the least of these would be American participation in the Organization for Economic Cooperation and Development, to which ultimately each nation would contribute in proportion to its capacity.

The entire world was listening, and the Soviet Union made no effort to jam even the Russian-language broadcasts of the Voice of America that dealt with Kennedy's speech. Russian news media gave it considerable attention, without commentary. Later, Moscow's *New Times* expressed Russian willingness to improve relations with the United States. In Germany, in Italy, in England, in Japan, even in neutralist India the speech won praise; at home, reactions tended to the partisan: Kennedy supporters stood behind what he had said without qualification, his opponents viewed his address as an unjustified jeremiad.

Meanwhile, the new President had to become acquainted with other leaders with whom he would have to work in the next eight years. Negotiations were already under way for meetings with Prime Minister Macmillan, President de Gaulle, Chancellor Adenauer, Premier Fanfani and other chiefs of government, in Asia and Africa as well as in Europe. At the beginning of February it was announced that Macmillan would go to Washington in April; Prime Minister John Diefenbaker of Canada was already expected within weeks, to be followed by Prime Minister Robert Gordon Menzies of Australia. Arrangements were being made to send former Governor Averell Harriman of New York on a mission for the President to confer with a number of national leaders abroad. At the same time, with the utmost secrecy, the first steps were being taken toward Kennedy's Vienna meeting with Khrushchev in June.

In the midst of this spadework an *opéra bouffe* incident occurred to provide a refreshing contrast between the behavior of the Eisenhower Administration and that of Kennedy in an unforeseeable, if minor, crisis. A group of Portuguese exiles, opposed to the Salazar dictatorship and led by a Captain Henrique Galvão, infiltrated among the passengers and crew of a Portuguese cruise liner out of New York, the *Santa Maria*. When the ship was in international waters the dissidents seized control, without injury to any of the passengers, and announced their determination to hold the liner in the name of General Humberto Delgado, whom they considered the head of a government in exile and who on January 24, the day after the seizure, demanded that the United States and other nations recognize a state of belligerency between his forces and the 32-year-old regime of Premier Antonio Oliveira de Salazar.

But United States and British naval vessels had already put to sea to track down the *Santa Maria* when she was first reported to have been seized by "pirates." The Navy, under the Defense Department, stuck to this view despite Delgado's statement that his men were engaged in an act of political insurrection; the Navy did not bother to consult the State Department. Here in the making was a typical bureaucratic bumble that could impair our relations with one or more friendly nations and threaten our international prestige. Meanwhile, satisfied that piracy had not occurred, the Royal Navy had signaled its tracking ships to return to port.

Portugal, a NATO partner, was urging the United States to board the *Santa Maria* and clap Galvão into irons. But the State Department's lawyers saw no question of piracy; now there was the question of American support for a recognized if dictatorial government as against assistance to its internal enemies. The United States therefore limited its concern to the welfare of the American passengers aboard the liner and promised that it would not interfere if the *Santa Maria* entered a Brazilian port to discharge her passengers and then put back to sea. Immediately unofficial rumors, denied by both Portugal and the United States, circulated in Lisbon to the effect that, unless Washington changed its mind again, Portugal would make trouble when the renewal of naval-base leases in the Azores came up for negotiation in 1962. But Kennedy stood firm in a position of honorable neutrality toward a political difference of another nation that was not an American concern. Portugal got back her ship, Galvão received asylum in Brazil and the United States, for once, brought off the rather difficult feat of maintaining its friendship with Portugal's Government without alienating the enemies of dictatorship around the world.

More serious matters, however, were occupying the President. On February 1 he held his first meeting with the National Security Council and met the press afterward. His review of the international situation was darker than the picture he had given in his State of the Union message.

The situation in the Congo, where Patrice Lumumba seemed to be gaining in his Russian-supported revolt against President Joseph Kasavubu, was steadily deteriorating and there was no real government control; the UN's representatives were consistently ignored. Russian intervention in Laos appeared to be increasing. Moscow and Prague alike were bolstering Castro's dictatorship with arms shipments to Cuba. Kennedy would not invite Khrushchev to attend the resumed session of the UN General Assembly in March, nor would he endorse UN Ambassador Stevenson's "personal" opinion that the President would be "happy" to see Khrushchev. And it was impossible even to consider normal relations with Communist China as long as she continued to hold American citizens in her prisons.

Though Kennedy did not touch on NATO—he had not mentioned it at all since his inauguration, to the great distress of those who could not forget that its emasculation was a basic objective of Soviet policy—it was at an advanced stage of what had come to be called its perennial crisis. Paul-Henri Spaak, its Belgian Secretary-General, had just resigned to return to political activity at home, leaving a mass of unsolved problems: Berlin; nuclear weapons for NATO forces and the increase of their number; revisions of command jurisdictions; national rivalries and aspirations within the organization, exemplified by de Gaulle's insistence on a "national character" for each of the forces within NATO, bitterly opposed by Adenauer; and the growing neutralist sentiment in Britain and many nations of the Continent. American support for newly created nations and colonies seeking independence was straining our friendship with the offended mother-countries (France, Belgium, the Netherlands). What Kennedy proposed to do about any or all of these questions was a mystery; it could not be otherwise until the evolution of his policies had progressed farther, and even then the ultimate effect on the alliance would not be unrelated to what the Russians decided to do.

In an effort to gain time to clarify his own thinking, Kennedy called Thompson home from Moscow for consultations. The President warned the Soviet Union to be guided by restraint during the transition period in Washington while this Government sought means to work toward a peaceful solution of such major East-West issues as Laos and the Congo. Moscow seemed, during those first days of February, quite amenable to a request that carried the implication that its rejection would arouse an even harder reaction than the Russians had experienced from the Eisenhower Administration. As long as the United States refrained from "provocations," whether verbal or physical, Russia appeared willing to wait for a position to be formulated from which negotiations might begin. "Provocation," in Russia's dictionary, included Kennedy's intention to build up the military arsenal and his concern for the freedom of the peoples of Eastern Europe. But Moscow could hardly have been expected to be pleased by Kennedy's pledge to increase our moral and material support of NATO as "our central and most important defensive alliance," or by the appointment of Dean Acheson, one of the founders of the alliance, to head a group advising Rusk on United States policy toward NATO.

The respite Kennedy sought was disturbed by the aftermath of his choice of Earl E. T. Smith as Ambassador to Switzerland. Berne's objection was based primarily on the fact that, during Castro's struggle for power, the Republican Smith, then Ambassador in Havana, had been considered actively pro-Batista. After the United States-Cuban diplomatic break, Switzerland had taken over American interests in Cuba, and she felt that in this role she would be handicapped by Smith's official presence in Berne. Secondarily, the Swiss felt that Smith was not "the best available candidate." No official rejection was made; but unofficial activity was forceful enough to stir considerable opposition in the Senate, which would have to confirm the nomination, and, a few days later, to impel Smith to ask the President to withdraw his name. This Kennedy did, to the relief of the Swiss.

A sudden stupid brutality in Africa drove the minor matter of Smith from the world's attention. The forces of Kasavubu, who was the more or less pro-Western faction's leader in the Congo, had captured Lumumba, who had promptly escaped. Immediately there were rumors that he had been killed; these were steadfastly denied until his body was discovered. The Soviet Union raised so savage an outcry in the UN, virtually accusing Secretary General Dag Hammarskjold of the murder, that Stevenson, for the United States, sprang warmly to his defense and hope for a truce in the cold war seemed futile. The new crisis lent point to Kennedy's message to NATO's Permanent Council in Paris, pledging the United States to maintain its military commitment despite the rumors that American troops would be withdrawn from Europe, and promising further United States cooperation in the field of economics, politics and propaganda. At the same time, the Central Treaty Organization—Turkey, Pakistan, Iran and Britain; the United States was only an observer, though represented in some committees—asked that, on his way home from the meeting of the Southeast Asia Treaty Organization scheduled for late April, Rusk attend the CENTO session.

Late in February Prime Minister Menzies arrived in Washington to confer with Kennedy, principally on matters affecting Southeast Asia. The two men appealed jointly for support for King Savang Vathana's peace plan for Laos, which called for a neutralist policy, the end of the insurrection and of foreign interference, and the help of Burma, Cambodia and Malaya to organize a commission to restore peace and end intervention. Soviet opposition was expected; most other nations remained silent. Both Kennedy and Menzies were perturbed by the revival of the Russian arms airlift to the Laotian rebels. These activities and the undiminished strife in the Congo were too pressing to permit Kennedy to act at this time on his campaign pledge in August to use "all the authority and prestige of the White House . . . to call into conference the leaders of Israel and the Arab States to consider privately their common problems, assuring them that we support in full their aspirations for peace, unity, independence and a better life." The United Arab Republic's firm opposition to the role of the UN in the Congo—supported by the United States—made it reasonably apparent that President Nasser would not listen to any American proposals that entailed the acceptance of Israel's existence. And, less than a month later, Saudi Arabia notified Washington that she would not renew the contract for American use of the strategic Dhahran air base on the Persian Gulf when it expired in April of 1962. The move was not unexpected; discontent within Saudi Arabia over the existence of this American military base only 1000 miles from the Russian border had been mounting, The announcement of the cancellation promised the end of a minor annoyance for Washington, that of continued domestic protests at American acceptance of Saudi Arabia's edict that no Jews must be included in the American forces at Dhahran.

Though Kennedy had said in September of 1960 that "the great struggle in foreign policy in the next decade will not be directly between the Soviet Union and the United States" and, in August, that "the Congo, Cuba, Latin America, Africa, Asia—these are the great areas of the struggle, not Western Europe," it was apparent that at this time Western Europe was the sole quarter to which the United States could look for active friendship and help. Harriman was dispatched on February 26 to visit London, Paris, Bonn and Rome to acquaint leaders there with the Administration's plans and to sound out their views on such matters as the future of the UN, East-West relations in general, disarmament, the advisability of a summit meeting and the prospects for NATO. From Europe Harriman went on to New Delhi, where, after several days of talks, Indian officials grew more optimistic that American thinking would line up more closely with theirs, even at the expense of some of our other allies.

The merit of this view seemed underlined by the stand

taken by the United States in the UN on Portuguese repression of autonomous aspirations in the African colony
of Angola and Harriman's hint that Washington would
favor Portugal's relinquishment of its colonies of Goa,
Damno and Diu on the west coast of India. Nor was American reaction to the actions of the Dutch in Netherlands
New Guinea well received in The Hague, which resented
Washington's refusal to send a representative to the inauguration of the colony's Legislative Council. The Netherlands still felt that the United States had unduly hastened
its loss of Indonesia in 1949 and it believed now that Kennedy had snubbed the Council invitation lest he offend
President Sukarno of Indonesia on the eve of the latter's
visit to Washington: Indonesia had always claimed that
Netherlands New Guinea was a part of Indonesia and did
not belong in what was left of the Netherlands Empire.

Basically, however, Kennedy found that the long alliance
with Britain, strong ties with France and Germany, the
maintenance of the UN's authority and the strengthening
of NATO were, at least for the foreseeable future, his surest
if not his only reliance in coping with the crises that are
explored in greater detail in other chapters. Much reliance was placed on the meeting with Macmillan scheduled
for April, to be followed within days by a visit from Adenauer and, at the end of May, a state visit by Kennedy to de
Gaulle. But Macmillan and Kennedy met several days
ahead of schedule when the Laos civil war sharpened rather
frighteningly at Easter. That meeting was devoted solely
to Laos; the originally scheduled conferences of early April
resulted in the tightening of the Anglo-American alliance
on all issues except the admission of Communist China to
the UN, which Britain continued to endorse.

Both Kennedy and Macmillan agreed above all on the
need for better coordination of political, economic and military planning among all the Western allies. Fears expressed
on both sides of the Atlantic that Macmillan's close relation

with Eisenhower and the difference in age between the
Prime Minister and the new President would militate
against the establishment of immediate rapport proved
baseless. American views and policies on the need for ending colonialism aroused no opposition from Macmillan or
his Foreign Secretary, the Earl of Home, whose own programs and acts in this sphere were entirely consonant with
Kennedy's goals. While little of a specific nature was made
known when the conferences ended, there was asurance of
a greater common effort by both nations in support of the
UN, NATO and the economic and political unity of Western Europe. Kennedy and Macmillan shared beliefs on the
need to maintain world trade "at the highest level," to make
aid to under-developed areas more effective, and to strive to
resolve the manifest obstacles to better relations with Russia and to the achievement of a permanent ban on nuclear
testing. In this respect France was viewed as a continuing
problem because of her insistence on attaining equal nuclear rank with the United States, Britain and Russia and
her unceasing testing in the Sahara. This French intransigence spurred Kennedy and Macmillan to agree at least in
principle on the need to develop a unified nuclear force
within NATO preventing the spread of nuclear weapons to
an increasing number of countries.

While Macmillan was in Washington, Vice President
Johnson was in Paris and Geneva on behalf of Kennedy
after serving as the President's representative at the independence ceremonies of the Republic of Senegal, where
Johnson had been impressed by the way in which the French
had handled the transition in Senegal's status and by the
"responsibility" of the local leadership. In Geneva he observed the dragging talks on banning nuclear tests and in
Paris he conferred with Premier Michel Debré, who had
become increasingly restive over American insistence on
French cooperation in international efforts to maintain the
neutrality of Laos. Like his chief, de Gaulle, Debré seemed

to couple America with Russia as a threat to French *gran-deur* by reason of Washington's support of former and emerging French colonies and of Algerian independence. To de Gaulle, this was foreign intervention in internal French concerns. Yet Johnson was able to predict a growing cordiality in French-American relations.

Kennedy himself was continuingly preoccupied with NATO, which, with the Organization for Economic Co-operation and Development, he hoped could bring about a strong political and economic Atlantic community developing common means to meet common problems. As the community's economic vigor increased, he hoped, it might prove more and more attractive to the uncommitted nations and even to some oriented toward the Communist bloc. Addressing NATO's Military Committee, shortly before Adenauer's arrival in Washington, Kennedy re-emphasized his commitment to "the full defense of Europe" with men and more and better weapons. At the same time he bore heavily on the point that NATO's problems were never solely political or solely military but always mixed. He did not touch on the growing view in Washington that the United States should be the chief, if not the sole, custodian of NATO's nuclear arms. His point on increasing conventional armaments for NATO underlined the generally accepted objective of "raising the threshold of violence"—that is, the level at which warfare could be confined to non-nuclear arms in order to minimize the likelihood of nuclear attack or defense. Both Macmillan and Adenauer stood with Kennedy; de Gaulle's attitude was still problematic but it was believed that his concurrence would guarantee the adoption of the view. De Gaulle's inflexibility, particularly on the subject of France's place in the community of nations, led many observers to think of his forthcoming conference with Kennedy as the most important of all the President's meetings with foreign leaders. Increased hope for its success was afforded by the statement in New York by Ambassador Hervé Alphand that there were no essential differences between France and the United States on either goals or policies. Nonetheless, the French remained deeply disturbed by the American fiasco in Cuba and Washington's determination to increase its aid to the Laotian government forces.

The scope of NATO, of course, reached far east of the Atlantic Ocean, as was evidenced by the membership of such a remote country as Greece. Her Premier, Constantine Karamanlis, visited Kennedy in April not only to reaffirm his country's allegiance to NATO and to discuss common problems with the President, but also to detail Greece's continuing need for American aid. But, in his preoccupation with NATO and its components, Kennedy had not lost sight of Asia. Not only was he weighing the advisability of asking Johnson to undertake a special diplomatic mission to countries on that continent; he was planning an experiment: to determine whether diplomatic relations could be established with Outer Mongolia. If it was found that Outer Mongolia was a truly independent nation and not a Soviet mandate, she could then be considered for UN membership; whether an affirmative finding would alter the American position on Communist China, however, could not be inferred. Meanwhile, conferring with Sukarno in the White House, after the unusual step of going to the airport to welcome the Indonesian, Kennedy won his support for Laotian independence and neutrality (nothing was said of Sukarno's earlier criticism of the American adventure in Cuba). Sukarno, who was to stop in Moscow on his way home from Washington and who had always enjoyed friendly relations with Russia, joined Kennedy in an unequivocal condemnation of "imperialism in all its manifestations." This was generally interpreted to mean that, like Kennedy, Sukarno stood firmly opposed to Russian and Chinese expansion by force.

As the time neared for talks between the French Govern-

ment and the Algerian rebel leaders, the United States
moved into the situation. Walter N. Walmsley Jr., Ambassador to Tunisia, formally received two ministers of the
Algerian Provisional Government for a two-hour conference. The State Department explained that the invitation
had been issued in consonance with the American desire
to expedite the solution of the Algerian question and that
the United States was striving to persuade both sides to
adopt a peaceful settlement with minimum delay; a
similar *démarche* had recently been made to the French
Government. The latter's plan to include in the negotiations representatives of an Algerian faction contesting the
Provisional Government's claim to represent all Algeria
was threatening to cancel the talks altogether, and a few
days later they were indefinitely postponed.

The result was a sharp upsurge in the fighting in Algeria and, toward the end of April, an abortive attempt by
four French generals to defy de Gaulle, seize control of
Algeria and attempt a coup in Paris. To the surprise of the
mutineers, the great majority of the armed forces in Algeria
remained loyal to de Gaulle and the threatened airborne
attack on Paris was never launched. The generals fled; two
of them were later imprisoned pending trial. But France
was vibrant with rumors that they had acted with the full
support of individual agents of Washington's Central Intelligence Agency, if not the CIA's own advice and backing,
despite the fact that in the midst of the preparations for
the defense of Paris Kennedy had sent an urgent message
to de Gaulle offering whatever help the French President
might need and the American President could constitutionally give. Those who believed the rumors about the CIA—
which were actively furthered by Moscow—reasoned that
the anti-Communist position of the agency was so violent
that, exactly as it had actively assisted those who professed
to seek the overthrow of a Communist government in
Cuba, it would naturally lend backing to anti-Communists

elsewhere: and the insurgent generals had made much of the danger of Communism in an independent Algeria. The rumors became so strong, so circumstantial and so widely repeated that in the first days of May the French Foreign Minister, Maurice Couve de Murville, found it necessary to tell the National Assembly's Foreign Affairs Committee that there had never been the slightest question as to the attitude of the American Government. Couve de Murville insisted that his Government had had nothing to do with the rumors; but it was noteworthy that he did not deny them.

It was against the background of the Algerian affair, the Cuban fiasco and the Laotian stalemate that, as his first hundred days ended, Kennedy injected a new note of wariness in reiterating his pledge of this country's help to all peoples who wished to keep their freedom. He did not mention Algeria, Laos or Cuba; but he strongly implied an impending curb on the rash evangelism and the unauthorized individual initiatives that had characterized so much of American foreign policy in the preceding two decades. "We are prepared to meet our obligations," Kennedy warned, "but we can only defend the freedom of those who are determined to be free themselves."

7. Foreign Aid

Like Truman and Eisenhower, Kennedy was committed to
a broad program of foreign aid, by conviction as well as
by necessity. But for Kennedy this commitment was
coupled with a new problem that had arisen toward the end
of Eisenhower's tenure: that of a balance of payments. The
imbalance had arisen not only from the massive loans and
grants abroad but also from a tremendous increase in imports and a decline in exports, as well as constantly rising
expenditures of dollars abroad by Americans and their dependents stationed in foreign countries. In the months after
the election there had also been a sharp crisis in gold, as
investors and speculators were caught up in a completely
groundless fear that the new Administration would devalue
the currency. It was Kennedy's task not only to maintain
a high level of aid where it was needed but also and simultaneously to redress the balance of payments and to halt
the flight from the dollar.

When Kennedy proposed that nations formerly aided
by the United States and now in a sound economic position
bear part of the burden of general international economic
assistance, he was thinking primarily of Germany, whose
economy was the envy of Europe. Germany's balance of
international payments showed a $7 billion surplus, in con-
trast to the $10 billion deficit of the American balance,
and Bonn signified its willingness to cooperate in bearing
the Western man's burden. The offer that followed, however, was disappointing, though it exceeded anything that
had come from Bonn in the talks on the subject that had
begun earlier under the Eisenhower Administration. The
Germans offered $1 billion, but they refused to commit
themselves beyond the current year and imposed conditions
on the $1 billion offer that stirred hostile reactions. These
included a further reduction in the balance owed for post-
war aid, which now amounted to $1 billion. Bonn proposed
to accelerate payment of $600 million and to deduct $187
million from the balance to compensate for German assets
seized here during the war. The Germans also agreed to
purchase $450 million in arms in the United States, pay-
ing in advance; to prepay $150 million of existing arms-
purchase contracts; and to assume some of the burden of
military aid to Greece and Turkey and of general economic
aid in under-developed countries. Washington had suggested that Bonn commit itself to annual arms purchases
of $400 million in the United States (the current average
was $250 million), similar procurements for other NATO
countries at $100/200 million annually, grants and loans
of $100 million a year to underdeveloped nations and liber-
alized rules on agricultural imports to increase American
earnings by $15/20 billions a year. The total was expected
to slash $600 million annually from the American imbal-
ance.

At the same time the plight of the dollar was receiving
attention throughout the West. Jean Monnet, a leading

French economist, called on major European nations to act with the United States in ending the "crisis of confidence" in the dollar. He associated himself with the views of the chairmen of some of Britain's greatest banks as well as his own Finance Minister and Chancellor of the Exchequer Selwyn Lloyd. Like the others, Monnet offered no specifics. But, as events proved, he was correct in contending that "the simple declaration that a common effort is in progress to stabilize the currencies of the West would transform the psychological climate." Within a week European speculation in gold had begun to diminish; for the first time in three months its price fell below $35.35 an ounce—the figure above which, under the rules of the International Monetary Fund, central banks buying gold could not go into the free market but could purchase only from official American stocks. Once the price dropped below the magic figure buyers could and did make their purchases in the free market and end their inroads on the American reserve, so crucial to confidence in the dollar.

It was, no doubt, in part the widespread concern for the soundness of the dollar that contributed to the check in speculation; but the principal cause was Kennedy's State of the Union message with its stress on maintaining the currency and restoring the balance of payments, as well as its promise to free more gold for international obligations. In effect, he was saying that $22 billion in gold stood behind the dollar. This guaranty of stability obviated alarm at a comprehensive program of American aid to other nations that was also embodied in the message.

Its most dramatic aspect was a proposal for assistance to countries in the Soviet bloc, American concern for which had always infuriated Khrushchev. Kennedy proposed that $365 million of American funds frozen in Poland be used for projects that would benefit that country. The final success of the suggestion would depend on amendment of the Battle Act, which forbade aid of any kind to any country dominated by Russia. As a Senator, Kennedy had sought such an amendment in 1959 and, while it had passed the Senate, it had been killed in the House. For both Communist and non-Communist countries, Kennedy urged legislation to empower, on a scale about double the $2 billion in the last Eisenhower budget, "more flexibility for short-run emergencies, more commitment to long-term development, new attention to education at all levels, greater emphasis on the recipient nation's . . . purpose, with greater social justice, broader distribution . . . and more efficient public administration." For this Kennedy also expected America's allies to share the cost: "each nation will contribute in proportion to its ability to pay." Finally, he called for a "food-for-peace" mission for Latin America to develop methods by which American surpluses could be "used to help end hunger and malnutrition in certain areas of suffering throughout the hemisphere."

Another immediate source of concern was Korea. Early in February she halved the value of her currency as her economy weakened; the United States planned a prospective rise of $43.7 million over the $201 million already allocated for aid to Korea in the current year. Neither Korea's need nor her gratitude could be matched by Poland, which had no petitions pending in Washington and little intention of altering her goals and methods to suit the conditions that might be imposed with any American aid. Her Communist Government would have much preferred American legislation permitting it to borrow commercially in New York. Still studying the terms of Bonn's aid offer, Kennedy could not avoid dissatisfaction with the harsh terms under which a defeated enemy was attempting to impose its own deal for the settlement of its obligations; and his views were so strong that it was not long before Bonn gave ground and conceded that modifications might be possible. To the degree that these were made in the subsequent conferences between Kennedy and Foreign

Minister von Bretano, who ultimately agreed that Bonn would contribute not a lump sum of $1 billion but that amount annually to the foreign-aid program, the victory was clearly the President's.

First he allowed Secretary of State Rusk and Secretary of the Treasury Dillon to present the American case and point out that the crisis was not acute. The solution, they added, following Kennedy's strategy, was not a bilateral one limited to the United States and Germany, because there was an imbalance among all the major industrial nations resulting from varying rates of economic growth and differences in help to under-developed areas. Ending the American gold deficit this year would be of little value if next year some other country faced a similar adverse balance. There were, the Germans were told, two fundamental principles: the problem was a permanent one and Germany could help to solve it only by making long-term commitments. The German delegation accepted Kennedy's view and Rusk proposed a memorandum to embody the harmony of views. It was so vague that George Ball, his Undersecretary for Economic Affairs, would not allow it to be submitted; then Kennedy intervened and, with Ball, redrew the document to express his views without equivocation. Von Brentano accepted it immediately.

Kennedy's advocacy of American membership in the new Organization for Economic Coordination and Development encountered considerable domestic opposition, based on the erroneous contention that it would strip Congress of its powers over tariffs and commercial policies and would thus lead to even more unemployment. Rusk launched the campaign for acceptance of what he called the West's answer to the Soviet threat of burial by economic competition, pointing out that the OECD was designed to conform with American Constitutional requirements and to expand our export markets, not to contract our economy. Dillon argued that approval of United States membership in the OECD was essential to the continuance of economic cooperation between the United States and Europe. Had it been in existence a year earlier, he added, it could have prevented the gold panic and minimized the trade deficit. He pointed out that, when the Federal Reserve Board cut its discount rate in 1960, the Bundesbank and the Bank of England had raised theirs, making Germany and England much more attractive than the United States to short-term capital; only when the two foreign central banks had reversed themselves and aligned their rates more nearly with that of the Federal Reserve Board was the flight of capital stemmed. The OECD, he said, would have provided a method of preventing such an episode.

But the three-year deficit in the foreign-trade balance "arises wholly from [American] commitments and actions in the common defense of the free world," Washington pointed out in a note addressed to Bonn but intended for all its allies. Concrete proposals on the sharing of the burdens of aid would be put before the ten-nation Development Assistance Group at its March meeting. Gold was mentioned, too: the Kennedy Administration proposed that no one nation should hold a sustained accumulation of gold reserves but rather that reserves should be used on a communal basis. It was made clear, as far as Germany was concerned, that Kennedy would not follow through on Eisenhower's pledge to seek Congressional compromise of the controversy over seized German assets and thus this subject was eliminated as a lever in the allocations of pro-rata contributions for help to under-developed countries.

Brazil was eager for assistance under the promised Latin-American program, for which Eisenhower had previously asked $500 million. But the House Appropriations Committee not only deferred action on that request but refused to authorize a $150 million increase in the lending authority of the Development Loan Fund, which had been requested by both Eisenhower and Kennedy. The House was moving favorably, however, on two of the measures Kennedy had requested with respect to the payment-balance deficit: the reduction in tourists' duty-free imports from $500 to $100 and the elimination of taxes paid by foreign banks on interest from United States Government bonds held by them. Kennedy was also moving to put into effect a voluntary savings plan for American personnel overseas that he hoped would achieve the same reduction in dollar outgo that had been envisaged in Eisenhower's order, repealed by Kennedy, to cut the number of military dependents abroad. Kennedy also proposed that service men be allowed in their spare time to take over non-military jobs held by foreign nationals. A further problem was labor's opposition to imports, and Kennedy warned that such action as the proposed refusal of the Amalgamated Clothing Workers to cut cloth imported from Japan could result only in retaliatory measures abroad that would injure the American economy far more than any imports could under the existing voluntary restrictions. A new, if minor, tension arose between the United States and Germany when Bonn announced a proposal to raise the value of the mark from 23.8 to 25 cents and the Treasury Department described this step as "useful but modest." That clearly implied that Washington wanted further revaluation, Bonn said, and hence, instead of shifting capital from Germany, speculators were leaving funds there in the hope, which Bonn insisted was vain, that there would be a further change in the mark's value to please the United States.

Preparing to send Congress an urgent request to appropriate the $500 million in aid for Latin America authorized under Eisenhower but still held up in committee, Kennedy made a major innovation: in all areas, the countries that most effectively helped themselves would receive the most assistance. Kennedy, like the acknowledged experts on the subject, believed that year-to-year foreign aid was conducive not only to poor planning at home but also to inefficiency

and often to waste in the recipient countries; he wanted
such help put on a long-term basis. Thus, if an under-
developed country committed itself to a long-range economic reform, the United States would in turn pledge itself
to a correspondingly protracted aid plan. The obstacle to
the realization of Kennedy's goal was the House Appropriations Committee, which would not relinquish its yearly survey of aid funds. One possible solution was believed to be
that of couching long-range aid plans in terms of annual
appropriations; another was the "back-door" method of
creating authority to borrow, which did not require action
by the Committee. The introduction of the self-help motif
was expected to do much to relax Congressional opposition
to long-range aid planning.

In mid-March Kennedy offered the first of such proposals,
making good on his promise to make it directly proportional
to self-help in the recipient nation. This was a ten-year program for Latin America to improve living standards and
education, further economic self-sufficiency, support moves
toward larger markets, promote inter-American scientific
cooperation and set up educational exchange programs. The
proposal also embodied a reaffirmation of the determination
of the United States to defend any American nation whose
independence was threatened. In addition, Kennedy asked
a special $100 million fund to help Chile rebuild after its
shattering 1960 earthquakes. Generally, Central and South
American reaction was favorable, despite some pessimism
in Mexico; but Chile indicated that, since the whole $100
million would not be needed to restore the quake area, the
balance should be made available for general development
of the country, a view shared by the mission of the International Cooperation Administration at work in the country.

Congressional reaction to the plan for Latin America and
to the five-year aid programs for other areas that soon followed was unusually cautious. The Senate, however, ratified

the treaty giving the United States membership in the OECD and, as a preliminary to the London meeting of the Development Assistance Group, which would become a subsidiary of the OECD, Under Secretary of State Ball initiated conferences in Bonn and Paris on the suggestions that would be made in London for international allocation of the costs of foreign aid. These talks resulted in the proposal to Western Europe and Japan that each of the industrialized nations contribute 1 per cent of its annual gross national product, totaling on the basis of current forecasts about $8 billion, of which the United States alone would pay in $5 billion. The primary purpose of such aid, Kennedy said in a special message to Congress, should be economic growth rather than defense. Therefore he requested legislation authorizing development loans for countries in Latin America, Africa, Asia and the Middle East for periods running up to fifty years, to implement his philosophy that this country owed to less fortunate nations an economic, political and moral obligation that could not be avoided and that would be sloughed only at the cost of disaster. More specifically, he also requested the creation of a new agency for foreign aid, authorized to borrow $7.3 billion from the Treasury over five years and to lend the proceeds to nations under development that pledged social reforms. The passage of the bill he sought would—for five years—relieve both the Executive and Congress of the annual foreign-aid battle.

Kennedy did not try to estimate the over-all cost of his five-year program. Observers expected it to entail several times the lending authority for which he had asked, exceeding the $12.5 billion in loans and grants issued during the three and a half years of the Marshall Plan. Kennedy proposed that in the first year Eisenhower's $4 billion figure be retained; but he asked that the military-aid allocation be reduced from $1.8 to $1.6 billion and the $200 million difference be allotted to economic assistance. Candidates for five-year aid would be expected to submit five-year development plans; wherever possible, loans repayable in dollars would replace grants. Substantial help to the domestic economy was envisaged from the adoption of the legislation, which would also consolidate in the proposed new aid agency the functions of the ICA, the Development Loan Fund, the Food-for-Peace program, the Export-Import Bank's local currency loans, the Peace Corps and grants of agricultural surpluses and excess equipment.

While the initial Congressional reaction was broadly favorable—except in those quarters whose resistance to all foreign aid was automated—it was reasonable to expect major objections to be raised to a number of aspects of Kennedy's plan. The most obvious target, of course, would be the cost. Valid practical objections to even considering a fifty-year program in the light of the extreme fluidity of existing world conditions were sure to be raised. The rather Messianic concept of an American moral imperative to improve the world was certain to evoke criticism, not only philosophically but also with respect to what constituted improvement for other countries and what qualified the United States to determine what was best for them. The most immediate peril to speedy enactment of any foreign-aid legislation lay in Rusk's order to his staff to withhold from Congressional investigators all information relating to allegations of waste, mismanagement and other scandals in the administration of foreign aid, all of which were already under investigation by the executive branch of the Government. Similar executive privilege on the same subject had been exercised by the Eisenhower Administration.

Kennedy blamed the waste, as well as the failure of some assisted nations to achieve self-reliance despite the great sums allocated to them, on the handicaps arising out of Congressional insistence on annual rather than long-term appropriations for foreign aid. If Congress rejected his plans for long-term planning, he said, it alone would have to accept the responsibility for continuing waste. It was impossible, the President contended quite rightly, to plan intelligently in a field that was by its nature a long-range operation if the planners could never be certain that they would have the means to translate ideas into acts; certainly there was not a well-managed corporation anywhere in the world that embarked on inherently long-term development without having assured itself of long-term financing.

The long-term concept was not limited to Washington's own foreign aid; it was proposed by Ball as one of the major points of the international program under discussion in London. He proposed also that a greater proportion of the assistance given should be rendered in the form of "soft" loans—that is, loans that could be repaid in other than freely convertible currencies—when the financial position of the recipient country required it. The general formula under which an industrial nation would be expected to contribute 1 per cent of its gross national product per year to the international effort was not intended to be rigid: account would be taken of each country's military budget and living standard: a nation whose military demands were unusually great would pay somewhat less than 1 per cent, while a country enjoying a very high living standard would pay rather more. An individual nation's balance-of-payments position, he added, should not determine the amount of its contribution; on the other hand, a nation with a deficit balance would be entitled to impose the condition that a major share of its contribution be spent on its own products.

In principle, the American proposals won acceptance by the ten nations of the Development Assistance Group: the United States, Britain, France, Germany, Italy, The Netherlands, Belgium, Portugal, Japan and Canada. They accepted a permanent American chairman. Kennedy felt satisfied that he had successfully initiated the realization of one of his major objectives: a "decade of development."

At the end of March Kennedy received from George S. McGovern, director of the Food-for-Peace program, a report urging him to make agricultural surpluses "an instrument of national policy." Though McGovern did not consider it a major objective, he noted that the adoption of his proposals would rid the United States of unwanted surpluses of food and fiber; what interested McGovern was the use of these materials to help areas interested in improving their lot. He suggested, for example, that road and irrigation workers in Indonesia could receive part of their wages in food instead of currency; the diets of needy peoples all over the world could be enriched with nutritious items that would otherwise be beyond the reach of their countries. He asked Kennedy to back a five-year program, costing $11 billion, that not only would provide the raw materials for food and clothing to areas that could not import them but also would supply technical assistance to teach the recipients how to process the basic supplies. Wherever possible, the surpluses would be sold to the recipients; the needier nations would get the help on credit or in out-and-out barter deals, and the neediest would receive farm products as outright gifts. McGovern proposed a $2 billion maximum for total shipments in any one year.

In mid-April Kennedy drafted a number of leaders from outside the Government to assist in reorganizing the whole aid program and in persuading Congress to adopt the ensuing changes. The basic objectives were two: to shift the emphasis from short-term grants and loans to a predominant system of long-term loans only; and to revise the structure of the affected agencies in order to make possible more centralized direction in Washington. Their work would ultimately be dovetailed with the OECD, which was just opening its official life in Paris. Walter H. Heller, chairman of the President's Council of Economic Advisers, led the American delegation, which was charged with the task of persuading the new organization to make detailed studies of the three principal economic problems of the West:

1. Economic growth in general and the reasons for great disparities in the rates of growth of various Western countries.
2. The perennial imbalance of international payments.
3. Monetary and budget policy.

The United States itself was still plagued by its own payments deficit as the hundred days ended, though it had shrunk almost melodramatically since the beginning of the year. The deficit for the first quarter of 1961 was running at the rate of $1 billion annually, against almost $4 billion in the final quarter of 1960. What Kennedy had described as the "hemorrhage of gold" had been virtually coagulated for nine weeks. All the customary indicators pointed to a continuing high rate of exports and to a gradual diminution of the deficit, though Dillon considered the situation remained "touchy." Early action by the ten nations that had agreed to share more of the load of foreign aid was expected to alleviate the situation further.

Nowhere more effectively than in this sphere of foreign aid had Kennedy laid a solid groundwork for the accomplishment of his objectives. It might be argued that his demand for fifty-year planning was unrealistic and impracticable; but his specific proposals for modestly long-term activity were not only statesmanlike but businesslike. He had won international acceptance of the principle that no one nation could be expected to carry the entire load of strengthening the non-Communist world and that all who hoped to benefit must be prepared to contribute. It was increasingly evident that both the principle and the utilization of foreign aid would be an increasingly important arm of American foreign policy.

8. The Peace Corps

On March 1, President Kennedy issued an executive order establishing a Peace Corps, which he described as a "pool of trained men and women sent overseas by the United States Government or through private institutions and organizations to help foreign governments meet their urgent needs for skilled manpower." He also sent a message to Congress asking legislation to make the Corps permanent. "Life in the Peace Corps," the President said, "will not be easy. Members will work without pay, but they will be given living allowances. They will live on the same level as the inhabitants of the countries to which they are sent." In his message to Congress he said: "There is little doubt that the number of those who wish to serve will be far greater than our capacity to absorb them." He said by the end of the year he hoped to have 500 to 1,000 trained corpsmen working abroad.

The news ignited greater public enthusiasm than any

other program sponsored by the new Administration. Two days after the message, 8,000 letters had been received. Rarely had a Presidential directive evoked such universal approval. George Meany, president of the American Federation of Labor and Congress of Industrial Organizations, offered immediate cooperation and assigned Henry Pollock, a staff specialist in foreign affairs, as liaison officer to study the use of trained workers in countries where skilled labor was scarce. Building-trades unions said the likeliest source of their volunteers would be two age groups. The first would be apprentices, finishing their work-and-education phases. Most of these were in their early twenties and had high school educations. The second would be older workers whose children had married and who were already serving as teachers in apprenticeship programs. Applications were requested by many young skilled construction workers who had wide experience in living under the rugged conditions of dam-building in Colorado or constructing the Distant Early Warning system across Arctic Canada.

Students and educators also gave swift support to the program. Arthur S. Adams, president of the American Council on Education, declared after a survey that 300 colleges and universities would cooperate in training members for the Peace Corps. Replies to a questionnaire that went to 468 institutions of higher learning showed that 441 approved and only 27 disapproved the Corps in principle. The National Student Conference endorsed the Peace Corps but opposed loyalty oaths for volunteers. The Administration declared it had no loyalty data requirement.

The reaction from the diplomatic corps was favorable and sound. Nigeria received the news "warmly"; Brazil called it a "very imaginative move that would add dynamism to programs already under way . . . public opinion in our country would be very sympathetic." Dr. Carlos Samz de Santamaria, the ambassador from Colombia, said it was "romantically and pragmatically good from all angles.

I am wonderfully well impressed." Britain gave the Peace Corps a hearty reception. *The Yorkshire Post* explained that the program "would appeal only to the most dedicated of young people or those with a large allowance from a millionaire parent. America being what it is, both these types are likely to be represented in the Corps." A government spokesman in Bonn said: "The idea would certainly find a potent echo among the Western allies." Italian officials said they favored the idea so much that their country might wish to start similar projects.

This "spiritual mobilization" of American youth was first broached to Kennedy by Senator Humphrey and Representative Henry Reuss of Wisconsin, who felt that the present generation needed a romantic and dramatic challenge to match earlier generations that helped Roosevelt revamp the economy and destroy the Fascist threat to liberty. Kennedy first introduced the plan in a campaign speech at San Francisco's Cow Palace on November 2, 1960, saying that, while "we cannot discontinue training our young men as soldiers of war, we also want them to be ambassadors of peace." No single utterance in his campaign drew more mail or a greater response. There were, of course, dissenters after the President sent his message to Congress. Representative Otto E. Passman, Louisiana Democrat and chairman of the House Foreign Aid Appropriations Subcommittee, objected on the ground of cost, and the Daughters of the American Revolution objected tremulously that this might lead to a universal civilian draft and job assignment.

The President named his brother-in-law, R. Sargent Shriver, 45, former president of the Chicago Board of Education, who had headed the planning of the Peace Corps since January, as director. There was no salary with the job. In an interview with Senator Kenneth B. Keating, New York Republican, Shriver declared that "anybody who joins us with the idea that this will be a glorified joy ride is doomed to disappointment. No Americans in modern times will have been asked to do harder work. It's going to be work carried on in the underdeveloped part of the world, under difficult living conditions, different diet, different culture, different language, sometimes in remote places."

The White House created a nucleus staff to assist Shriver in carrying out his program. Some would remain permanently with the organization, others would serve as temporary consultants. They were:

Bradley Patterson, 39, career Civil Service official, former Assistant Secretary of the Cabinet during the Eisenhower Administration. John D. Young, 41, an executive with McKinsey & Co., management consultants. Lester Gordon, 38, deputy assistant managing director for planning and economics of the Development Loan Fund. Forest Evashevski, 43, of Iowa City, Iowa, University of Iowa athletic director and former football coach. Lawrence E. Dennis, 40, of University Park, Pa., former Iowa journalist and vice-president in charge of academic affairs for Pennsylvania State College. Dr. Arthur S. Adams of Harvard, president of the American Council of Education, who accepted supervisory responsibility for the Peace Corps training program. Thomas H. E. Quimby, 42, East Lansing, Mich., business executive; he set up a recruitment program. Louis E. Martin, 48, of Chicago, editor of *The Chicago Defender*, a Negro daily, working on the development of programs with the United Nations and other international agencies. Dr. Howard A. Rusk of New York, professor and chairman of the Department of Physical Medicine and Rehabilitation, New York University Medical Center. Albert G. Sims, 43, of Riverside, Conn., vice president in charge of operations for the Institute of International Education, in charge of the development of university programs. Gordon Boyce, 43, of Putney, Vt., president and international secretary-general of the Experiment in International Living. Morris B. Abram, 42, Atlanta lawyer and Rhodes scholar, who was to set up a legal office. Edwin R. Bayley of Madison, Wis., 42, former reporter for *The Milwaukee Journal*. Warren W. Wiggins of Washington, 38, assistant deputy director for programs of the International Cooperation Administration.

To add some luster (as if it were needed) to the group, the President appointed a National Advisory Council, a 33-member bi-partisan group, headed by Vice President Johnson and including Supreme Court Justice Douglas, a renowned traveler, explorer and outdoors man; Mrs. Roosevelt, John D. Rockefeller 4th, Dr. Mary Bunting, president of Radcliffe; David E. Lilienthal, former chairman of the Atomic Energy Commission; the Reverend James Robinson, director of New York's Morningside Community Center, and Thomas J. Watson Jr., president of the International Business Machines Corporation. The other members included representative of the arts, sciences, business and various hues of political opinion, demonstrating a national unity rarely achieved in any piece of legislation.

The first financing of the program came through already appropriated funds of the Mutual Security Agency. Subsequently special funds would have to be set aside by Congress to cover the estimated cost of $10,000 to $12,000 a year for each overseas worker, including training, transportation, medical care and administrative overhead. With about 2,000 workers overseas, the cost would run to about $24 million, considered a modest sum in the more than $80 billion Federal budget.

In presenting the fiscal portrait of the Corps, the Administration stated its official purpose: The Peace Corps volunteers of both sexes would operate as teachers and technicians in the fields of education, agriculture, public health, English-language instruction, urban renewal and public administration. The first emphasis would be on teaching. The volunteers would work only on projects that by Peace Corps standards showed the need as well as the possibility of improvement. They would work only at the invitation of the host country and largely under its authority. The plans called for the volunteers to fill the void between technical advisers already in the field and the unskilled local labor. One official explained that the volunteers were not expected to perform tasks that could be done by native manpower.

The Peace Corps was organized as a semi-autonomous agency under the State Department, but the workers would also function in approved programs undertaken by private universities, voluntary private agencies, the ICA and United Nations groups. Ambassador Stevenson suggested to UN Secretary General Hammarskjold that the idea of an international Peace Corps be considered. He said it was Kennedy's hope that other countries would join in a similar effort so that the American program would be only one step in a major international drive in the sharing of knowledge and techniques with underdeveloped areas. Stevenson noted that the British Voluntary Overseas Services group already had 89 workers in 25 countries teaching, training and working with youth clubs. Only a few, he said, were university graduates; most were secondary-school graduates with plans for college after they had completed their overseas duty of a year or so. Voluntary Services Overseas was founded by youth and religious organizations, is supported largely by grants and pays for the transportation of its workers. Host countries are required to supply food and lodging and $2.80 a week in pocket money.

In his recruiting drive, Shriver made it clear that men and women with trade skills, in construction or home economics, were just as welcome as those with college degrees. While the minimum age was set at 18, it was expected that the majority of those accepted would come from the 22-to-35 age group. Candidates would be thoroughly screened for intelligence, skills and emotional stability, the plan being to fit volunteers into projects already designated. The screening procedures would include a security check by the F.B.I.,

written tests and carefully annotated interviews. The training program would begin in a number of universities and
continue in Peace Corps staff centers and overseas stations.
Each candidate would have three to six months of intensive
instruction in language, foreign culture and his chosen
occupation. The training period was also expected to evolve
into a further screening process where the recruits would
be observed under conditions as close to actual assignments
as possible.

In order to ease the anxieties of parents of some of the
younger workers, especially the women, the Peace Corps
gave the assurance that experienced supervision would be
the foundation of the overseas units. Depending upon the
place of assignment, a Peace Corps volunteer would spend
two to three years abroad. He would get only a basic allowance sufficient to equal local living standards. For example,
a teacher would get only enough money to live as the local
teachers do. Technical helpers would work under the guidance of ICA technical advisers and would be expected, for
example, to follow through a demonstration of malaria control by remaining in the area, mapping the mosquito-in-
fested marshes and doing the field testing required. It was
stressed that the Peace Corps was not designed as a propaganda agency or a means of spreading the American influence on the local political scene. This, of course, did not
preclude the setting of the best possible example of the
American way of life, which could be considerably more
influential than a publicity release or a speech. It was stated
as a fixed policy that the Peace Corps could not be used for
religious missionary purposes or by the Central Intelligence
Agency. The legal status of the volunteers would be governed by treaties now covering ICA personnel abroad. Some
countries give the agency diplomatic immunity, others do
not. At the end of his tour of duty, a volunteer would get
travel expenses home and an accumulated "bonus" of $50

to $75 for each month of overseas service. In addition, a Peace Corps career board would seek to develop job opportunities for its veterans.

Volunteers of draft age were not promised automatic exemption. General Lewis B. Hershey, Director of Selective Service, said that, barring some national crisis, the corpsmen would be able to get indefinite deferments (de facto exemption) if they worked on some occupation "in the national interest." It was presumed that the Peace Corps could be construed as in the national interest.

The President was so gratified by the reception the Peace Corps proposal received that he announced later that he was studying the establishment of a Peace Corps Foundation to channel aid to private United States groups working overseas. These would include projects that did not meet official United States criteria; proposals by several Roman Catholic and Mormon organizations to couple missionary efforts with work projects, and those countries that would prefer non-governmental help from the United States. Congress was empowered to create such foundations, and even state governments could grant them charters. Funds would come from private sources, but the United States might also provide some money. The Peace Corps received a number of private donations, which had to be returned.

Another facet of Kennedy's program came to light in a television conversation he had with Mrs. Roosevelt. He announced that the Administration was seriously considering methods of using the Peace Corps concept in slum and depressed areas at home. He referred to the "reservoir of talent" that had been uncovered in the applications for jobs sent to the Corps. He mentioned retraining and education in blighted sections of the country as needing the same kind of attention as was planned for foreign nations. "I think that we have hundreds of thousands of people in this country who genuinely want to be of service," he said.

The organization of the Peace Corps moved ahead so

rapidly that by April 21 the President was able to announce definite plans to send the first group of 28 volunteers to Tanganyika in east central Africa. The group, consisting of surveyors, geologists and civil engineers, was scheduled to arrive in Dar-es-Salaam in September to help local technicians and construction workers to plan and build roads. "There is nothing more important in Tanganyika," the President said, "than the development of roads to open up the country." Tanganyika was a British-administered United Nations trust territory with a population of 9 million, scheduled to gain its full independence on December 28. The country's Ministry of Communications and the Ministry of Commerce and Industry had promised to provide the American volunteers with native armed game scouts, transportation, tents, mosquito netting and other non-technical supplies. During the dry season the volunteers would camp out three weeks at a time and labor on farm-to-market road surveys, on engineering of main bridges and roads and on geological research and mapping. Sir Ernest Vesey, finance minister, described as vital the three-year development program undertaken by the Peace Corps. He dramatized his statement by saying that his country could train only two surveyors in the next five years. The need was for simple dirt roads that would change the country's farmers from living under a barter economy to a cash economy. After the dry season, when rains made outdoor work impossible, the American volunteers would teach the Tanganyikans engineering and surveying techniques. Two- and three-man teams would fan out from Mount Kilimanjaro to Lake Tanganyika in a romantic and practical trek that should make for excellent reminiscence in the future.

The United States began negotiations with United Nations groups, such as the World Health Organization, and with foreign governments for the most effective use of the Peace Corps. Ten nations almost at once expressed an interest in the program. Among the first possible host countries were Brazil, the Philippines, Nigeria, Pakistan, Colombia, Chile and India. There would be more as the Peace Corps demonstrated its abilities. It promised to be a long and arduous assignment of trial and error, failure and success. This was emphasized by Shriver in his report to the President when he warned that "no matter how well conceived and efficiently run, there probably will be some failures and some disappointments. These could be costly and have serious effects both at home and abroad. Nevertheless the Peace Corps over the long run may create a substantial popular base for responsible American policies to reward the world. Thus the Peace Corps could add a new dimension to America's world policy—one for which people here and abroad have long been waiting."

There were many who regarded the Peace Corps as Kennedy's dynamic reply to the Birchers, the right-wing students, the security-conscious conformists and their bewildered fathers and mothers.

9. Swords Into Plowshares

The Anglo-American-Russian talks in Geneva designed to bring about a cessation of nuclear testing were in adjournment when Kennedy took office; their resumption had been set for February 7. In order to gain time to familiarize himself with the background of the problem and to enable himself and his staff to deliberate on policy, Kennedy decided to ask the other powers for a brief postponement. This, he believed, was a particularly promising area for negotiation. The outgoing chairman of the Atomic Energy Commission, John A. McCone, had submitted a report warning of danger in the existing unpoliced moratorium on testing, which, McCone said, was preventing technical progress by the United States while perhaps the Soviet Union was clandestinely violating the gentlemen's agreement.

Britain backed Kennedy's request for a postponement, and the Russians agreed to defer the resumption of the talks until March 21. At the same time, however, Moscow refused the American invitation to join a Washington conference for developing a program for the international use of weather satellites; no explanation was given. In the new interval before the talks on nuclear testing should resume, American hope for progress grew. To a considerable degree it was fed by the fundamental policy difference between Moscow, which still advocated co-existence, and Peiping, which rejected it out of hand. While technical and political staffs prepared their proposals, substantive and procedural, another hope was rising: that success in reaching an accord on a supervised nuclear-testing moratorium would provide a solid foundation for the exploration of limitations on conventional armaments. Khrushchev, in a message thanking Kennedy for the President's congratulations on the Soviet rocket probe toward Venus, called for "strict international control" of all armaments. Until such a compact should be achieved, however, the State Department believed with the Pentagon that both the conventional and the nuclear arsenals of the non-Communist worlds should be substantially strengthened. Kennedy had ordered a complete review of the whole arms problem and did not expect its findings to be available before the summer.

It was Kennedy's idea, as it had been Eisenhower's, that disarmament negotiations should be conducted directly among the major powers. Apparently taking advantage of the length of time required to complete the study ordered by Kennedy, the Soviet Union tried to have disarmament included on the agenda of the UN General Assembly session resuming early in March; Stevenson, for the United States, replied that "a period of relative quiet would contribute to a better international climate for serious negotiation," and his view ultimately prevailed: with Soviet consent, the UN talks were postponed until autumn. Kennedy then suggested to Khrushchev that formal disarmament talks be resumed on September 11, but Khrushchev declared that six months was too long a time to wait. Another issue between the two leaders was the size of the negotiating group. The United States wished it to be limited to the ten nations that had originally participated: the United States, Britain, France, Italy and Canada for the West and the Soviet Union, Poland, Czechoslovakia, Rumania and Bulgaria for the East; but the Russians wished to add five ostensibly neutral countries: India, Indonesia, Mexico, Ghana and the United Arab Republic, of which all except Mexico had generally tended to support Russian views on arms. The United States wanted to compromise by accepting only India and Mexico. Ultimately an August start was agreed on but the question of additional participants was left unsettled. Meanwhile Russia had emphasized the necessity for speedy accord because of the effect it would have on China, which, Moscow argued, could not stand alone against the worldwide endorsement that was sure to be given to any general East-West agreement on arms.

On the eve of the resumption of the nuclear talks in Geneva, both Britain and the United States expected Russia to stall. The negotiations were now thirty months old. Moscow had made it plain that it was growing cool toward any nuclear accord that was not tied in with general disarmament, and it had not retreated from its position—which had motivated its withdrawal from the earlier disarmament talks—that the United States was not acting in good faith. A more cogent explanation of possible Russian temporizing lay in the fact that an agreement giving the West access to control points in Soviet territory from which to check adherence to a nuclear-testing ban could be exploited in the general disarmament talks. In addition, Khrushchev was believed to hold the view that a ban on tests would increase Peiping's pressure on him for nuclear weapons, to which he claimed thus far to have been cold. Furthermore, Khrushchev was concerned with the likelihood that France, which was determined to become a nuclear power, would flout any ban arrived at in Geneva without her participation.

By contrast, the Americans under Arthur H. Dean were entering the parley prepared to make concessions—not on basic issues, but on points that had been stumbling-blocks in the past. Kennedy had modified the stand of the Eisenhower Administration, for example, to propose that Soviet scientists would be allowed to inspect outmoded atomic weapons that this country intended to use in its research for improving seismic detection of underground blasts—a move that would require a joint Congressional resolution to become effective. Washington was also ready to revise its earlier insistence on a maximum 27-month moratorium without inspection for small underground tests and to specify a time closer to the Russian demand of three to five years. Kennedy had also instructed the delegates to agree to Moscow's proposal for a ban on high-altitude and outer-space tests and for parity of representation on the seven-man control commission that would be set up. But the United States stood firm in demanding at least twenty inspections of Soviet testing sites per year, against Russia's offer of three; however, it appeared, if the Russians raised their figure, the Americans would be willing to lower theirs. On one other point there was no sign of compromise: American insistence that Britons or Americans head control posts in Soviet territory and Russians head those in the West. Moscow had demanded that each post should be headed by a national of the country in which it lay.

It was vital to Kennedy that agreement be reached. Like Eisenhower, he was under mounting pressure to resume nuclear testing unilaterally. Some of this pressure came from scientists who genuinely feared that inactivity would prove immeasurably costly; but most of it was emotional and political, brought to bear by extreme nationalists and Russophobes and exploited by leaders inside and outside Congress. The first day of the talks did nothing to ease Kennedy's problem, for, though he must have known that Britain and the United States were ready to create a climate of compromise, the Soviet delegate, Semyon K. Tsarapkin, insisted on opening the meeting by backing down on an old agreement governing the secretariat of the control organization. "A single, competent, impartial and objective administrator" had been agreed on earlier; now Tsarapkin revived the Russian position that there must be a three-member council representing the Soviet bloc, the West and the neutral countries. He coupled this demand with a warning on the continuation of testing by France: as an ally of Britain and the United States, he said, she might act merely as their agent while they abstained from making tests of their own —a statement received with sardonic grins by the intransigent French, who had no intention of sharing their atomic progress with the bigger nations.

In subsequent sessions Tsarapkin listened to the detailed explanations of the concessions offered by the West but said nothing. Outside the conference room he would come back to the subject of France, insisting that her continued testing could imperil the whole negotiations. Then Dean asked the Russians to accept an agreement for peaceful nuclear testing—as distinguished from testing for weapons— by both sides in order to further scientific progress. The Russians had previously indicated that they might accept this on the basis of one Russian test for each Western test, but Dean insisted that there must be no limitation on either side. Tsarapkin replied that his Government opposed all nuclear testing, whatever the purpose. Dean also rejected Russia's terms for staffing the control posts. A new stalemate supervened, which an American spokesman called "the most deliberate stalling" yet encountered. Kennedy therefore asked Johnson, who was representing the United States at Senegal's independence celebrations, to go to Geneva and try to assist in breaking the deadlock.

The Vice President spent two days in Geneva, working with Dean. Three days later, on April 10, some limited agreement was reached on one point: Russia accepted the

West's proposal for a control commission consisting of four Western nations, four from the Soviet bloc and three neutrals. This met the Russian demand for "parity" of representation; but the West emphasized that its offer was conditioned on "satisfactory agreement on the totality of other treaty provisions, including assurance of an effective, reliable and fast-acting control system." It was primarily Britain that had been responsible for all the Western concessions that Kennedy had accepted because, should it become necessary to break off the talks and resume nuclear testing, it was essential that the neutral nations recognize that the West had exhausted in the best of faith every possible hope of accord and that failure would be the fruit of Russian obstinacy. After three weeks of Tsarapkin's obduracy, Dean called on him to make some constructive contribution to the success of the negotiations. The only reaction was a Russian refusal to open Soviet territory to inspection until four years after the ratification of any treaty on banning tests. A week later the United States began to consider the advisability of breaking off the negotiations, which the Russians were evidently trying to prolong until they could be merged into the general disarmament talks scheduled for August. But such an interruption as the Americans were considering would compel the formulation of a policy on the resumption of tests, a move that would be sure to evoke important minority opposition in the United States, particularly in the liberal wing of Kennedy supporters, and much broader antagonism in other countries. The dilemma was, as usual, intolerable: whether to tell the world that the United States was going back into the business of devising cheaper and better mass-killing instruments or to allow the Russians to fix American policy simply by sitting on their hands.

The Soviet Union was well aware of the advantage it enjoyed; it refused to be swayed by Dean's statement that its attitude on nuclear testing could jeopardize the August parley on general disarmament. Nonetheless, Kennedy had finally decided not to break off the test talks despite the rapidly waning likelihood of concrete achievement; and once more the West proposed a concession—it offered Russia complete parity in the staffing of each control post as well as in that of the supervising commission. But Tsarapkin stood firm in insisting that each post be headed by a national of the country in which it was established. In such countries as China, of course, the effect of Tsarapkin's proposal would be to give the Soviet bloc a decisive majority and thus to negate any hope of effectiveness. As Dean observed, the Russian position was hardening as that of the West softened.

At the end of the hundred days the Geneva conference had got nowhere. Kennedy rightly continued American participation, if only for the record, while he wrestled with the advisability of proclaiming American freedom to resume some kinds of nuclear tests even while the meeting continued. It was most probable, however, that such a step would be rejected because of the obvious propaganda tool it would give to those who were always ready to challenge American good faith.

10. The Enemy

"Let us never negotiate out of fear," President Kennedy
urged in his inaugural address. "But let us never fear to
negotiate."

He took office determined to make every honorable effort
to arrive at and maintain harmonious relations with his
country's major antagonist, Soviet Russia. At no time did
he lose sight of this objective, even when the Russians tried
hardest to obscure it. At no time did he allow the objective
to supplant the greater purpose: the best interests of his
own country.

A Russian initiative just after the inauguration was most
auspicious. On January 25, at his first press conference,
Kennedy announced that Moscow had released uncondi-
tionally the two American fliers captured in 1960 when their
RB-47 was downed north of the Arctic Circle, over what
the United States had always contended were international
waters. Though the Russians had set no terms for the release

of the two men, Kennedy coupled his disclosure of their liberation with the statement that he was continuing the ban on flights over Soviet territory that had been invoked by Eisenhower after the notorious U-2 incident, in which an American airman was forced down some 1200 miles within Russia and imprisoned for espionage. Kennedy made it clear that the U-2 case was in no way similar to that of the RB-47. Ambassador Thompson, he added, was still seeking some definite facts on the whereabouts of eleven other Americans whose C-130 transport was shot down over Soviet Armenia in 1958 and who were supposed to have landed safely by parachute and then been arrested.

Kennedy did not mention the fact that four companions of the two freed fliers had been killed when their plane was shot down; nor the further fact that, until their release, the survivors had been held incommunicado since July. Yet Khrushchev's personal decision to order them freed could not be denied a certain reluctant gratitude. Five days later, unfortunately, another RB-47 was sighted over the Kara Sea, not too far from where the first had been shot down; but this time Moscow filed no formal protest, nor did the Russians attack the American reconnaissance-bomber. The diplomatic technique invoked by the Russians to bring the matter to Washington's attention was that known as raising questions concerning the incident; and the President renewed his assurance to Khrushchev that there would be no repetition of American flights over Soviet territory. The matter was thereupon dropped.

Kennedy had made it plain that the United States was going to eschew the kind of gutter-epithet outburst that had characterized so much of Russian-American interchange in the past. Two days after the release of the RB-47 fliers, Kennedy ruthlessly struck out of a speech prepared by Admiral Arleigh A. Burke, chief of naval operations, a number of violent denunciations of Russia as untrustworthy and bent on world conquest. The President insisted, with great justice, that the military had no authority to jeopardize international relations. But there was no reason to believe that Kennedy planned a softer policy toward Russia; the difference was to be made apparent only in methods and in a restoration of dignity to international intercourse.

His State of the Union message made it plain that the "unfavorable tide" of the cold war made it imperative to reinforce the military machine while exerting new efforts to render its use unnecessary. His emphasis on doing everything possible to bring about "the ultimate freedom and welfare of the Eastern European peoples" was further indication of a position toward Russia at least as strong as Eisenhower's. In Kennedy's view, the conflict between East and West had very nearly reached ultimate crisis: over the ensuing four years, he declared, "we shall have to test anew whether a nation organized and governed such as ours can endure. The outcome of this struggle is by no means certain."

At the end of January Kennedy asked Ambassador Thompson to return to Washington from Moscow to present his views on Russia. At the same time the President made it clear that this was not a preliminary to the replacement of Thompson. Immediately there were rumors that one purpose of the Ambassador's return was to initiate steps leading to a meeting between Kennedy and Khrushchev; but these were forthrightly squelched (though much later confirmed). Kennedy believed that meetings between heads of government were of little value without much preliminary groundwork and a reasonable assurance that some agreement might emerge from such consultations. For the conference with Thompson, Kennedy called in not only Johnson and Rusk but also three men who had preceded Thompson in Moscow: Harriman, George F. Kennan and Charles E. Bohlen. McGeorge Bundy, the President's special assistant for national security, also attended the meeting with his deputy, Walt W. Rostow. It was not expected that any policy decisions would be made immediately; rather, the conference was called in order to present to a variety of trained minds the needed information on which policy might be founded. The tone of caution predominated as Thompson reviewed and appraised the events of the past months and the probable trends of Russian policy. It would have been folly to dismiss as rhetoric Khrushchev's frequent references and rarer (and minor) contributions to the easing of the cold war; it would have been equal folly to accept them on faith. It could certainly be assumed that Russian pledges of peaceful co-existence could hardly be expected to be unaffected by American determination to break Moscow's hold on other nations and its acquisition of more.

American hope that Khrushchev would match Kennedy in disciplined restraint, even during a brief transition period, was severely shaken in mid-February when the Russians lashed out at Hammarskjold and the UN after the murder of Patrice Lumumba. On the same day, however, Kennedy made a point of sending Khrushchev a congratulatory message on the Soviet launching of an unmanned space vehicle aimed at Venus; in addition, the President was debating whether to put at Russia's disposal the American tracking network.

Before Thompson returned to Moscow late in February he held a long final conference with the President. Presumably Thompson would try to confer with Khrushchev as soon as possible; he was charged to convey to him Kennedy's desire to evolve solid agreements on major issues. Kennedy also wanted it made plain to Khrushchev that the United States considered it advisable to avoid public disputes that contributed to tension and bad feeling; Thompson's most immediate task would be to develop unimpeded avenues for the continuing practice of the new Administration's "quiet diplomacy." The most important barometer of Khrushchev's intentions, Kennedy believed, was not the

Premier's declarations but his substantive actions and programs in existing crises: the Congo, Laos, the UN. American alarm at the attack on Hammarskjold was certain to be communicated to Khrushchev. While Thompson carried no warrant to negotiate detailed accords, he was expected to stress as the major issues for prior attention the questions of nuclear testing and general disarmament, as well as the broad positions of the Administration. In addition, he was to invite the Soviet Union to enter into negotiations, often envisaged but indefinitely postponed after the U-2 and RB-47 incidents, for the establishment of reciprocal airline service between New York and Moscow. This was hardly of major moment, but a favorable Russian reply might help to improve the general climate and facilitate subsequent negotiations on more sensitive subjects. There was a vaguely hopeful indication in the Soviet accession to the request of the United States to televise films of two of Kennedy's press conferences. The films were edited, ostensibly because of considerations of time, and all dialogue was translated into Russian; still it was the first time that the Soviet Union had given so much attention to an American President's press conference.

Khrushchev was about to leave for central Russia when Thompson returned to Moscow. The Ambassador asked for a meeting "anywhere and at any time" to transmit his message from Kennedy; but Khrushchev indicated no intention of changing his schedule. This was interpreted as a deliberate rebuke for Kennedy's unenthusiastic reaction to the thought of an early meeting with the Premier. Kennedy's firm views on Laos and the Congo were also thought to have contributed to Khrushchev's behavior. He took no notice of alterations in Washington's attitude toward trade with the Soviet Union. While there was to be no major policy change—indeed, it was not unlikely that shipments of strategic materials would be even more tightly controlled—there was a general tendency to relax curbs on other American exports to Russia.

But the basic mutual suspicions underlying Khrushchev's coquetting with Thompson would not abate. America's suspicions were grounded, for example, in Russia's attachment to subversion, sabotage, propaganda and even "just wars" on a less than global scale in order to further world Communism even while protesting her devotion to peaceful co-existence and friendly economic competition. Russia claimed justification for her wariness in Kennedy's determination to strengthen the military establishment and to tighten the bonds between his domestic social and economic program and his country's ability to stand against Russia, as well as in his reluctance to rush into an embrace with Khrushchev on some summit.

It was more than a week after Thompson's return to Moscow that Khrushchev agreed to receive him two days later in Siberia—Khrushchev insisted on secrecy as to the actual meeting place, but it was later identified as Novosibirsk, 1,700 miles east of Moscow. Premier and Ambassador spent four hours together. Thompson presented Kennedy's message and listed the specific issues, such as nuclear tests, arms, Laos, the Congo, the UN, on which Kennedy hoped that substantive agreement could be reached. Unexpectedly, Khrushchev injected the twin problems of Berlin and the two Germanys, on which the Premier placed major emphasis, though he set no time limit for either the acceptance of his views or the execution of the alternative threats. Khrushchev repeated that peace treaties must be signed with both East and West Germany and that Berlin must be made into a free city from which all troops would be barred; otherwise he must unilaterally conclude a treaty with East Germany, which would then have sole control over access to the former capital. His position was "fixed." Thompson replied that the Administration was studying the problem, but that no basic change in American views was probable. Kennedy was as deeply committed as Eisenhower or Truman to the defense of West Berlin.

Neither side had made progress. The stalemate was not eased by the signing of an agreement in mid-March to extend the exchanges of scholarly activities in the humanities and the sciences between the two countries, or by the Moscow radio's allotment of "prime time" to a new program on American scientific and technical advances, prepared by the United States Information Agency. By this time Gromyko was in the United States for the UN Assembly session, and he went to Washington for a five-hour conference with Rusk, in which the major topic was Laos (it was at this time that Gromyko had his exchange with the President on the same subject). The atmosphere, at least for public consumption, was genial enough, and the talks were followed by the usual pious invocation of "better mutual understanding" as a result of the "open and frank" conversations. But neither side could claim any concrete result.

Developments in the UN and abroad, and the Russian attitude as the nuclear-testing talks began in Geneva, indicated that Kennedy's restrained overtures had been made to an audience as unreceptive as any that his predecessors had faced. It was not only that Khrushchev was viewed as having been over-vulnerable to the seduction of the advantages he enjoyed in Cuba, the Congo and Laos; now it was believed that he sought much more than a mere personal humiliation of a rival, such as he had seemingly attempted to impose on Eisenhower at the summit meeting of May, 1960. Khrushchev, in the view of expert observers, was determined to undermine the authority of the American Presidency itself for the foreseeable future. Kennedy, for his part, was proceeding quietly and determinedly along the course that he had concluded to be most beneficial for his country and its position in the world; if he continued to hope and even to act for the maintenance of contact with

Khrushchev, it was not from any naive belief that the
Premier could be cozened but rather from the conviction
that events and the role of America in shaping them must
compel Khrushchev ultimately to fall back on rational
realism.

Hence it was important to eliminate minor irritations as
far as possible. On March 24 a Federal Court in Chicago
acceded to a request by the Attorney General and dismissed
a charge of espionage against Igor Yakovlevitch Melekh, a
Russian diplomat formerly employed by the UN, on condition that he leave within thirty days for Russia. No Russian-American negotiations had preceded the motion to dismiss the charge; Rusk had asked the Justice Department
to take the action "in the belief that it would best serve
the national and foreign-policy interests of the United
States." Every suggestion that the release of Melekh had
any connection with either the RB-47 fliers or the continuing imprisonment of the U-2 pilot was categorically
denied. Since Melekh had not yet pleaded to the accusation
that he had obtained military information and photographs
for the Soviet Union, the court observed, there was little
choice about granting the dismissal motion. Moscow expressed its gratification at the result and remained silent
on fears expressed in Washington that, had Melekh gone
to trial, Russia would have taken reprisals on "trumped-up
charges" against some American in the Soviet Union.

But the Russians were less concerned than the Americans
about reducing irritations. The Soviet Embassy in Ethiopia
vexed the United States by reporting in one of its current
news bulletins a wholly manufactured report on restrictions
alleged be imposed on representatives of African nations
in Washington. The truth was bad enough, but the Russian fabrications were almost too clumsy to be believed
anywhere. The technique was an old one in propaganda:
while ostensibly giving credit to the State Department for
seeking means of easing, if not ending, discrimination

against non-white diplomats, the article sought to leave ineradicably in the reader's mind the implication that the efforts were half-hearted lip-service and that the United States was insincere.

All such episodes vanished in the shock of the invasion of Cuba. Kennedy must certainly have known that Khrushchev would react promptly and vigorously. "I earnestly appeal to you, Mr. President," Khrushchev's message of April 18 said, "to call a halt to the aggression against the Republic of Cuba." The appeal was followed with the expected warning: "We shall render the Cuban people and their Government all necessary assistance in beating back the armed attack on Cuba." On the same day Kennedy replied: "I have previously stated and I repeat now that the United States intends no military intervention in Cuba. In the event of any military intervention by outside force we will immediately honor our obligations under the inter-American system to protect this hemisphere against external aggression." The President concluded with unqualified moral endorsement for the Cuban revolt.

As these messages were being exchanged, a tremendous demonstration broke out before the United States Embassy in Moscow with that efficient spontaneity for which Soviet mobs have so long been renowned. Thousands of students paraded, shouted and flung stones and inkpots against the building, while more than a thousand unarmed soldiers and militiamen tried to keep them away and, after two hours, succeeded in backing off the rioters. Washington filed a formal protest with Moscow, but it was almost ignored in the Russian city's official and unofficial jubilation at the defeat of the Cuban rebels.

On April 22 Khrushchev replied to Kennedy's message of April 18. Unfortunately, the facts lent a certain support to the Premier when he said: "It has now been proved beyond doubt that it was precisely the United States that prepared the intervention." Turning to Kennedy's argument that Cuba might very likely become a base for Communist aggression against the United States, Khrushchev pointed out that countries hostile to and bordering on Russia had made their territory available for American bases "and your military say openly that these bases are spearheaded against the Soviet Union." It was one of those sad ironies in which history delights that once again all the morality was on the side of the immoralist; and Khrushchev, studiously avoiding threats, concluded with renewed assurance of his desire for relations with the United States such that neither of "the two most powerful states in the world would engage in saber-rattling or push their military or economic superiority to the forefront" because of the inevitable consequences.

There was always the possibility that Khrushchev meant what he said. Above all there was the inescapable truth that international law and morality had been flouted by the nation most dedicated to their support. It was not pretty to see them defended, even hypocritically, by the nation most dedicated to their breach.

Kennedy did not reply directly to Khrushchev's message of April 22; he did approve a statement that branded it a polemic and a "distortion of the basic concepts of the rights of man." But it could not be denied that the immediate prognosis for Russian-American relations, after the tragedy of Cuba, was anything but favorable.

The astounding announcement, barely a month later, that President and Premier would meet in Vienna early in June, immediately after Kennedy's visit to de Gaulle, raised hope only among the most unsophisticated. The initiative for the meeting had been taken when Ambassador Thompson returned to Moscow late in the winter; the need for it had been considered steadily greater as the various crises deepened. Kennedy made it plain that he was going to Vienna with the most sober appreciation of the probable outcome: the conference would be purely exploratory, giving each leader the opportunity to take the measure of the other.

The President arrived in Vienna with the assurance of French backing for the firm American position on the preservation of West Berlin. In Vienna as in Paris he was greeted by hundreds of thousands whose genuineness could not be doubted, in contrast to the dutiful and curious welcomers who turned out for Khrushchev. But neither Khrushchev nor Kennedy came away with more or less than he had taken to the meeting: on Berlin, Germany, nuclear testing, disarmament, each leader reiterated uncompromisingly the positions his Government had assumed for years. "I found this meeting," Kennedy reported to the nation afterward, "as somber as it was to be immensely useful."

The most somber aspect of the talks, the President said, was the question of Berlin and Germany. Nonetheless, he insisted, the meeting's usefulness lay in the opportunity it had presented for making plain to Khrushchev exactly what the United States stood for and how determined it was to realize its ideals. "The gap between us was not, in such a short period, materially reduced," Kennedy said, "but at least the channels of communication were opened more fully."

He added that Khrushchev had joined him in endorsing the concept of a neutral and independent Laos and the importance of an effective cease-fire. But the President had hardly returned home when the Geneva conference on Laos was forced to break up by reason of the repeated and aggravated rebel attacks in defiance of all agreements. Communication channels may have been opened, but realists were inclined to believe that, however high-minded Kennedy's intentions in conferring with Khrushchev, the meeting had done nothing to alter the prognosis of April.

11. Laos: Confusion Into Crisis

The first statement made by Kennedy as President on the subject of Laos emphasized his desire to see that country independent and uncommitted to East or West, "not dominated by either side but concerned with the life of the people inside." The civil war between the pro-Western Government and the pro-Communist rebels in the north was continuing, and the rebels, supplied by Soviet planes, were gaining ground; Britain had proposed the re-establishment of the International Control Commission, comprising Canada, India and Poland; in the capital of Vientiane and in the farm country outside, Laotians were carrying on their daily lives in complete indifference to the skirmishes in the north. Ambassador Winthrop G. Brown was called home at the end of January to report to the President.

Various courses designed to end the fighting were under study: an outright appeal for the cooperation of Moscow, a request for UN intervention, increased action by non-

Communist nations to aid the Government. Reports from Laos itself were rarely immediately credible. It was said that the rebels had set up their own government, and the loyalist forces claimed the recapture of a town held by the rebels; but no one could be sure. Truth had not been forwarded by the confession of the Laotian Government that it had vastly exaggerated, if not fabricated, its reports of massive foreign intervention on behalf of the rebels. If Kennedy was going to select Laos as the test of Soviet sincerity in professing a desire to cooperate in peaceful settlements, he would not find it easy to get at the facts.

Britain was still, in the beginning of February, awaiting a Russian reply to her proposal on the control commission. Kennedy viewed favorably the suggestion that Laos invite a commission composed of neutral Burma, Cambodia and Malaya to make a study of the legitimacy of Boun Oum's regime. A few days later King Savang Vathana of Laos issued the invitation to these countries and reiterated his determination to keep his country neutral. Suddenly the airlift of supplies to the rebels ceased, and hope rose. Rusk called Russian Ambassador Mikhail Menshikov to his office and asked him for his country's support of the King's invitation. On the face of it there was every reason why the Soviet Union's reply should be favorable: the King offered to eliminate all foreign bases in his country and declared his willingness to put an end to "camouflaged" aid to his own forces as well as to those of the rebels: American military personnel in civilian clothes had long been training his army and the rebels had the assistance of technicians from North Vietnam. The King had also indicated his readiness to accept a more broadly based government, and both Boun Oum and the rebel Pathet Lao were hoping they could persuade the exiled former Premier, Prince Souvanna Phouma, to join it.

But the official Pathet Lao spokesmen, echoed by Communists outside, denounced the King's proposal as an Amer-

ican conspiracy. It was believed that this attitude might
alter if Prince Norodom Sihanouk of Cambodia accepted
the Laotian invitation, and Kennedy made his first venture
in personal diplomacy near the end of February, when he
addressed a letter to Sihanouk urging the Prince to assume
the key position in bringing peace to Laos. Sihanouk curtly
refused; at the same time Premier U Nu of Burma rejected
any part in the proposed commission. Both leaders felt that
the commission would be only a device for bolstering Boun
Oum, whose government they considered illegitimate. In
the face of this initial failure by Kennedy the Soviet Union
renewed its suggestion for an international conference of
the kind that had ended the war in Indochina in 1954. But
the West was reluctant to enter such another propaganda
arena.

Hope stirred again when Phouma consented to negotiate
with General Phoumi Nosavan, representing Boun Oum.
They agreed that Laos should be truly neutral and, despite
the rejections by Cambodia and Burma, endorsed the King's
plan for these countries to join Malaya in a commission to
put neutrality into effect. Rusk, meanwhile, told Britain
that the United States could not support the appeal to Moscow to revive the Canada-India-Poland group as long as
there was a chance for success in the negotiations with
Phouma. Phouma himself contended that the United States
held the key to peace: he demanded proof of the genuineness of American support for neutrality. In Laos itself, the
rebels continued to advance, the capital maintained a re-
markably active social life, and the peasants paid no attention to military movements or even fighting on the
roads that ran through their fields. A government land surveyor named Tong Sai told a correspondent of *The Wall
Street Journal*:

"The reason you can't find strong views among our people is that most have none. We Laotians are real neutralists. We have no interest in the cold war between the

United States and Russia or even our neighbor, Communist China. We don't understand why this struggle was brought to Laos and we want no part of it . . .

"We just want everybody to leave us alone. To many of us this is mostly a struggle between different Laotian political cliques and families, and we don't understand how all the foreigners got mixed up in it."

But the foreigners were mixing in more deeply. The Russians resumed and increased their arms aid to the Pathet Lao; Kennedy had appealed without success to Khrushchev to remove Laos from the cold war, and now the President began to consider augmenting his help to the Laotian Government. Even Phouma, after a visit to the rebels' territory, conceded that Soviet aid to them was some twenty times as great as Western help to the Government. But, instead of taking a post in the Government, Phouma was preparing for a journey abroad and it was feared that his absence from Asia would vitiate the effect of his agreements in principle with Nosavan. By mid-March, when Russia was still avoiding a reply to Britain on the control commission, Kennedy was ready to make a public pledge of more assistance to the Government, in the hope that the mere promise would move the Russians to halt their intervention. The possibility that, at its meeting at the end of March, the Southeast Asia Treaty Organization would send troops into Laos at the King's invitation—which had not yet been issued—was openly admitted as Phouma began a world tour to muster support for a fourteen-nation peace conference. Washington was not on his itinerary because, he said, the United States had not invited him. The conference he urged was backed by Sihanouk, whom Phouma had made no attempt to persuade to change his view on Cambodian participation in a survey of Laos, as well as by the Communist bloc and Britain and France. But the United States, very possibly because Communist China and North Viet-

nam were included among the proposed conferees, would
not accept the plan.

While Washington insisted it had no intention of en-
gaging in an arms race with Moscow on Laotian soil, it
lost no time in sending more weapons, fuel and instructors
to the Royal Laotian Army. Rusk and Russian Foreign
Minister Andrei A. Gromyko conferred on the Laotian
question as a curious echo of the Laotian surveyor's appeal
to be ignored came from Prime Minister Nehru of India, to
whom King Savang Vathana had appealed to ask the nations "not to interfere." As if neither Nehru nor the King
had spoken, Rusk told Gromyko that the United States
insisted that Laos must be made and kept independent and
neutral. He added the obvious point that the growth of aid
to both sides in the civil war could easily lead to a major
war, but at the same time he underlined Kennedy's determination to do everything in his power to help the King.
Finally, he told Gromyko frankly that the outcome of the
Laotian crisis would prove the genuineness or sham of professed Soviet desires for an improvement in East-West relations. Phouma, who by now had reached India, expressed
pleasure at Kennedy's emphasis on independence and neutrality for Laos; he also clarified the reasons for his continuing exile: he challenged the legitimacy of Boun Oum's
regime as the choice of a fraudulently elected Parliament
and he insisted that peace could be achieved only after new
elections under the supervision of an impartial international
commission selected by the United States, Britain, France,
Russia, Communist China, Laos, Cambodia, North and
South Vietnam, India, Canada, Poland, Thailand and
Burma.

At least on the surface, Phouma's position sounded eminently reasonable, and on closer examination it stood up
well. How then could the United States justify its rejection
of a rational proposal that had the support of its two major

allies with its determination, after Kennedy conferred on March 20 with his top advisers, civilian and military, to incur all the risks of a test of wills with Russia? The alternative to exposing this country and the world to the danger of a major war, according to Kennedy, was to allow Laos to fall under Communist rule. To Kennedy this alternative was inadmissible, and his view was gaining ground among some members of SEATO, notably the Philippines, Pakistan, Thailand, Australia and New Zealand. But Britain and France still opposed Kennedy's view, if only for the excellent military reason that the hilly, primitive little country of Laos was an eminently unsuitable battleground on which to draw the line against Communism. Undoubtedly, too, Britain and France, with their first-hand knowledge of the rigors of war, were somewhat more reluctant than the United States, which had not known war on its own soil for a century, to court such destruction again. It appeared, too, that a sense of purpose might be over-balancing a sense of reality. So the President accelerated his just-issued orders for greater help to the Laotian Government and, in a highly secret exchange with Gromyko, reiterated and underlined what Rusk had told the Russian. Gromyko did not like it any better when it came from the President of the United States.

Neither Kennedy nor his advisers could determine what Russia sought in Laos, in her long-standing efforts to get the West out of Berlin, or in her attempts to unseat Hammarskjold. Was Khrushchev trying to set the stage for negotiations in which the United States would be on the defensive? Was he testing Kennedy? Was he seeking to force new advances in the belief that the West would not resist? No one in Washington could be sure; hence Kennedy was prepared for the worst. Over the weekend of March 18/19, after the failure of his meeting with Gromyko, the President ordered extensive precautionary measures that would make it possible for Western troops to be in Laos in force on twenty-four hours' notice. It was reported—and never confirmed or denied—that an American aircraft carrier escorted by two destroyers had sailed out of Hong Kong for Laos.

On March 22 Kennedy abruptly reversed his field, announcing that a new peace plan for Laos would be presented next day to Moscow by the West; this was viewed as the final test of Russia's peaceful intentions. The new plan turned out to be merely American acceptance of two basic steps that Kennedy had previously refused to countenance: the revival of the Canada-India-Poland control commission and the convocation of the fourteen-nation conference on the future of Laos. Certain conditions were imposed, however: an immediate cease-fire and the prompt cessation of all foreign military shipments to Laos must be verified before the big conference could begin. Britain acted as the emissary of the West in presenting the proposals to the Soviet Union. At the same time, Harriman was in New Delhi, where he delivered to Nehru a letter in which Kennedy asked the Prime Minister to assume a major part in arranging the cease-fire and in the ensuing negotiations for insuring Laos's independence. Capitals around the world relaxed, though none could be sure whether Moscow would now accept what were in essence its own once rejected proposals.

The reason for Kennedy's sudden change of position was a cruelly practical one: no major power would join the United States in military action in Laos, and the UN was fully committed in the Congo. Neither Britain nor France was willing to chance a war for the sake of Laos, which had never, after all, asked any help whatever from anyone. If Kennedy had stuck to his original pledge to help the Laotian Government at all costs, his country alone would have had to bear them all. Now he had at last embraced the only possibility for an honorable non-military solution; if the Russians turned it down, he would have the insupportable choice of either writing off Laos completely despite all his pledges or else defending her alone. For, though he had ordered weapons speeded to strategic SEATO depots, there was every reason to believe that at the SEATO conference opening March 27 Britain and France would vote against SEATO members' taking military action in Laos. London and Paris believed that if even only Thailand and the Philippines intervened in Laos the United States would have to bail them out and that Communist China would almost certainly intervene full-scale on the other side.

In the evening of March 23 Kennedy held a televised press conference to explain the danger in Laos and the means he had adopted for dealing with it. Always a serious speaker, he was preternaturally grave and even harassed as he delivered his exposition with the aid of specifically prepared maps, and then answered questions from reporters. He avoided direct responses as to the dispatch of American forces, but he made it plain that he had not delivered an ultimatum to Khrushchev. While "no one should doubt our resolution" to keep Laos independent, for the alternative was the loss of all Southeast Asia, he set no time limit for the end of the fighting or the start of negotiations. Once more the United States had reached the brink that had seemed an integral part of policy under the late Secretary of State John Foster Dulles, but this time the country had got there almost by accident.

On March 24 Kennedy telephoned Eisenhower in California when he heard that the former President was about to issue a public statement on foreign affairs. On the telephone, as later at his press conference, Eisenhower unqualifiedly supported Kennedy's position; further affirmations came from Nixon and even from Barry Goldwater, the farthest right of Republican Senators. A day later Kennedy flew to Florida to meet Macmillan, who was making a special trip from the West Indies in advance of his April conference with the President. A personal message from Kennedy to de Gaulle elaborated the American position.

All three were awaiting the meeting with Kennedy that Gromyko had requested for March 27, when he proposed to deliver a message from Khrushchev. This would not, in all probability, be a direct reply to the conference and cease-fire proposals, since these had been made by Britain as spokesman; but it was thought that the message to the President would indicate by its tone, if not in substance, Moscow's reaction. Meanwhile, the Pathet Lao troops continued their advance toward the south, and the flow of supplies from Russia and the United States was unabated. It was doubtful whether the Russians would agree to a cease-fire as long as the rebels were advancing so steadily. Macmillan and Kennedy announced that they had reached "absolute agreement" on the Laotian crisis, but they gave no indication what they had decided to do if the Russians should reject their proposals. Questioned on their course, they said merely that "the situation in Laos cannot be allowed to continue to deteriorate." Macmillan resumed his official tour in the Carribean and Kennedy returned to the White House to receive Gromyko.

When Gromyko was ushered into the President's office the first session of the SEATO conference was under way in Bangkok and Rusk had laid the groundwork for an appeal for the use of force if Laos requested it. Reflecting the tenor of the previous day's talks between Macmillan and Kennedy and their telephone exchanges with their ministers in Bangkok, Lord Home told the conference that, while Britain would continue to seek a political solution, "the Communists would be extremely foolish to presume too much on this restraint . . . There is a limit beyond which free men cannot go." Even the French delegate indicated that his country would ultimately concur. These facts were known to both the President and the Soviet Foreign Minister when they sat down together.

Their meeting lasted almost an hour. While Gromyko's message from Khrushchev turned out to be oral rather than written, general rather than specific, it promised at least a hope. Gromyko said his Government was still studying the British message and would reply "in the very near future." He agreed with Kennedy on the need for Laotian independence, neutrality and development, but nothing was put forth from either side as to means, though Gromyko cautioned the West against any action that might expand the Laotian fighting. He did not reply to Kennedy's question as to Russia's attitude on an immediate cease-fire and the cessation of intervention. While Kennedy and Gromyko were meeting, Khrushchev was receiving from Indian Ambassador Menon the request by Nehru for the implementation of the Allies' proposals. *Pravda* was saying that there was an opportunity for a peaceful settlement provided the United States did nothing to extend the war and withdrew its personnel. In fact, the always leisurely pace of the fighting had slowed, in part because the West found it advisable not to make any major moves against the rebels' advance until Russia's answer had been received. By March 28 the Pathet Lao held about one-third of the country.

The next day the SEATO conference adjourned with a warning to the Communists that, if diplomatic moves could not bring peace, it would "take whatever action may be appropriate." SEATO also expressed concern over fighting, virtually unnoticed in the excitement over Laos, in South Vietnam, where Communist-led guerrillas were killing about 500 persons a month—far more than the casualties in Laos; and it was feared that the Laotian conflict was only a prelude or a screen for an attempt to seize the free portion of Vietnam. Kennedy, while gratified that there had been no abstentions in the vote to issue the SEATO warning, was not entirely satisfied with its tone and privately caused a much more blunt message to be sent, advising the Kremlin that the United States and its Allies would not long temporize.

From day to day the world waited for Moscow's reply

on the armistice proposals. Phouma, in London, declared
that he would ask Russia to halt her arms shipments to Laos
provided the United States would do so simultaneously. He
was convinced, he said, that it would be possible to form a
genuine coalition government embracing the Communist-
led Pathet Lao, what he called the pro-Americans and, he
added, the genuine neutralists who were his supporters.
The British were trying to persuade the Prince to end his
tour and go home, but this he refused to do; he was going
to Moscow in April.

In a note remarkable for its mildness of tone, the Soviet
Government announced on April 1 that it was calling for
an international conference as soon as possible in Cambodia
to end the Laotian war and suggested that Russia and Britain issue an appeal for a cease-fire. Though Moscow did
not mention the United States, it added on a minatory note
that "threats of interference" and "tactics of saber-rattling
used of late by certain powers, far from promoting a settlement, may seriously aggravate the matter of settling the
Laotian problem." The Kremlin also made plain its support of Phouma as the head of the legitimate Laotian Government. Ignoring the allusions to his threat of force, Kennedy expressed restrained gratification at the Soviet note,
though he foresaw protracted negotiations before peace and
stability were achieved. One obstacle was obviously the
Russian insistence on the legitimacy of Phouma's claim to
the Premiership; both the United States and Britain recognized Boun Oum as head of the Government. But the para-
mount issue was American determination, in which Britain
was expected to concur, that a verified cease-fire must precede the opening of the fourteen-power Geneva meeting to
settle the future of Laos. In fact, it was six weeks after the
Soviet note of April 1 before both sides could agree that
the fighting had stopped and the conference could begin.

While the bickering and dickering over the cease-fire continued, the United States invited Phouma to visit Washing-

ton and the Prince accepted at once, aware that he would arrive in the United States with the backing not only of the Russians but of most of Western Europe as the logical choice to head the new Laotian Government. He said nothing about the continuation of the fighting and a new increase in Soviet airlift activities, in which Western observers saw hints that the truce negotiations might well collapse. Kennedy himself was inclined to minimize these reports, though he instructed Thompson to inform Gromyko, who had returned to Moscow, that the United States was "disappointed and concerned" at Russia's delay in accepting the cease-fire procedures and ending her airlift. On April 16 the Russians agreed that the cease-fire must be verified before the fourteen nations could meet, but they left uncomfortably vague the effective time of the cease-fire and their concept of the methods for verifying it. While the diplomats of both sides tried to evolve some solution, Phouma took umbrage at word from Rusk that, because Phouma had changed the schedule for his visit to Washington so that it conflicted with other Rusk appointments, it would be helpful if Phouma delayed a few days more. Thereupon Phouma declared that he would not come to the United States at all.

Still the Soviet Union delayed acceding wholly to the original British procedures for the cease-fire. Boun Oum's Government asked the United States to disband the civilian advisers it had sent to Laos and install a military group —a simple matter of changing clothes and designations, which would result in much broader powers for the same 300 men who thus far had not worn uniforms. The United States agreed—the request seemed to have primarily a symbolic value—though discounting new Laotian reports of a major rebel offensive. On April 21 Moscow reached agreement with London on the technicalities of the cease-fire and agreed to request it formally three days later. The Canada-India-Poland commission would be re-activated to verify compliance and invitations to the Geneva meeting would be issued. On April 25, after another seeming reversal by the Russians on the timing of the truce, it was announced that the rival commanders in Laos were ready to stop firing.

But two days later no progress had been made, and Kennedy summoned his principal advisers and the leaders of Congress to discuss steps to be adopted if the truce effort collapsed. The National Security Council met the President again the following day, and faces in Washington were grave. Kennedy's uncomfortable position was aggravated by the fact that the Laotian Government had yet to put up a real fight against the rebels, even when they launched a fresh offensive on April 29. By then, too, the President himself had declared publicly that "we can only defend the freedom of those who are ready to defend themselves"—a criterion that the Laotians miserably failed to meet. The Laotian Government's own seeming indifference to its fate gave Kennedy little ground for asking the United States to risk war for its defense. Now, however, there was also the question of international prestige: the United States had taken first a threatening position, then a kind of middle ground; it had yet to implement any of these stands.

On the hundredth day of Kennedy's term the crisis appeared to be as bad as it had ever been, despite the rebels' offer to meet loyalists' representatives three days later to arrange the cease-fire. The Pathet Lao had cut deeply into southeastern Laos, driving for two towns that controlled the major road leading into South Vietnam. Increased American aid to that country was one of the measures that the Administration was considering as a further means of indicating to the Communists, without actual combat, the seriousness of our intentions. Those who recalled the President's approval for Theodore Roosevelt's old slogan, "Walk softly but carry a big stick," reflected that Kennedy had been striding harshly until he found he was not carrying much of a stick at all. In all the allied capitals doubt was eating away what was left of the high hope with which the West had greeted the beginning of the Administration. As the Laotian cease-fire dragged well into May before it was finally verified and the new mutual pettifogging of the Geneva conference could begin, our Allies were asking where was the purposeful direction that was to have been the hallmark of the Kennedy Administration's New Frontier in foreign affairs?

12. The Cuban Adventure

The revolution by which Fidel Castro made himself the ruler of Cuba had never enjoyed uncritical enthusiasm in the United States. Some Americans distrusted Castro because he had the reputation of being an intellectual, and Americans have never understood the European concept of the political intellectual. Many feared that anyone who sought to overthrow an established government must necessarily be a Communist. There was a general indifference to the enormities of the regime of Fulgencio Batista; there was also a preoccupation with the importance of trade with Cuba. Castro's personal idiosyncracies—the undisciplined beard, the unkempt uniform, the incredible verbosity—alienated many Americans. Washington recognition of the Government he headed evoked controversy and considerable criticism of Eisenhower from the Right.

The Left clung to its image of Castro long after his accession to power had made it clear that he was not the liberator he professed to be. By the summer of 1960 his increasing contempt for parliamentary democracy, the brutality of his repressions and the irrationality of his tirades against the United States had left him relatively few American supporters; only the irreducible nucleus of these continued to back him as he took his country quite deliberately farther and farther into the ambiance of the Soviet bloc. The Cuban Communist Party, which had long had a working arrangement with Batista and had been represented in his Government before it parted with him, at first looked down on Castro's movement as bourgeois but later began to recognize its possibilities and, by the time Castro took power, the party was well entrenched in his organization. One after another of the anti-Batista leaders who had joined Castro and taken high positions in his Government were forced out by Communist pressure and replaced by loyal party men. By the time Castro visited Washington in the spring of 1959, it was becoming evident that his brother and close associate, Raul, was, if not a card-carrying Communist, strongly dominated by the party. Finance Minister Ernesto Guevara was also suspect.

What disturbed Americans most at this time was Castro's reluctance to hold elections, though he had promised them on his accession in 1958. Nonetheless Washington emphasized its willingness to discuss his country's needs and the help it could give him. But Castro himself rebuffed every approach, refusing for a long time even to receive the United States Ambassador. Though in August, 1959, Cuba signed the Declaration of Santiago as a member of the Organization of American States, thus subscribing to the pledge of free elections, human rights, due process of law, freedom of speech and information and economic cooperation within the hemisphere, Castro refused to permit elections, imposed a series of repressive decrees that abrogated the most fundamental individual rights, imprisoned and executed increasing numbers of old associates as well as enemies, suppressed public expression and ignored the other American nations in order to increase his economic ties with the Soviet bloc. By the end of 1959 he was regularly denouncing the United States as the enemy of freedom not only in Cuba but throughout the hemisphere.

By then the State Department was sharply divided. Vice President Nixon had submitted a proposal that the United States help Castro's opponents to overthrow him, but most of the Eisenhower Administration opposed it. In March of 1960, however, opinion had swung round to Nixon's view and steps were begun to train the thousands of Cubans fleeing daily to the United States. The task was given to the Central Intelligence Agency, which selected as the leader of the rebel movement Dr. José Miró Cardona, a Batista foe who had been Castro's first Premier until he chose exile in preference to Castro's Soviet orientation. For some months the CIA's work was successfully kept secret, but in the fall of 1960 it became public and United States newspapers openly published photographs and detailed accounts of the training operations at bases in Florida and in Guatemala, which, like the United States, firmly opposed Castro. The Cuban leader, in the interval, had initiated a number of anti-United States measures, principally the expropriation of American-owned properties and restrictions on the activities of Americans living in Cuba; he had also threatened in his interminable public harangues to seize the United States naval base at Guantanamo Bay despite the long lease held on it by Washington.

Soviet intelligence had learned by the summer of 1960 that the CIA was preparing the rebel forces and the information was transmitted to Castro. In July, Khrushchev pledged full assistance to Cuba, including the use of rockets, "if aggressive forces in the Pentagon dare to start intervention against Cuba." In the UN Assembly session that autumn, Castro himself took the floor to denounce the United States as an aggressor and was warmly supported by the Soviet delegations inside and outside the UN. By the end of the year Castro had bound himself to Russia and the more industrialized satellites by a complex of economic and technical assistance agreements.

In addition, Cuba was seeking to extend the Castro revolution to other Latin-American countries. Cuban diplomatic missions were serving as channels for propaganda and arms, as well as recruiting of local dissidents. There was hardly a day in Havana without summary executions of a half-dozen "enemies of the people" after pro forma trials— a fact that was more important than any other single element in rousing United States hostility, official and unofficial. But the only action taken by the Eisenhower Administration, fearful not only of driving Castro closer to the East but of alienating the Cuban people themselves, was to obtain from Congress authorization for the President to suspend United States imports of Cuban sugar. The United States was Cuba's largest customer and took by far the greater part of the crop under a price agreement that artificially inflated the island's revenues. The hoped-for minatory effect of the embargo failed; Castro grew only more violently anti-United States and diplomatic relations between the two countries were broken shortly before Eisenhower left office. Six other American nations took the same course; several others asked Cuba to call home her diplomats because of their flagrant activities in the affairs of the countries where they were serving.

The jingoes and the professional Red-haters in the United States had long demanded that Washington send troops into Cuba, arguing that the presence of a pro-Communist regime within ninety miles of the Florida coast was too great a peril to be dealt with otherwise than by overwhelming force. But during the early weeks of the Presidential campaign both Kennedy and Nixon specifically rejected armed intervention of any kind on the uncontestable ground that it would violate every canon of international law and morality. Kennedy argued for collective action by the Organization of American States. But on October 20 he issued a special statement on Cuba that caused grave concern by its implication of a disguised intervention. "We must attempt," he declared, "to strengthen the non-Batista democratic anti-Castro forces in exile, and in Cuba itself, who offer eventual hope of overthrowing Castro." Sober Americans hoped that this was mere campaign talk; perceptive Europeans were disturbed; and the Cubans and the Soviet bloc seized on the statement as corroboration of their contention that the United States wanted to destroy Cuba's independence.

Nonetheless, after Kennedy's inauguration, Castro made some tentative explorations of Washington's willingness to extend economic help and to resolve the disputes arising out of Castro's anti-United States measures and the resulting embargo and diplomatic rupture. Kennedy replied through the State Department that, while the United States endorsed the professed aims of Castro's revolution, it was concerned with the "capture" of the revolution by anti-democratic forces. Only the full restoration and guaranty of freedom "so that the Cuban people may freely choose their own destiny," the United States said, could establish the climate for the resumption of normal relations. Castro, of course, imperiously rejected such an attitude. The United States was further rebuffed when Brazil's new President, Janio Quadros, refused to support Washington's attitude.

The rumors of more intensive United States preparation of an invasion force of Cuban rebels were by now accepted as fact throughout the world, despite official silence. Late in March a Cuban exile went on trial in New York, charged with the killing of a child during a restaurant brawl over Cuban politics, and a witness was testifying to the tenor of the political discussions that preceded the shootings when the prosecuting attorney told the court that "an agency of the Federal Government," which he refused to identify, had requested that no witnesses be questioned or allowed to testify to "activities in the Miami area." These activities were the accelerated operations of the CIA among the anti-Castro Cubans, which were known to every Floridian and must certainly have been reported in detail to interested foreign governments. In Havana, meanwhile, Guevara and Castro made vituperative attacks on the United States, insisting that it was involved in a fight "to the death" with Cuba, while huge audiences of workers and students cheered without restraint. Castro's support had come initially from the peasantry and the proletariat, augmented by the intellectuals; but these last had rapidly grown disaffected as his initial economic reforms, which unquestionably improved the living conditions of the mass of Cubans, were followed with the suppression of all basic civil liberties, a mounting terror, and an obvious crusade to destroy the minority middle and upper classes on the island. It was from these groups that the great majority of the refugees in the United States came.

At the end of March Congress extended for fifteen months the embargo on Cuban sugar; individual members were urging a total economic embargo and steps to persuade the entire hemisphere to join in economic sanctions to bring Castro to heel. He retaliated a few days later by ordering a gunboat to intercept and detain a cable-repair ship owned by Western Union and sailing outside the three-mile limit. Her captain radioed to the Guantanamo base and a United States destroyer and a number of airplanes sped out at once. They took no action, merely keeping the Cuban boarding-party under surveillance, and after a few hours the repair ship was released. Through the Swiss Embassy in Havana the United States immediately demanded an explanation.

That night the State Department published a lengthy review of the history of Cuban-American relations since Castro's revolution. It warned Cuba that she must at once

"sever her links with the international Communist movement" and "restore the dignity" of the original revolution.
Pledging the help of the United States to this end, acknowl-
edging past errors of omission and commission by Washington, the document warned that, if its appeal went unheeded,
the United States was confident that the Cuban people, with
its help, would unseat Castro's regime, which, the State
Department charged, "offers a clear and present danger to
the authentic and autonomous revolution of the Americans
—to the whole concept of spreading political liberty, economic development and social progress through all the
republics of the hemisphere." The State Department was
careful not to say how or when the struggle against Castro
would begin. The President had carefully supervised the
preparation of the document and fully approved it.

The Cuban reaction was to have been expected. Out of
the mass of epithets emerged an unshakable determination
to continue the present course, confident of every assistance
from Russia and her satellites. Cuban Foreign Minister
Raul Roa, in New York for the UN Assembly, called the
publication of the State Department's pamphlet a part of
the undeclared war of aggression that he accused the United
States of preparing against his country. He charged that the
Government had recruited about 5,000 "counter-revolution-
aries, mercenaries and adventurers" of a half-dozen national-
ities, including former Nazis, to lead the invasion of Cuba,
and he threatened to ask the Assembly's Political Committee to act on recruiting centers in New York City, the
existence of which was an open secret, and on the Florida
training camps. In Havana, his Government rejected the
United States' protest on the detention of the cable ship
and countercharged that United States military planes
had violated Cuban air space and a United States warship
had fired on a Cuban plane. Almost fifty other violations
by the United States were listed in the note, which described
all the incidents as preparation for aggression.

The State Department refused comment. It also refused comment on the unscheduled visit of former Premier Miró Cardona, now head of the Cuban Revolutionary Council in New York. Miró Cardona paid another call on the department the next day, April 6, when it was finally admitted that the Government was maintaining the closest contact with all anti-Castro exile groups. Miró Cardona's Council embraced the Democratic Revolutionary Front, headed by Dr. Manuel Antonio de Varona, Premier in 1948 under Batista, and the smaller Revolutionary Movement of the People, led by Castro's former Public Works Minister, Manuel Ray. But Miró Cardona had come to Washington, it was announced, merely to see old friends in the department.

A few days later Washington's remaining shreds of secrecy were blasted away by open dissension within the Government on the Cuban problem. The Administration was divided not only on what it should do but on with whom it should act. The CIA had favored only de Varona's conservative group, which included a considerable number of Batista backers; Ray's followers were considered potentially "crypto-Communist." It was de Varona's sector in the Council that wanted invasion; Ray's faction preferred to try to organize revolt within Cuba. A decision for an invasion would in effect be an endorsement of the right wing of the rebels. The Pentagon and the CIA wanted action, even if this were limited to financing and training Cubans to make the landings, since Kennedy had specifically vetoed the use of American troops. The activists argued that the withholding of help for an invasion would strengthen Castro not only at home but in other Latin-American countries and encourage the Soviet bloc to increase its activities in this hemisphere.

The intellectuals recruited into the Administration countered, first of all, that any such help to the Cuban rebels would clearly violate the OAS treaty, of which the United States was a signatory, for its Article 15 stated: "No state or group of states has the right to intervene, directly or indirectly, for any reason whatever, in the internal or external affairs of any other state. The foregoing principle prohibits not only armed force but also any other form of interference or attempted threat against the personality of the state or against its political, economic and cultural elements." In addition, it was argued, United States backing of a Cuban invasion would vitiate Washington's stand on the proxy armies in Laos; it would impair the nation's standing in the UN, whose Charter prohibits the use of force in settling international disputes; it would, if Russia fulfilled her promise of military help to Castro, create another Spain. Such men as Rusk and Bowles and Schlesinger, citing the many American pledges to abjure force and establish the rule of law, went farther and baldly raised the moral issues of obligation to uphold treaty commitments and of the dichotomy of opposing the use of force only when it was an enemy who used it.

For a moment it looked as if reason, law and honor would prevail. On April 10 a Federal Grand Jury in Miami indicted former Cuban Senator Rolando Masferrer Rojas on a charge of conspiracy to violate a federal statute prohibiting anyone in the United States from knowingly participating in a military expedition against a nation with which the United States is at peace. Masferrer was accused of the major part in organizing the landing of a tiny force in Cuba in October, 1960, whose activity at the time was regarded as a private adventure and given little significance. Two days later Kennedy not only repeated his pledge not to send American troops into Cuba but added unequivocally: "I would be opposed to mounting an offensive" by Cubans from the United States. He also promised to make every effort to "make sure that there are no Americans involved in any [anti-Castro] activities inside Cuba." But he did indicate, rather contradictorily, that he would continue supplying aid and military training to non-Batista Cuban refugee groups; and he did not say whether he would prevent Cuban invasion groups from leaving the United States. It was not a wholly consistent position.

On April 15, three days later, a number of Cuban airfields were bombed at dawn and Roa protested the same day in the UN. He insisted the pilots of the attacking planes were not disaffected Cubans but "mercenaries" of the United States. Stevenson countered not only by denying Roa's charges but also by reading a statement given in Miami by one of the bomber pilots, who had landed there after the raid and claimed asylum as a defector from the Castro regime. Stevenson documented his statement with a photograph of the pilot's plane, which had the markings of Castro's air force. Roa retorted that they were easy enough for anyone to paint on. The plane itself was an American-built B-26, a number of which were transferred to Cuba after the Second World War.

No one in Washington would comment on the incident. The three airmen who had landed in Florida received asylum, but their identities and whereabouts were kept secret. One of them had said, before going into hiding, that all the planes involved in the raid were manned by defectors; one was admittedly lost to ground fire. The defectors had planned their act for a later date, the flier said, but acted when they did only because they feared one of their number was about to betray them. But then it was learned that Miró Cardona, before leaving New York for Miami, had had advance knowledge of the raid. American officials questioned about this simply refused to answer. Miró Cardona said, too, that no invasion was planned; his Council hoped to achieve its goal through a succession of small landings by guerrillas who would immediately establish contact with the strong anti-Castro forces that, the Council insisted, were hiding in the interior. The strength of these internal opponents of Castro was to prove the deciding force that would assure the success of any action, the CIA insisted, for Cubans backing Castro could not, it said, claim a majority.

Sometime in the night of April 16/17 CIA agents took Miró Cardona and the other leaders of the Council to an old house near Miami and held them there incommunicado in order to prevent them from having any part in what was to follow. In the next few hours a number of small power boats set out from Florida, carrying perhaps 1500 armed men who were to set up beachheads and link forces with the presumed troops of the underground. What Miró Cardona and his colleagues might not have known was that, for weeks before their own confinement by the CIA, seventeen other anti-Castro recruits had been isolated in a remote CIA camp in Guatemala because of their opposition to pro-Batista elements in the leadership of the projected invasion (these men were not freed until several weeks after the fiasco). What Miró Cardona and his colleagues did know, because their CIA guards allowed them to listen to radio broadcasts, was that their names were being used to authenticate communiques from the rebel forces. No one knew—or would admit—what had happened to several thousand trained refugees who were not used in the landings and who, three weeks later, were still held incommunicado by the CIA.

The landings were a minor debacle. Some of the attackers were killed; 1200 were wounded and captured; some wounded were evacuated with the uninjured survivors to a United States Marine Corps base on an island near Puerto Rico and detained there for the next fifteen days while all access to the base was forbidden. Meanwhile the rebel leaders imprisoned in the Miami area demanded release; enraged by its refusal, they insisted they would leave even if their guards shot them. The CIA men were not prepared for this intransigence; Miró Cardona got to a telephone and complained bitterly to the State Department, which sent Schlesinger and Adolf A. Berle Jr. to Florida to hear his protests. The Council leaders were then taken to Washington, where Kennedy received them and attempted to restore amity. After a succession of meetings with the President, Miró Cardona made the astounding declaration that the United States had afforded no help of any kind to the invaders at any time, that there had been no attempt at invasion, and that a few boats had merely landed supplies and reinforcements for rebels within Cuba.

In the weeks after the event it became increasingly difficult to descry truth on any side. Castro charged that the CIA had recruited paid Batista killers into the invasion force; Roa told the UN that the United States had sent at least one tank into Cuba and produced a photograph to prove it, but the picture showed a Russian tank; *Izvestia* accused the United States of having sought to annex Cuba. What remained indisputable was the fact of American assistance in the training of the landing forces and the direction of the actual attack by the CIA; what remained to be determined was whether the President of the United States had authorized its cooperation in an attack on a Government with which his country was at peace or whether the Central Intelligence Agency had arrogated to itself the power to determine foreign relations and make war.

Rusk, in his first press conference after the collapse of the assault, was unusually cautious. He reiterated that no American troops would be sent into Cuba; he insisted that the operation had been wholly in the hands of the Cuban leaders who had been held at gunpoint while it was going on and that the force involved was negligible; he declared the sympathy of the nation for the rebels but he added that it was for the Cuban people to decide the fate of their country. It was a sorry performance. But it was a tragic day for those to whom for so long Adlai Stevenson had represented political decency when, in the UN, he had to rise to defend an action countenanced by his Government in which he had never concurred.

The fighting had virtually ended when Khrushchev and Kennedy exchanged their threats and warnings on further intervention in Cuba; the President refused to halt help to the rebels. But he ordered the cancellation of naval maneuvers off the coast of Florida, scheduled long earlier, lest the exercise be seized on as a provocation. He called emergency meetings with his chief advisers as he began to prepare a major declaration of policy on Cuba. Should it ever appear, he warned, that "the nations of this hemisphere should fail to meet their commitments against outside Communist penetration . . . we do not intend to be lectured on intervention by those whose character was stamped for all time on the bloody streets of Budapest." The issue, he insisted, went beyond Cuba itself to the fate of the entire western hemisphere; and the President concluded: "Let me then make clear as the President of the United States that I am determined upon our system's survival, regardless of the cost and regardless of the peril."

But no rhetoric, no rallying cry to freedom could undo the illegality and the immorality of Washington's active assistance to the overthrow of another Government. To the allies of the United States it raised not only the moral question but the practical one: how long could the United States be depended on as an ally if another nation chose a regime repugnant to Washington? For more than a century the United States had been recognized as one of the handful of great powers that never violated a treaty. Arguments of "political realism" were advanced to defend the Cuban adventure—but it was a realism of the moment, not of the long view; any argument of expediency could be only specious against the clear canons of international law and morality. Observers after the event wondered: when Kennedy, with his unquestioned high sense of honor, came into

office in January with the knowledge of the preparations
initiated by his predecessor to assist in an assault on another state's internal government, why had he not had the
foresight and the moral courage to order the operation
disbanded?

But it was only in other countries that the legal or the
moral implications were raised. Domestic criticism was
limited to the failure, not to the attempt. It was disturbing
that even the harshest critics of method and result stood
with the vast number of Americans, prominent and anony-
mous, whose emotions impelled them to shower praise and
support on the President for the stand he had taken against
Communism on the doorstep of the United States. That
Kennedy himself, in afterthought, might have been less
certain of the wisdom of his course was to be inferred from
the speed with which he called in for consultation in the
emergency not only Truman and Eisenhower but Nixon,
Goldwater and Governor Rockefeller of New York. Yet each
of these men emerged from his conference with the President to declare his unshakable support of what had been
done and what might have to be done; even outside public
life no authoritative voice dared to question the basic principles involved.

Kennedy, characteristically, refused to accept the exoner-
ation for the failure that his supporters tried to find for him.
The decision had been his alone, he insisted, as the responsibility had been his alone. He had listened to every view, he
had assessed every datum and he had judged badly. Even the
severest critics of his judgment had to respect his courage.

Even while the President was refusing to accept absolu-
tion, however, the repercussions were growing. The Cuban
conflict would continue; and, the Soviet Union warned, it
might yet bring war to the United States. In an effort to
minimize any danger of war, the United States delegation in
the UN endorsed a proposal by seven Latin-American nations to refer the dispute with Cuba to the members of the

OAS, but Washington declared its opposition to a Mexican draft resolution appealing to all nations "to insure that their territories and resources are not used to promote a civil war in Cuba." It was a strange stand for a nation dedicated to the principle of the right of every people to decide for itself the form of government it wanted.

Economic consequences of the Cuban crisis began to become apparent almost immediately after its climax. American trade with Soviet-bloc nations was threatened with new restrictions from the East as a matter of reprisal. In Latin America, many nations had retained their sympathy for Castro and others had been thrown reluctantly toward him by the apparent revival of "Yankee imperialism." Kennedy's Administration, in its search for a new direction in its policy toward Cuba, was beginning to study a total embargo on trade with the island, which would be bound further to antagonize not only Castro but other leaders in both hemispheres.

Looking into itself, the Administration called for a complete investigation of the CIA. Kennedy appointed his brother, the Attorney General, to work with General Maxwell D. Taylor, former Army Chief of Staff, in a nonpartisan study designed to produce recommendations for the complete reorganization of the agency in order to minimize the fallibility of this important intelligence arm. The President made it plain that the study was not to be made into a personal weapon against the agency's chief, Allen W. Dulles. Cuba, Kennedy believed, had sharply pointed up the problem of effective intelligence operations in a free society. Kennedy did not intend to convert the CIA into a policy-making agency; he did seek to make it far more valuable in the service it was supposed to perform for those agencies that do shape policy.

The policy-makers' problem was becoming more acute as Moscow's strategy on Cuba evolved. The firmer Khrushchev's stand on Cuba, the softer he grew on Laos; it was in the bitterness of the recriminations over Cuba that Russia agreed to the cease-fire in Laos. Cuba took priority because she was so much farther advanced than Laos in what was known to Muscovite theorists as Socialist evolution: Cuba had overthrown a reactionary government, she had (with Soviet help) eliminated the influence of the "imperialist" United States, and she had launched an indeterminate period of ever-increasing movement into Socialism, with continuing economic, military and technical help from the Communist nations. In the UN, Russia reiterated and reinforced her promise of all-out military aid to Cuba if that country were attacked; the pledge, Zorin emphasized, was even more earnest that Britain's to Poland before the German invasion of 1939. Two days later, Moscow denounced Kennedy for concocting a new "plot" against Cuba with the help of Truman, Eisenhower and Nixon.

It was on that same day, April 26, that the United States turned its back on an effort by Cuba to obtain a resumption of diplomatic relations and a discussion of the differences between the countries. "Communism in this hemisphere is not negotiable," the State Department replied curtly, disdaining to reply to a charge by Cuban President Osvaldo Dorticós Torrado that the United States was planning a new and bigger invasion of Cuba.

What Washington was planning was collective action by all the American republics against Cuba and Communism. Kennedy sought to persuade all American nations that had not already done so to sever diplomatic and trade relations with Cuba. Under his plan, the wartime Committee for the Political Defense of the Hemisphere would be revived in order to provide a constant check on the activities and movements of Cuban and other Communist agents within the hemisphere. But this collective venture was being forwarded with great circumspection because of the number of American nations that could be expected to balk at any overt action against Castro. Some, like Haiti and Argentina, condemned any intervention; others were so divided internally on the question that their governments dared not take a position. Unless informal exploration showed that Kennedy's proposal could command the required two-thirds majority in the OAS, it would not be formally presented.

On April 26, for the first time, Castro declared Cuba a "Socialist state"—the accepted Soviet-bloc term. On May 1, the 101st day of the Kennedy Administration, Cuba officially proclaimed her alignment with Russia.

The alliance had become inevitable long before Kennedy entered the White House. Nothing within the power of the President of the United States could have prevented it; it is even doubtful whether the ill-considered invasion accelerated it. What was immeasurably more significant was the position that the United States had taken on the conflicting claims of the principle of self-determination and of its own concept of its security, and the consequences of this position in the community of nations.

13. Africa: The Red and the Black

Reluctantly granted independence by Belgium, the Congo was an economic and political chaos at the beginning of 1961. Four men claimed or sought the governing power: President Joseph Kasavubu, former Premier Patrice Lumumba, secessionist President Moïse Tshombe of the former province of Katanga and another secessionist, Albert Kalonji. Kasavubu, whose Government was recognized by the UN, was generally pro-Western; Lumumba was backed by the Soviet bloc and many Afro-Asian nations; Tshombe was pro-Belgian; Kalonji had no clear allegiances. The troops of each—Kasavubu's 7500 under General Joseph Mobutu, Lumumba's 7000, Tshombe's 5000 and Kalonji's 1000—battled the forces of the others at will and opportunity. Lumumba's strength, even though he was imprisoned early in the year, seemed to be growing as a result of his contention that he alone could keep out the "white colonialists." Kasavubu employed Belgian nationals in his administration and Tshombe was accepting aid from Belgian army officers and business men. All foreign intervention in the Congo, from whatever source, had been condemned by a resolution of the UN. A UN force of 19,000 men had succeeded in keeping warfare under some control, but a number of Afro-Asian nations were threatening to withdraw their units.

Hammarskjold asked the Security Council for new powers to disarm all Congolese troops; the pro-Lumumba nations asked that only the other leaders' forces be disarmed and Lumumba be restored to power. The UN was badly divided and hence static. President Kennedy and his advisers addressed themselves to the first international crisis of the Administration and evolved a compromise formula that they hoped would bring at least a truce to the Congo. It contained four recommendations:

1. The release of Lumumba and his eventual inclusion in a new coalition government.
2. General agreement by all powers to send no arms or other aid to the Congo except through the UN.
3. The disarming of all Congolese soldiers.
4. The reconvening of the Congolese Parliament, suspended in September by Mobutu.

Secretary of State Dean Rusk added an appeal for a stronger mandate for the UN. The general prospect was not unencouraging, since the Soviet-Afro-Asian bloc had already expressed its advocacy of the first point in the compromise formula. Belgium objected to it in toto on the ground that the only need in the Congo was a program that would bar Communism there. Britain and France were dubious of a coalition as a threat to Kasavubu's authority, but they did not rule it out. But, before any decision could be reached, Lumumba escaped and was killed by Tshombe's men.

The Soviet bloc reacted violently, implying that the West had murdered Lumumba and denouncing the UN's entire record in the Congo. Antoine Gizenga, a follower of

Lumumba, immediately claimed the title of Premier and was recognized at once by the Soviet Union and the United Arab Republic; the Russians made a disguised threat that they would step in to maintain Gizenga in power. Kennedy reacted firmly: massive unilateral intervention by any one nation, he declared, would carry "risks of war," for the United States would fulfill its obligation to defend the UN Charter. His statement was issued with the full backing of the major Western powers, who hoped that it would deter Moscow from going beyond words. The West would continue to accept Kasavubu's as the legitimate Government; but Ghana, Guinea, Yugoslavia, East Germany, Morocco, Mali, Cuba and a number of European satellites accepted Gizenga. The UAR was actively supplying Gizenga's troops.

In the next few days the United States found it necessary to bring pressure on Belgium in the hope that that country could persuade Tshombe to lead Katanga into a new Congo Federation. Kasavubu was proving a poor rallying point for Congolese allegiance. UN action had watered down the compromise formula proposed by the United States and its allies so that it merely "recognized the danger" of outside intervention and called for the expulsion of foreign military and semi-military personnel. The United States, however, had prevailed on the UN to declare that force should be used only as a last resort to prevent civil war in the Congo. Now it was seeking action by the UN to condemn the use of assassination—a gesture that seemed hardly required or effective.

The UN's position was not helped by the attitude of the man whose regime in the Congo it was striving to support. Kasavubu violently attacked Rajeshwar Dayal of India, the chief UN representative in the Congo, for what he called bias in favor of his opponents and for acting without "proper" consultation with him. Tshombe and Kalonji, who had somewhat consolidated his position as president of the secessionist South Kasai Province, had joined Kasavubu in

making it plain that they would resist by force any effort by
UN troops to disarm their forces. Kasavubu also resented
the refusal of the UN to act against his 2000-man garrison
at Luluabourg, which to a man had defected to Gizenga's
army. Parliament was to be reconvened, but under conditions that stirred serious doubts of its effectiveness. Still,
Kasavubu assured G. Mennen Williams, Assistant Secretary
of State for African Affairs, that he was always willing to
cooperate with the UN provided its officials consulted and
worked with his Government.

In the midst of the Congo crisis Williams had created an
unexpected embarrassment for Kennedy by his behavior on
his mission to Africa for the President. Williams was visiting
both the new African nations and the colonies—predominantly British—that were being prepared for ultimate
independence. The United States, Williams declared, stood
for a policy of "Africa for the Africans"—an announcement
that was immediately seized upon by black nationalists and
white imperialists alike for their own purposes. The one
side immediately claimed American support for its efforts
to drive out all Europeans; the other criticized America for
interfering in what was none of her business. Britons in
particular were incensed, to the point where one editorialist
asked: "Would any British minister in any party government be so tactless or short-sighted as to interfere in Little
Rock?" Williams hastily added a qualification to his original
statement, to the effect that "Africa for the Africans" meant
"all people in Africa regardless of their race and color."
Kennedy himself was questioned on Williams's statement
and gave it unqualified endorsement in its amended form,
saying he recognized as Africans "all those who felt that
they were Africans, whatever their color might be, whatever
their race might be." By implication he was excluding those
residents of Africa who considered themselves primarily
British, French, Belgian or Portuguese—in other words, he
was underlining his own anti-colonialist stand. Neither the

envoy nor the President had smoothed the nation's road in dealing with any faction involved in the continuing Congo problem.

Among the leading critics of the UN's role in the Congo was President Kwame Nkrumah of Ghana, who had already begun to reduce his contribution of manpower to the UN forces. Early in March he asked Kennedy for an appointment, and arrived in Washington a few days later en route to the resumption of the UN's General Assembly. The United States Navy had directed a task force of four ships to enter Congolese waters and stand ready with whatever support might have to be lent to the UN troops, but twenty-four hours later the order was reversed and the ships were diverted on the ground that they were not needed. The pretext for the first order was the surrender of Matadi, the Congo's only seaport, to Congolese troops by UN soldiers after a two-day battle; negotiations were under way for the restoration of UN control of the port and the UN had threatened to recapture it by force if the talks failed. On the eve of Nkrumah's arrival in Washington, however, Kennedy apparently had grave second thoughts as to the advisability of involving American warships and their contingent of 500 Marines in military action.

At the same time the Congolese Government was hamstringing the UN's aerial access to the country. Though UN troops retained control of the principal airport, at Leopoldville, the Congolese were imposing their own control on takeoffs and landings. The negotiations for the return of Matadi were made contingent on the UN's removal of Dayal, but the UN had refused to accept the condition and persisted in its intention to airlift more Tunisian and Indian troops into the Congo via Leopoldville despite the Government's announcement that it alone would authorize or refuse clearance for all planes. It was against this background that Nkrumah arrived at the White House on March 8.

In dealing with Nkrumah Kennedy was talking to a chief of state whose Parliament was almost admittedly a rubber-stamp body. Any stand taken by Nkrumah alone would have the force of law for his country, and it was important to erode at least in part the adamant anti-American and anti-UN position that Nkrumah had been developing. The first steps had been taken in preliminary talks between Stevenson and Nkrumah. The official welcome at the airport was replete with pomp and panoply far above and beyond the call of protocol.

Kennedy's one-day talk with Nkrumah bore some immediate fruit. While the Ghanaian remained unshaken in his contention that a Congo solution was impossible without the withdrawal of all Belgian military units, he agreed that the UN must use force if necessary. Of his own country, which he intended to make the leader of the new African nations, Nkrumah said: "We are trying to create a society in which private capital and certain state-controlled agencies can cooperate. . . . Don't equate Communism or being Communist with African nationalism." From this it was to be inferred that he hoped to use his influence with the Congolese leaders, once a stable regime had been installed, to follow a similar policy.

As Kennedy and Nkrumah were meeting in Washington, Gizenga was restating his claim to the Premiership of the Congo, but now he announced his willingness to accept Kasavubu as the constitutional head of state. The Congolese factional chiefs were preparing to meet in Tananarive, in the Malagasy Republic, in an effort to work out their own solution. Gizenga had gone to Cairo, where he enjoyed the support and advice of Nasser. The controversial Dayal had gone back to New York to report to Hammarskjold and for the moment, at least, there were no further demands for his ouster. In the Tananarive meeting the Congolese, without Gizenga, who had refused to attend, agreed to replace the contested Republic of the Congo with a confederation of states that would re-integrate Tshombe's Katanga and Kalonji's South Kasai in the whole, though they would retain their sovereignty. Kasavubu and his Premier, Joseph Ileo, considered this a victory, but much remained to be done before the confederation could become operative. The United States took the view that the decision required careful study before it could be ratified by the Security Council, but it rejected the stand of the Congolese leaders that the time had now come to withdraw the UN's troops. Washington believed that until Gizenga accepted the confederation civil strife would continue. The Soviet bloc, on the other hand, denounced the Tananarive group as "traitors" working to "dismember" the Congo to please "colonialists."

One fact was certain: fighting among the rivals continued in the Congo. The United States tightened its restrictions on unauthorized shipments of military supplies to the Congo aboard American-owned ships or planes from any point of origin; only shipments licensed by the UN would be permitted. Meanwhile Stevenson and Williams voiced, presumably with Kennedy's clearance, approval for some form of Congolese confederation—not necessarily that loosely decided on at Tananarive—whose separate members would be willing to surrender substantial control of finances, foreign policy and the military to a central government that would gain in power as time passed. Despite American hostility to Gizenga, Washington was now prepared to concede that his participation in the Government was inevitable if peace was to be established. At the end of March it was reported that Kennedy and his advisers had at last worked out a plan to be offered to the United Nations for the pacification and development of an independent Congo.

The problem was aggravated by fiscal trouble within the UN. Its involvement in the Congo was draining its budget at an annual rate of $120 million, and the Soviet bloc had cavalierly refused to pay its assessed share of these costs.

Without funds the UN mission and troops would have to be withdrawn and the area would be left defenseless against a full-scale renewal of internal warfare and the growing danger of Soviet intervention leading to full control. While Stevenson was urging the UN to assist actively in drafting a new Constitution for the Congo that would enable the country to make its way toward nationhood and thus accelerate the feasibility of ending UN intervention, the United States voluntarily assumed—for the second time; the first occurred in 1960—virtually half the total burden. France had joined the Soviet nations in refusing to pay her share of the costs of the Congo operation (the French action was generally attributed to the fear of eventual UN intervention in Algeria if a peaceful settlement were not worked out). The United States therefore paid in not only its $32.5 million assessment for the Congo operation but a voluntary contribution of $15 million as well.

While the Congo offered the most immediate and dramatic evidence of Kennedy's quick implementation of his promises to devote increasing attention to American relations with Africa, he was constantly concerned with many other aspects of the situation. In Washington itself the emergence of Africa was creating problems; the new nations were sending diplomatic representatives and staffs and they were too often running up hard against the bigotry of the South. One of the first acts of the new chief of protocol of the State Department, Angier Biddle Duke, was to create a special staff to help the Africans to find housing, office space and schools for their children. Everyone in the Government was acutely aware of the impact in an African country when its diplomat, arriving at a restaurant for breakfast, was given the food in a paper bag and told to eat outside.

But this was only the beginning. Kennedy's interest in Africa embraced the entire continent. Early in his term it became known that he would invite President Habib Bourguiba of Tunisia to visit Washington—a move linked with Bourguiba's important role in efforts to settle the Algerian war and the respect he enjoyed on both sides. Kennedy's own stand for Algerian independence was well known. He did not find it inconsistent with the warning he caused to be sent to Morocco when that country accepted military aid from Russia: continuance in this course would make it impossible for Morocco to obtain spare parts for military equipment of Western origin. Rabat was advised that it would do well to limit Soviet aid to the purely economic.

Such actions could not be expected to help the United States in Africa as a whole, where high hopes had been aroused by Kennedy's election. Three Democratic Senators —Frank Church of Idaho, Gale McGee of Wyoming and Frank E. Moss of Utah—reported after a 22,000-mile tour that "the gravest possible injury to our positions and influences" in Africa could be expected if the Administration did not evolve positive new policies toward it and put them into action without delay. The line that the Administration had begun to take was directed toward "independence" as against "neutralism" for the new countries, but on examination the difference turned out to be largely semantic. Kennedy's aides were well aware that Marshal Tito of Yugoslavia had prefaced his impending visits to African countries with an appeal to them to remain clear of both the Eastern and the Western blocs, and true neutralism could hardly be the subject of condemnation.

But the new nations were not the limit of the Administration's concern in Africa. During February there was an outbreak of racial violence in Angola, an African colony belonging to Portugal, and the Security Council was asked to order an inquiry with a view to compelling Portugal to effect reforms in race relations in Angola. When the inquiry resolution was put to a vote—which proved unsuccessful—the United States joined the Soviet Union, Liberia, Ceylon and the United Arab Republic in the affirmative.

Britain voted against the resolution and France abstained,
both accepting Portugal's view that there was no legal basis
for UN intervention.

The decision to vote for the resolution was the President's. He was supported by Rusk, whose own department
was sharply divided on the question. Some of the opponents
of the resolution believed that normal diplomatic pressures
should first have been brought to bear on Portugal in the
hope that she would initiate improvements in Angola without external pressure. All those who disagreed with Kennedy's action believed that, whatever his decision, he should
first have consulted, not merely notified, those friendly
colonial powers whose reactions were bound to be antago-
nistic. But others felt that the affront to our allies was more
than offset by the good will gained in Africa and Asia by the
American vote, even though it was unsuccessful. The advo-
cates of this view had in mind the upsurge in anti-American
sentiment on those continents late in 1960 when the United
States abstained from a General Assembly vote on a resolution calling for immediate action to give independence to all
remaining colonies.

The vote on Angola was only part of the new face of
American policy. The Security Council was also grappling
with the Apartheid policy of the Union of South Africa and
had before it a resolution calling on the Union to moderate
its extreme segregationism. Again the United States voted
to adopt the resolution. On both issues this country had for
the first time taken a stand that could provide a logical
foundation for an ultimate movement within the UN
toward an abridgment of national sovereignties, for in both
cases the United States was in effect demanding international action on a purely internal problem of another
country. At least theoretically Washington had sacrificed
its best defense against any possible call in the UN for investigation of or action on racial relations in the United
States. American endorsement of the right of the UN to act

in a domestic situation that offered no threat to international peace and security was in effect American rejection of that section of the UN Charter that expressly protected the rights of national sovereignty. Hence the two votes on Angola and South Africa were most important not because of the risk of tension among allies created by the former, but because of their clear indication of a new American concept of the powers and responsibilities of the UN. Nor was this altered by the subsequent refusal of the United States to vote for the Assembly resolution to impose economic sanctions on South Africa. But in the eyes of Portugal the United States had betrayed her in favor of "black Communists" and a mob attack on the Embassy in Lisbon soon followed.

Kennedy's commitment to Africans was not swayed. Williams returned from his tour of the continent with a recommendation for more and quicker economic aid and the news that African enthusiasm for Kennedy's Peace Corps was high. Stevenson called on the leaders of the African countries to draw long-range development plans to which the Administration could give its help and in which the UN could assist. The program, he said, should be "by, of and for Africans" and help should be multilateral as a guarantee against political strings. It was reported that the project had undergone preliminary discussion with a number of Asian and African representatives before Stevenson proposed it in the Assembly, but it was attacked at once by Jaja Wachuku, Nigerian Minister of Economic Development, because it lacked a "statement in dollars." Africans, he said, wanted nothing to do with a plan designed to "hoodwink" or "mesmerize" them. The United States replied that a rigid program had not been presented precisely because it was preferable to allow its beneficiaries to present their own thinking on their needs. In a subsequent private meeting between Stevenson and African leaders a more cordial reaction was elicited even in the face of Stevenson's warning against waste and inefficiency. Important American help, he said, could be counted on by nations showing themselves capable of careful and realistic thinking.

Many of the nations to be aided wanted to attach to any industrial-development project a rider calling for the immediate liberation of remaining colonies. They insisted that the UN Assembly impose "target dates" for such action; but with this the American Government was not prepared to agree despite some advocacy for it within Administration ranks. Nonetheless it was now unmistakably clear that Kennedy was committing the United States to a gradual but unremitting drive for the end of colonialism at the risk of wounded feelings but stopping short of fundamental damage to American alliances.

14. Germany and China

Germany and China might well be said to represent the positive and negative poles of American policy since the end of the Second World War. In the fifteen years before Kennedy became President the United States had worked resolutely to cement new and strong ties with West Germany; in the same period it had adamantly refused to admit the existence of Communist China. Nothing in Kennedy's Congressional or campaign record indicated any intention to alter either stand.

Within a week of the inauguration it was announced that German Foreign Minister Heinrich von Brentano would visit Kennedy in Washington. Chancellor Konrad Adenauer had hoped to make the trip then but had deferred it when persons close to the President had told him informally that it would not be wise at that time. Von Brentano was due in the United States in mid-February in any case for a conference on relations with Germany; but the utmost secrecy was

maintained as long as possible on his meeting with the
President, which was expected to cover Berlin, the continuance of American troops in Europe, nuclear arms for American allies, and other subjects. The United States had its
own demands to make, too: German help to ease military
and financial burdens on the United States, including the
early payment of German dollar obligations. The West
German economy was the soundest on the Continent and it
was felt that Germany should bear part of the burden of
mutual-aid and security programs.

Shortly before von Brentano's departure from Germany,
Kennedy sent a private message to Adenauer that reassured
the Chancellor on this country's intentions with respect to
Berlin and German unification. In addition, Adenauer was
pleased with Kennedy's emphasis on NATO, which en-
hanced Adenauer's position in his forthcoming talks with
de Gaulle and took some of the sting out of American views
on the inadequacy of German plans to help alleviate the
American imbalance of payments. Hence the climate for
von Brentano's trip was not unfavorable. Before seeing the
President, the Foreign Minister had a preliminary session
with Rusk in which they discussed American reactions to
Bonn's plan to remit $972 million in prepayment for arms
purchases and post-war debts and to contribute $750 million
for loans to underdeveloped countries. The Germans had
refused any grant funds. Rusk made it plain that von
Brentano's hope for a credit of $200 million in "reimburse-
ment" for German assets in the United States seized during
the war was vain. Von Brentano had authority from his
Government to modify its stand and the major purpose of
his talk with the President, which was economic, was
accomplished with mutual satisfaction and the pledge of a
billion-dollar German aid allotment. The road had thus
been smoothed for Adenauer's visit in April, despite division
in his Cabinet on his accession to Kennedy's demands.

The question of Berlin was certain to be prominent on

the Chancellor's agenda in Washington. In that city, Harriman declared that the Kennedy Administration was not necessarily bound by decisions made by Eisenhower but preferred a completely fresh start on the problem. Harriman made it clear that this meant that Kennedy would be, if anything, firmer than his predecessor on the maintenance of the city's independence and on the American contribution to keep it free. This position was repeated in Washington by Rusk; the State Department emphasized that there would be no reduction of the American garrison in Berlin, then numbering about 6,000 men. A few days later, an article in *Foreign Affairs* by von Brentano emphasized Germany's attitude toward the United States by demanding that this country take a more leading role in NATO and in expanding the alliance to broaden its influence beyond the area it already covered. Before leaving Bonn, Adenauer questioned Dean Acheson for five hours on American NATO policy.

Arriving in Washington, Adenauer expressed his people's "great confidence" in the President. But their first meeting was formal and inconclusive, though relations warmed later, and Adenauer's initial fears of changes in basic American policies on Germany were dissipated. Reassured that the United States would oppose Russian proposals to convert Berlin into a demilitarized free city and to transfer control of land access to the city to the East German regime, Adenauer supported Kennedy's stand on the OECD and, at least in principle, on increased aid by both their nations to under-developed areas. The conferences concluded with an affirmation of plans to work for increased political unity in NATO, for new efforts toward disarmament, for "continuing attention to the balance-of-payments problem" (on which nothing specific was settled) and for self-determination for Berlin and for the two Germanys.

The approach to the problem of Communist China was the diametric opposite of that guiding dealings with Germany. Early in Kennedy's term the State Department made a virtually routine announcement that it would continue to press for Peiping's release of the Americans it held captive. The Chinese, rather surprisingly, admitted that Kennedy's program promised some "gestures for peace," but they insisted he was lying when he spoke of the "so-called Chinese 'menace' to Asia." The United States struck the next blow when Lord Home told the House of Lords that "the facts of international life" required Peiping's admission to the UN. The State Department reported that the question of admission "must confront the cold, hard fact of Communist China's own attitude." The American position was complicated by the long-standing commitment to Chiang Kai-shek's Nationalist regime on Formosa, whose abolition was demanded by Peiping.

American insistence on the threat posed by Peiping was embarrassed in February when the Burmese Government charged that Chiang was airlifting American arms and ammunition to guerrillas loyal to him who had been hiding out in Burma's back country since 1950. The Burmese were so incensed that 10,000 of them rioted outside the United States Embassy in Rangoon and had to be dispersed by the gunfire of Burmese troops. Premier U Nu said he held the United States directly responsible for the guerrillas' activity and threatened to bring the matter before the UN, which had prevailed on Chiang in 1953 to disown them. American aides in Burma inspected some of the material captured from the guerrillas by the Burmese and found that at least some bore United States aid labels; this tended to support the Burmese charge that Chiang was giving the jungle fighters arms that he was receiving from the United States. At the same time Peiping charged that this country was trying to widen the Laos war by introducing Chinese Nationalist troops into the loyalists' ranks; numbers of them had fled into that country, which had protested their entry and was trying to keep them out of its army. The question of the arms drop was never officially resolved, but early in March Washington ordered Chiang to disarm any Chinese Nationalist guerrillas in both Burma and Laos, and promised to help relocate them to other areas.

Of considerably graver concern was the Peiping arms buildup with the latest Soviet weapons. Kennedy and Prime Minister Keith J. Holyoake of New Zealand, who was conferring with him in Washington, jointly denounced Communist China's "hostile and aggressive attitude" as a threat to peace in Asia, Africa and Latin America. It was true that China was actively assisting Castro and some of the African states, but it was Russia that was bearing the load of intervention on behalf of the Laotian rebels. Nonetheless, Jacob D. Beam, the American Ambassador to Poland, resumed the intermittent seven-year conferences that had been held in Warsaw with Peiping's envoy, with instructions to take the initiative for at least the beginning of a rapprochement. He was, of course, going to pursue the long-standing request for the release of captive Americans; in addition, he was to offer an American-Chinese exchange of journalists on a reciprocal basis. For many years neither country had had journalistic representation in the other.

Peiping refused on the ground that negotiation of anything would be difficult as long as the United States continued to "occupy" Formosa. The Communists held that American support of Chiang amounted to intervention in internal Chinese matters. For the same reason the Peiping envoy refused to discuss the release of the prisoners or a suggestion that his country and the United States agree to settle their disputes without resorting to force. Kennedy replied at his next news conference that "we are not prepared to surrender" in order to treat with Communist China. Rusk amplified with the statement that Peiping would not accept the diplomatic recognition of "two Chinas"—Peiping and Taiwan. The Communists retorted that the attempt at negotiation in Warsaw had been sabotaged by American hostility; they insisted that they could see only "a lack of desire on the part of the United States to renounce the use of force or the threat of force."

The stalemate appeared unbreakable. When the Senate Foreign Relations Committee was questioning John K. Galbraith, Kennedy's Ambassador-designate to India, he insisted that American recognition of Communist China and her admission to the UN were essential to the establishment of peace in Asia. But he said Communist China would first have to demonstrate that she was a "peace-loving" nation by accepting the UN Charter and recognizing Chiang's Nationalist Government. When that would happen he was not willing to predict, and for the foreseeable future it was hard for any observer to descry any sign of compromise on either side.

15. The United Nations

Kennedy rightly viewed the United Nations as "our last, best hope" for ending the cold war. As his representative there he had chosen his greatest rival for the loyalty of the American intellectual, Adlai Stevenson, a man whose own views were not always in accord with Kennedy's. But Stevenson was thrust into his front-line position alone: behind him there was only a vacuum of policy. The international thinking of the previous Administration had proved its worthlessness; new international crises were arising before the Kennedy Administration could evolve a workable and durable policy. In the beginning Stevenson had to improvise and to temporize. The initial blunder of his excessive optimism about the President's willingness to confer with Khrushchev brought an immediate and rather crushing rebuke from Kennedy, who made it clear that he alone was deciding policy. One aspect of it had already taken shape, and on this both Kennedy and Stevenson had always thought alike: the Russians must be prevented from carrying through their proposal to replace Secretary General Hammarskjold with a three-member secretariat representing the West, the Soviet bloc and the uncommitted nations.

It was no lack of confidence in Stevenson but rather an awareness of the immensity of the task of the Ambassador to the United Nations that impelled Kennedy to materially strengthen the American delegation to the UN early in February. The delegation's work extended far beyond such dramatic public manifestations as the verbal battles on the floor of the Security Council or the General Assembly, and Stevenson believed there should be a moratorium on such public squabbles and a greater reliance on "quiet diplomacy." A UN delegation had to concern itself with much more than major political issues of a moment. There were the myriad continuing UN activities in which a nation could hardly afford to be represented by minor figures: international control of the narcotics trade, joint efforts at raising levels of education and literacy, protection of human rights, administration of trust territories and many more. Hence Kennedy gave Stevenson in effect five right hands:

Jonathan B. Bingham, a liberal New York Democrat, had served as secretary to Harriman when the latter was Governor. A veteran of Army Intelligence, he had later been deputy director of the Point Four program. Francis T. P. Plimpton, like Bingham a lawyer, was a director of the Foreign Policy Association. Philip M. Klutznick, another lawyer, had developed model suburbs in the United States and was creating a new port city in Israel; he had served in the delegation before. A fourth lawyer, Charles P. Noyes, had served the Lend-Lease Administration and the Rockefeller Brothers Fund. The fifth assistant to Stevenson was a career diplomat, Charles W. Yost, who had served in various parts of the world and taken part in the UN's founding convention. Stevenson welcomed the addition of these men to his high-level staff but let it be known that he was not yet satisfied.

The new Administration's first test in the UN arose when the Soviet Union refused any longer to recognize Hammarskjold's authority. The pretext for Russia's action was the murder of Patrice Lumumba and two colleagues in the Congo; the draft resolution submitted to the Security Council by Valerian A. Zorin, the Soviet Ambassador, declared it "essential to dismiss Dag Hammarskjold from the post of Secretary General of the United Nations as a participant in and organizer of the violence committed against the leading statesmen of the Congo."

This, Stevenson said in the Council, "is virtually a declaration of war on the United Nations and on the principle of international action on behalf of peace." The second phrase alluded to the resolution's demand for the UN's withdrawal from the Congo within a month. With the fine irony of which he had considerable mastery, Stevenson commended the Soviet Union for denouncing assassination as a political weapon, colonialism as an institution and foreign intervention in other nations' domestic affairs as a policy, adding that he hoped "we misinterpret the threat by the Soviet Government that 'it is ready to render all possible assistance and support'" to the *soi-disant* government of Antoine Gizenga, "which has no legal status." He would "pass lightly" over the "petulant attack" on Hammarskjold, Stevenson said, and he devoted very few words to it; but they were decisive, and the Soviet resolution failed.

The stand taken by the United States served an ancillary purpose: it squelched the rumors of a rupture between Kennedy and Stevenson that had arisen after Kennedy's rebuke to the Ambassador over the President's putative attitude toward meeting Khrushchev. As soon as Stevenson's speech was concluded, Kennedy telephoned his congratulations; he felicitated Stevenson publicly in his subsequent press conference. For the policy adopted by the

United States had been shaped by Stevenson himself as
well as by Kennedy and Rusk; all three had held repeated
telephone conferences in the developing Congo crisis.

Khrushchev renewed his attack on Hammarskjold in a
letter to Prime Minister Nehru of India. Stevenson reacted
by publicly declaring that Russia was trying to cripple the
UN, a view from which Kennedy did not disassociate himself. As evidence of his charges, Stevenson pointed out that,
when the United States had asked the Security Council to
adopt a resolution condemning executions throughout the
Congo, not merely in the secessionist provinces controlled
by anti-Communist leaders, Zorin had promptly exercised
his right of veto. Outside the UN, Stevenson made it plain
that Kennedy's endorsement of "Africa for the Africans"
applied to any efforts by Russia to implement her threat to
intervene in the Congo.

When the General Assembly opened on March 7, Foreign
Minister Gromyko rather than Khrushchev headed the
Russian delegation. Among the hold-over items on the
agenda for the session was a debate on disarmament. Without referring to Kennedy's earlier statement that the problem was the subject of an intensive study that probably
could not be completed before the summer, he asked that
the debate be deferred to allow a "period of relative quiet"
to "contribute to a better international climate." The
United States hoped that all cold-war bitterness could be
avoided during the session. But the Soviet delegation immediately insisted that the arms debate remain on the agenda;
in a private conversation a day earlier Gromyko had indicated to Stevenson that he would not yield. That talk dealt
with the American proposal to reduce the agenda to only
the few items essential to the conduct of current UN business, such as filling vacant council and commission seats and
financing the Congo operation. But there was to be no
bartering with Russia on items to be dropped.

For some months neutralist delegates had been urging

both the East and the West to avoid debate on four controversies. The first of these was the Soviet charge of "aggressive actions" by the United States because of the U-2 and RB-47 flights in 1960. Cuba had also asked for debate on her charges of aggression by the United States, based on the revelation that the Central Intelligence Agency was training exiles in Florida and Cuba for an invasion of the island. Two other items had been postponed from earlier sessions: the Soviet Union's 1956 intervention in Hungary and the Communist Chinese repressions in Tibet. The United States had submitted in the previous September a request for a debate on a program for African development, and Gromyko had hinted that, if the United States would drop this request, the Soviet Union might agree to a postponement of the arms debate.

Other nations' delegates were having difficulty in their efforts to determine what positions Kennedy would take on various issues related to the cold war. On some problems, such as the American attitude toward Russia, there was simply no indication at all; in other instances there seemed to be contradiction. For example, Kennedy's determination to build up conventional armaments appeared to revive the "toughness" of Truman. On the other hand, the President had taken a distinctly unprovocative, if firm, position on the Congo and Laos. The emphasis on American interest in underdeveloped and uncommitted countries seemed to indicate that Kennedy wanted to eliminate the brawls with Russia that had marked so many previous sessions. However, it was beginning to appear that on such matters as cutting the agenda the neutralists would go along with the United States only as far as the Russians permitted. After Stevenson's defense of Hammarskjold and his attack on the Soviet attitudes toward the Congo and the UN, *Izvestia*, the Soviet Government newspaper, began to complain that he sounded like Henry Cabot Lodge, who had been Eisenhower's Ambassador to the UN.

American policy in the UN did not take a really clear line until the Assembly began to debate the Portuguese repressions in Angola and Apartheid in South Africa. It was now manifest that Kennedy's anti-colonialism was not a gesture; it was a conviction that he was prepared to implement even in the face of harsh criticism and the threat of harm to America's relations with some of her allies. It was unfair to condemn Kennedy, as many observers did, on the false ground that he had ordered Stevenson to vote for Angolan self-determination and against Portuguese tyranny in the colony in order to win the support of the great number of Afro-Asian nations. That this may have been a secondary consideration is not impossible, but the basic reason for the American stand was one of moral belief. Similarly, American support for UN condemnation of South Africa's racial policies and practices arose from the deliberate conclusion that the protection of human rights transcended the preservation of national sovereignty. South Africa had contended that what happened within her borders could not, under the UN Charter, legitimately be a matter of UN concern unless it threatened international peace and security. American concurrence in the contrary view threw the prestige of the United States to the side of those who looked forward to the ultimate supremacy of an international government that would have the duty and the power to prevent injustices within national borders regardless whether they endangered other nations.

But the single gravest issue before the UN as the spring advanced was the Congo. It was made so by Russia, which, in the Assembly, renewed her attack on Hammarskjold for his conduct of UN operations in the Congo and repeated the accusation that he was the responsible murderer of Lumumba. Gromyko demanded that the UN recognize Gizenga and allow him to proceed unmolested to enforce his rule throughout the Congo without delay. Stevenson rose to denounce Gromyko for behaving in "the worst and most destructive traditions of the cold war" and for his "wild and irresponsible and absurd" personal attack on Hammarskjold. "The Soviet Union does not want the United Nations to succeed in the Congo," Stevenson charged, bolstered by the documentation of the bare facts; he added: "To use the unhappy state of affairs in the Congo for such insensate attacks on the Secretary General compounds the offense to the dignity of this body and to the very survival of the United Nations as an effective operating instrument for peace and progress."

The United States under Kennedy was determined to preserve and, if possible, to strengthen the UN; hence Stevenson exerted every effort in his successful defense of the Secretary General, the Congo intervention and, as he accurately indicated, the survival of the UN itself. When parliamentary maneuvers failed to hamstring the UN, the Russians resorted to outright refusal to pay their assessed share of the cost of the UN's intervention, undoubtedly believing that such a refusal, supported by their satellites and later, for other reasons having chiefly to do with Algeria, by France, would certainly have the practical effect of getting the UN out of Africa and letting the Congo go to Gizenga by default. Perhaps Moscow reasoned that Washington was either too short-sighted or too frightened by the plight of the dollar to resist. But at the end of March Kennedy declared that the United States, to "demonstrate its desire, and its faith, that the United Nations shall survive to serve the interests of mankind," pledged his country to assume as much as half the total cost of the Congo operation instead of its normal pro-rata share of one-third.

Against any errors of judgment or of action in international relations during his first hundred days as President, Kennedy made with this gesture a contribution to world stability that it would be difficult to overestimate. When the Soviet effort to unseat Hammarskjold and to vest the control of the UN in a committee failed, only the gamble of this projected sabotage could have been relied on to wreck the UN. Moscow knew that if the United States did not assume so disproportionate an economic burden the remaining members of the UN variously would not and could not make up the deficit created by the withdrawal of financial support by the Soviet bloc. Had Kennedy acted otherwise the Congo intervention would certainly have collapsed, and it was more than probable that the resultant tremendous gain in Russian prestige would have cemented to Moscow not only the Congo but many other states that still hesitated between East and West, influenced less by the thought of tangible immediate benefits than by the uneasy need to ally themselves with a winner. The influence of the UN would have been destroyed, for it would have become utterly impotent.

Kennedy's rescue of the UN was far more dramatic than it seemed; but from that time until the session closed at the end of April the rest was anti-climax. There was a renewal of the bitter Russian-American dispute over the revision of the agenda and the elimination of the arms debate, and the United States triumphed in the end only because the majority of the Assembly stood behind it despite Russia's unaltered position; unquestionably the resolution of the Congo budget crisis had something to do with influencing more than one neutral or uncommitted vote. But that was the last American victory in the session, partly because no major issues remained on the agenda, partly because the new prestige of the United States was almost immediately breached by its Cuban adventure.

A minor American defeat, in fact, occurred near the end of the Assembly's meeting. The Assembly's Special Political Committee had taken up the question of Arab refugees from Palestine. In mid-April the Arab delegations attached to a routine resolution for continuing aid to the needy refugees a clause calling for the appointment of a custodian for the property they had left behind. Such assets had been seized by Israel, which stood ready to compensate the former owners. In the Assembly, Israel also challenged the authority of the UN to concern itself with property claims. In weeks of private negotiation the United States had tried to prevail on the Arab states to abandon their insistence on the property clause, but they refused, charging that America seemed determined "to serve the policy and interest of Israel." Plimpton replied that it was the Arabs, with their injection of the property clause, who were inciting political discord in the UN.

The United States sought to achieve a compromise "devoid of controversy" by offering a new resolution providing for the repatriation of the Arab refugees. It omitted any reference to either their resettlement or their compensation. On this ground the Arabs objected to it, and Israel rejected it as being overwhelmingly one-sided—i.e., pro-Arab. The committee's vote was so small, however, that it was doubted whether the resolution would be able to command the two-thirds majority required for adoption by the full Assembly.

It was inevitable that the Cuban invasion should expose the United States to attack in the UN—attack that would have been even fiercer, and very likely more successful, if the invaders had accomplished their objective. To Russia, denounced with monotonous regularity at every UN session for her Hungarian repression, America's mistake was a godsend. But many of the Afro-Asian nations that so often sided with Moscow were estopped, by their own expressed view that the affairs of a given area should be handled by the countries of that area, from going very far in attacking the United States for its action on Cuba as long as most of the other nations in the American hemisphere withheld support from the assault; instead they offered a resolution to submit the matter to the Organization of American States. It fell short of the two-thirds majority, but the best that the enemies of the United States could gain from the Assembly was a resolution adjuring its members to do their best to ease the "existing tension." It was the good luck of the United States that the very emergence of competing blocs, which had so often handicapped American efforts, presented an immovable obstacle to the vote of censure or worse that might otherwise have been registered against the Kennedy Administration in the forum of the nations.

16. Reaching for the Moon

In April a photograph that appeared in almost all news-papers throughout the world showed the President watching television. He was standing in the office of his secretary, Mrs. Evelyn Lincoln, hands in his pockets. At his left was Mrs. Kennedy, leaning on a desk. Behind him stood his brother, Robert, McGeorge Bundy, Vice President Johnson, Arthur Schlesinger and Admiral Burke. Their eyes were fixed on the screen, which was showing them a Redstone rocket about to carry Alan B. Shepard Jr., a Navy commander, into space. It was America's biggest publicity gamble.

At this stage in the Kennedy Administration, American prestige and morale were at their lowest. The Russians had already sent a man into orbit; the Cuban tragedy was still fresh in the minds of the people, as were the retreats in strategic Southeast Asia. There had been strong voices that had urged Kennedy to postpone the shot indefinitely, fearing that failure would plunge America's position even lower,

if that were possible. There were the timid who had criticized the tremendous publicity buildup the space shot had
been given. A week before, a similar shot, unmanned, had
been destroyed shortly after blast-off, but, when the Cape
Canaveral command had looked to Kennedy, he replied:
"You may proceed when ready."

For 15 anxious minutes Kennedy and the nation watched
as the space capsule named Freedom 7 carried the 160-
pound Shepard in an arc that reached an altitude of 115
miles and set him down 302 miles away in the sea off the
Bahama Islands. The relieved nation cheered and the world
applauded. The London *Daily Telegraph* said: "Technically,
the Americans were runners-up. Morally, the cup is theirs.
Nobody can doubt that Commander Shepard really did it."

The triumph for the United States was not tarnished by
the technical difference between Shepard's feat and the
flight of Yuri Gagarin. Shepard had attained a top speed of
only 4,500 miles an hour and had traveled a short distance
in comparison with the Russian's total orbit of the earth
at a speed of 18,000 miles an hour and an altitude of more
than 188 miles. Gagarin was only a passenger in his capsule,
while Shepard was able to control some of the actions of his
vehicle. Both saw the earth and described it. Both suffered
no ill effects from their voyages. Both were enthusiastic.
Both were sportsmen. Gagarin said: "There's enough space
in the cosmos for all. American cosmonauts will have to
catch up with us. We shall welcome their success, but will
try to keep in front." Shepard echoed these sentiments.

The American triumph dramatically demonstrated to
the world Kennedy's avowed philosophy of free and un-
fettered information about United States activities. It
showed that this country felt sufficiently confident and
secure to embark on a dangerous gamble and that it could
survive in the event of a spectacular failure. This was in
pointed contrast to the secrecy surrounding the Russian
space shot. Questions were properly raised whether Gagar-

in's success was preceded by failures and death for earlier cosmonauts. Reporters and photographers from the United States and other nations crowded Cape Canaveral, recording every moment of the activities, delays and anxieties that surrounded Shepard's flight. The Administration had made it clear that all except classified information should be available to everyone. The universal expressions of approval from all the nations indicated that the result had been worth the gamble.

Kennedy took his calculated risk in the face of his awareness that the United States was competing with the monolithic Soviet Government, whose leaders did not have to answer to a Congress or an electorate. There were no budget battles, no fragmentation of authority and no vocal or organized opposition that insisted the money should be spent in other areas. Kennedy knew there were no exceptional geniuses working for the Russians, but their enviable achievements were the result of hard work and uncompromising concentration in the field of space conquest at the expense of other needs. Leon Trilling, professor of astronautics at MIT, pointed out that "scientific development is an effective tool of persuasion and power and therefore receives a high priority in the Soviet scheme."

Immediately after World War II, when Germany had proved the value of the rocket as a weapon, the Soviet Government assigned a high priority to missile development and proceeded with an admirable single-mindedness to pursue and develop all forms of boosters from liquid and solid fuels to atomic power. There was no interference from dissidents because there were no dissidents.

It was different, however, in the United States. Ironically, the first liquid-fueled rocket was launched in 1926 in America by Robert H. Goddard, who was casually assigned to the oblivion occupied by all men who live before their time. But, like Russia, the United States was impressed by the German rockets and proceeded in 1945 to initiate a program with the aid of German rocket experts who had been "induced" to come to America. Under the leadership of Wernher von Braun, 110 scientists, considered the cream of German rocketry, began to work on plans that were regarded with casual indifference by a military traditionally suspicious of innovations and "gadgets." Between 1945 and 1957 the American space projects suffered from pessimism and penny-pinching founded on pernicious complacency.

Vannevar Bush, director of the wartime Office of Scientific Research and Development, looked upon the idea of a 3,000-mile military missile as unrealistic. "I don't think anybody in the world knows how to do such a thing," he said. "I feel confident that it will not be done for a long time." In those days, the atomic bomb weighed 10,000 pounds, which was an inconceivable load for a rocket to carry. Big bombers such as the B-29 were regarded as the best system for delivering the atomic bomb. The attitude of the military and civilian experts began to change by 1951, when the Korean war was in progress and the cold war had brought demands for experimentation in advanced weapons. The Air Force began work on the Atlas missile, its booster scaled to the needs of carrying a nuclear warhead. A 360,000-pound thrust was provided as sufficient for the task. (Gagarin's vehicle was boosted into orbit with a thrust of at least 800,000 pounds. Were their Germans better than our Germans?)

The United States was forced into action in 1957 when Sputniks I and II went up. By this time the American program was woefully behind Soviet development. The National Aeronautics and Space Agency was set up a year later with orders to proceed at headlong speed "and never mind the cost," but officials sadly observed that money was not a complete subsitute for time.

After Gagarin's flight Kennedy appeared at a press conference and for the first time gave the impression of being visibly shaken by a Russian victory. His answers were slow and plodding and he repeated several times that the Russians had bigger boosters and we would try to catch up. No one doubted that the United States would catch up, but when was another problem. "The news," the President said, "will be worse before it gets better. It will be some time before we catch up . . . and I'm sure they [the Russians] are making a concentrated effort to stay ahead."

Shepard's success in his Redstone heartened those working on the space program. A big booster rocket, the F-1 Nova, was tested successfully on the ground and showed great promise. But the main hopes were centered on the Saturn, with a thrust of 1.5 million pounds, which was expected to be ready by 1964 and help the United States catch up with the Russians in 1965. In that year, the United States planned to launch Project Apollo, a three-man orbiting space ship that would ride atop the giant Saturn. Robert C. Seamans, associate director of the NASA, said the United States might be able to put a man on the moon by 1967. "It is a date that could be considered from a planning standpoint," he told Congress. The cost was placed at $5 billion.

There were, of course, many earth-bound thinkers who saw no sense or reason in the mad race for space. In a mass Washington interview, Commander Shepard neatly turned aside a question on how his flight was going to benefit the hungry and the needy of the world. But this was the historic argument against all scientific experimentation. Sociologists, scientists and historians had too many precedents to cite in rebuttal to make the argument even interesting. It was true that for the moment experiments in space travel were tied to military urgencies and ideological rivalries, but most people seemed to understand that man was following a cosmic destiny that had begun in the cave and had moved inexorably forward.

Time Magazine speculated that, "even if the deadly

Russian-American rivalry that now supports most space research should die out, men will surely continue their struggle to escape from their own globe. For, in the end, space victories do not belong to any particular nation. They are achievements of the science and technology of the human species, the result of man's urge to explore the unknown."

There was really no need to explain or apologize because there was sufficient evidence in the sky that some practical application of the space race had been achieved. The Russians and the Americans had sent up satellites covering various scientific requirements. In addition to sun probes, moon probes, a shot at Venus, instruments were orbiting the earth sending back weather data, information on cosmic rays and radiation zones, and other knowledge to be used in the pure as well as the applied sciences. Tracking stations throughout the world were keeping in touch, harvesting information from space in a manner that had become mostly routine and ordinary.

Practical application on a commercial level was not far off with the use of private satellites. The promise (or threat) that Americans could recline in their living rooms and watch the 1964 Olympics in Tokyo, the May Day parade in Moscow or the Paris Opera as they were in progress was made by the large communication organizations. All that was necessary was approval by the Government. James Webb, NASA administrator, said he was "taking a hard look" at the applications and they would be considered seriously as soon as the over-all space planning permitted.

The financial attractions in a private space program were literally cosmic. The Lockheed Corporation estimated that all revenues from space communications would amount to $3 billion a year. Richard S. Morse, Assistant Secretary of the Army, predicted that private satellites would yield income of "several billions of dollars a year by the late 1970's."

Lloyd V. Berner, chairman of the Space Science Board, of the National Academy of Science said satellite communication would be a $100 billion business within 20 years.

The American Telephone and Telegraph Company, leading the list of applicants, said it could have its own satellite in the sky within a year. Frederick R. Kappel, its president, said in three or four years his company could have a full-scale, privately financed satellite communications system that would include 50 satellites in polar orbit, 6,000 miles high, relaying messages throughout a ground network of 26 terminals scattered across the earth. Kappel said his firm was ready to spend at least $170 million to increase overseas telephone calls from 4 million in 1960 to 100 million by 1980.

The corporate gold mine in the sky was also discovered by General Electric, International Telephone and Telegraph, Radio Corporation of America, Hughes Aircraft, Lockheed, General Telephone and Electronics, Philco, Bendix, Thompson Ramo Woolridge, and Ford.

There were no doubts that on a physical plane the plans of these firms were sound. Echo and Courier, two satellites launched in 1960, were still orbiting and proving the feasibility of space communications. But the political and bureaucratic problems were highly complex.

Corporation lawyers outlined a tortuous legal road for private enterprise seeking to make its way into space. A company would first have to deal with the NASA to get booster rockets; then with the Federal Communications Commission to get frequency allocations; then with the Justice Department for approval on anti-trust grounds; then with the State Department because of international negotiations, and finally with the Defense Department on national security.

Of all the complications, the problem that confronted the President was who would get the first contract. The first and most practical solution was to give it to a consortium of all the bidders. NASA, still working for the Government alone, planned to launch the first of a series of new communication satellites within a year. The Pentagon was also working on Project Advent for armed-services communications. The private companies were eagerly following the progress of these two plans, hoping somehow to get into the space program with Government blessing and their own funds. In this commercial area there was no reason to believe that the Russians were ahead of the United States, which had long experience in the understanding of how to work for profit.

While almost everyone was looking up into space, the President, considering population growth and food problems, cast a look at the ocean and made it part of his "science for the future" program.

As a long-range investment in the future of all mankind, Kennedy asked Congress to consider the richness of "the seas around us." He presented an impressive statistical portrait—the Pacific, the Atlantic, the Indian and the Arctic Oceans accounting for an expanse of 130 million square miles; the Mediterranean, the Bering, the Malay, the Black, the Red and 13 other seas covering 10 million more square miles, and the depth of all making 330 million cubic miles. In a letter to Johnson, in his capacity as President of the Senate, Kennedy said: "We are just at the threshold of our knowledge of the oceans. This is more than a matter of curiosity. Our very survival may hinge upon it." He then urged Congress to appropriate $97.5 million for various ventures in oceanography designed to develop future sources of food and minerals. This basic research, he pointed out, would include new studies in weather forecasting and possible weather control. It would also be of immediate benefit to the Navy in its undersea operations.

Kennedy showed that at present about one per cent of mankind's food came from the ocean and more would be needed soon. "The seas offer a wealth of nutritional resources," he wrote Johnson. "They already are principal sources of protein. They can provide many times the current food supply if we but learn how to garner and husband this self-renewing larder. To meet the vast needs of an expanding population, the bounty of the sea must be made more available. Within two decades our nation will require over 1 million more tons (a year) of seafood than we can now harvest."

The program was received with elation by oceanographers generally and in particular by Dr. Harris B. Stewart Jr., chief oceanographer of the Coast and Geodetic Survey. "Nothing like it has ever come from the White House," Dr. Steward said. "Most of our resources on land are gradually running out. People are starving in the world, and the seas are full of food. Over the course of geological time the earth has been eroding into the sea, so the sea is now the great sinkhole of the mineral resources drained from the land, including such vital industrial necessities as salt, potassium, manganese, nickel and cobalt. Off the West Coast we photographed whole areas of the bottom of the sea littered with manganese nodules the size of an orange or grapefruit. These nodules are rich in nickel and cobalt as well. Here is untapped wealth. Through basic research we may be able to learn the mechanism by which these nodules are made."

Dr. Stewart emphasized the point made by the President that "this is not a one-year program or even a ten-year program. It is the first step in a continuing effort to acquire and apply the information about a part of our world that will ultimately determine conditions of life in the rest of the world." As a beginning, the President proposed that the money would be spent in the next fiscal year on ten new oceanographic vessels, laboratories, wharfside facilities and basic research.

If the President needed encouragement as he contemplated his future travails in the space race, in the advances of all the sciences and in striving for a richer and better life for his nation, he received it from a most unexpected quarter. It came from Nikita Khrushchev in the moment of triumph when Russia had sent the first man into orbit around the earth. He looked with wistful envy toward America when he told all the Russians: "The space flight must not distract the attention of the Soviet people from other targets, and these include catching up with the United States in the standard of living."

17. Arms and Men

The cold war was 14 years old when Kennedy took office and it showed no signs of abatement. There had been indirect armed conflicts between the Communist nations and the Western nations from Greece to Korea, varying in size, scope and fatalities, but the two major antagonists, Soviet Russia and the United States, had managed to stave off the final blast that would end modern civilization. The new President was able to examine and choose from such philosophies of his predecessors, Truman and Eisenhower, as containment, deterrence, limited war, balance of terror or massive retaliation.

The President regarded peace, not war, as the primary purpose of his arms program. He wanted to be certain that American arms would be used only to deter war, general or limited, nuclear or conventional, large or small. He wanted to make clear to all potential aggressors that any attack on the West would be futile and fatal. He sought to provide realistic support to diplomatic settlement of disputes, "to insure the adequacy of our bargaining power in the arms race." He told Congress that "diplomacy and defense are no longer distinct alternatives, one to be used where the other fails—both must complement each other."

Taking an attitude of cautious and calculated optimism, the President indicated that it was not likely that either side would embark on a nuclear war since both sides possessed the ultimate weapons such as the cobalt-hydrogen bombs that would lay upon the entire earth a shroud of radiation. While his clearly stated intention was to be prepared for such a war, he foresaw during his eight years in office an era of messy internal and international struggles where smaller countries could expect help from the two major powers in bringing opposing sides together. "The struggle," he said, "is changing. It's not a question of troops marching across a frontier. We face the problems of having 'Spains' all over in the next decade. Laos is an example—Vietnam, the Congo. It is a question of subversion and parliamentary techniques."

It was noted that all the catch-phrases adopted by other Administrations had omitted the word *win*. Kennedy's idea of winning the cold war did not carry the threat of massive preventive attack. Actually, he pledged that the United States would never launch such an attack. To him the word *win* meant a fusion of arms and diplomacy, a clearer concept of the use of weapons, and a strong authority in the White House binding the interests of the State Department and the Pentagon. He subscribed to a statement made by Admiral Hyman Rickover that "most of our people cannot understand that we are actually at war. They need to hear shells. They are not psychologically prepared for the concept that you can have a war when you don't have actual fighting."

The President emphasized in his message to Congress that America's strategic nuclear force was still the foundation of national security. The United States, he said, was still in the uncomfortable position of waiting for the surprise attack before it could retaliate, but the potential of retaliation was known to the enemy as being so formidable that it was expected to prevent the inital blow. Kennedy put a major burden on the submarine-borne Polaris missile, which, in the event of attack, would be at sea and thus be able to survive and take the offensive. He asked for ten more Polaris submarines to bring the total to 29 by 1963; and, in order to give them a larger range so they would not have to lie close inshore in order to reach Soviet targets, the missiles range would be increased from 1,500 miles to 2,500 miles. To support the Polaris, Kennedy proposed 150 additional Minutemen, the Air Force's long-range, solid-fuel missiles. There were to be at least three additional fixed installations. Studies were continued on putting the Minutemen on railroad cars.

The life and range of the B-52, considered the backbone of the American deterrent, were to be increased. Kennedy also asked for a speedup in the 1,000-mile air-to-ground Skybolt, a nuclear-tipped missile of frightening power. The price to be paid for these advances was curtailment of the liquid-fueled, obsolescent Titan Intercontinental Ballistic Missile; the "low-reliability" Snark; the Air Force's pet bomber of the future, the controversial, 2,000-mile-an-hour B-70, and the experimental nuclear-powered airplane.

Plans were proposed for more non-nuclear field weapons and ordinary ammunition, an increase of 50 to 129 long-range aircraft for airlifts, more tactical aircraft and some 13,000 more men for Polaris, the Strategic Air Command, the Marines and guerrilla forces. The request for guerrilla forces was significant in light of a new policy formed by the Administration. Kennedy said: "The free world's security can be endangered not only by a nuclear attack, but also by being nibbled away at the periphery, regardless of our strategic power, by forces of subversion, infiltration, intimidation, indirect or non-overt aggression, internal revolution, diplomatic blackmail, guerrilla warfare or a series of limited wars." This was the President's permanent burial of the Dulles doctrine of replying on a massive scale to attacks of relatively minor magnitude. The Administration foresaw innumerable "conflagrations" in Southeast Asia, in Africa and possibly even in South America, where the beachhead storming by derring-do Marines would be far more effective than total obliteration of an offending nation. This was regarded in capitals of the Western as well as the Communist world as a substantial step toward peace and personal survival and was received with gratifying if unspoken approval.

This did not in any way diminish the Administration's concern with preparations for a total war. The plans were not only to survive but to be able to operate effectively during the chaos that would follow an attack and to conduct some sort of offensive. However, the matter of fall-out shelters, which, some said, would reduce casualties, was not discussed in detail. To remove the fears of an accidental war, in which, through error or blunder, the nuclear weapons would be unleashed, the Defense Department detailed the system of meticulous care and foolproof checks that were already in operation and that were dramatically demonstrated when the rising moon was mistaken for "unidentified aircraft" and a secret alert was in being before the correct reading could be made. The nation was assured that, even in the most dire eventuality, only the President of the United States had the authority to press the fateful button that would release our counterattack, and he would not do so without the combined advice of the Chiefs of Staff and other highly trained, highly reliable technical experts. To further reduce possible error to absolute zero, Kennedy asked for improvements in communications and warning systems so that "our retaliatory power does not rest on decisions made in ambiguous circumstances or permit a catastrophic mistake."

The Administration was troubled by an unhappy inheritance from the Eisenhower years in missile bases, whose slow construction had been the bottleneck in the development and testing of the missiles themselves. The delays were caused by many factors, chiefly too many managers, repeated changes in design and the lack of a policy of urgency. Strikes, labor stoppages and slowdowns contributed largely. When Kennedy took office the available missiles were strategically placed and ready for the horrible eventuality. In Britain there were 60 Thor intermediate-range (1,725 miles) missiles; 30 Jupiters were almost ready in Italy, and 15 were delivered to Turkey. About 12 Atlas missiles, with an intercontinental range of 5,750 miles, were ready in the United States and about ten more were on their way. Comforting as these installations were, they posed the gnawing question of the missile gap between the United States and Soviet Russia.

When the Minuteman (admitted range, 6,000 miles) became operational in February, 1961, after a successful first test, the Air Force was so pleased that it predicted that the test program would be cut by months. By 1962, the Air Force hoped to spot this missile in 55 squadron areas buried in steel and concrete silos around the United States sufficiently far apart to frustrate any concentrated attack designed to paralyze retaliatory weapons. The advantages of the Minuteman were that it cost less to produce and required a smaller crew. Once armed, it could be stored indefinitely, ready for count-down—an ideal weapon for the split-second, push-button warfare that all hoped would never come. All scientists in all departments in the Defense establishment were working intently on what America wanted sorely and the Soviet Union already had. This was the "big booster," a propellent made of either liquid or solid fuel that

had enabled Russia to send bigger satellites higher into space
and that by simple inference, could be used on gigantic,
maximum-range armed missiles. The possibility that this
unknown propellent might be nuclear was not discounted,
especially in the face of inspired rumors that the Russians
had successfully tested an atomic-powered airplane. *U.S.
News and World Report* quoted *Flying* magazine, which
quoted Korean underground sources as saying that the
Soviet atomic bomber on its first test flew 21 days without
refueling and reached an altitude of 85,000 feet. United
States officials doubted this high-flying story.

The fact that the missile gap existed was recognized in
the figures presented by Kennedy on his defense message
when he asked Congress for $41.8 billion which was $1.9
billion over the Eisenhower budget request. He proposed to
spend $1.3 billion on the Polaris and $96 million on the
Minuteman. Quantitatively, the United States planned to
have 1,298 long-range missiles beneath the waves, on the
ground or under the ground. If the qualitative difference
between the two nations was known to the Pentagon, it
did not say.

In order to effect some economies, the President ordered
the Pentagon to close down 52 military installations in the
United States and 21 more abroad. Among those shut down
in 25 states were storage depots, ordnance installations and
ship facilities, as well as three air bases: Presque Isle in
Maine and Laughlin and Harlingen fields in Texas. Defense
Secretary McNamara told the Senate Armed Services Committee that many of the domestic bases already were idle
or on a caretaker basis and that efforts would be made to
find new jobs for the 9,000 civilian workers who were dis-
placed in the closing of the others. Many Congressmen,
already plagued by unemployment in their districts, balked
at this move but were swayed by the potent reference to
necessary economies.

Kennedy managed to maintain a balance in his handling

of civilians in the armed forces. In the shutting of the bases, which, among other benefits, was a move toward greater efficiency, Kennedy realized he had made many people unhappy. But in another move, sentimental and dramatic, he had made many happy. President Eisenhower, in what appeared to be one of his rare acts of impulse, had ordered more than half of the 500,000 dependents of service men overseas to return to the United States. The Eisenhower move was based on a desire to stem the flow of gold from the United States. It was one of the few times in his career that Eisenhower was severely criticized for heartlessness and thoughtlessness in wrenching the loved ones away from the soldiers, sailors and marines who were serving their country in foreign lands. What he had hoped to accomplish was to keep in the United States the money used by these families abroad. Kennedy decided he could achieve the same objective in another way. He rescinded the "back home" order, and, instead, asked the members of the armed services and their families overseas, about 1 million of them, to cut their spending of American dollars by $80 a year each. This was about the same amount of money Eisenhower had hoped to conserve. It was an early Kennedy move that won for him the plaudits of the civil servants in general and the armed forces members in particular.

While the people appreciated the "sacrifices" made by our armed services overseas, they approved of Kennedy's swift action when typical Pentagon waste of taxpayers' money was exposed, even if it was only in minor matters. An American woman in France, worried about the United States economy and the outpouring of its gold, cabled the White House that perhaps it ought to look into the $200,-000 earmarked for expansion and refurbishing of a United States officers' club just outside Paris. Within two hours, President Kennedy killed the project and invited all Americans to report to him personally when they had evidence of waste. Later the President canceled a trip by the Army band to Brazil that would have cost $200,000. Later, Secretary McNamara received a visit from Senator Douglas of Illinois, whose pet peeve was Pentagon prodigality, and who had frequently sounded off in the Senate against such items as shuffleboard equipment for Marines and United States-supported diaper services for dependents of soldiers. He cited to McNamara the little items that could blossom into big scandals. The Air Force, he said, paid $10.67 apiece for four-foot sections of electric cable with a plug at each end. "A member of my staff paid $1.50 for the identical item in a retail store," he said. "Another example is a small wrench-set, with case, which the Army bought at $29. The same thing is being advertised in an auto-supply store for $3.98. And then there was that small lamp socket for which the Navy paid $21.10. I had a similar item priced at 25 cents."

The President of the United States, as commander-in-chief of all the armed forces, could easily be tempted to play soldier and every so often there had been interference in the internal affairs of the various branches. Truman, an obscure captain of artillery, always stood in awe of the generals and admirals he commanded as President, but he never interfered. Eisenhower, the great general, was an expert in all the inter- and intra-service politics but never interfered even though as a general he had expressed the belief that the Marines were not needed in the defense scheme. He kept silent on this when he was President. Kennedy, a Navy lieutenant and a combat hero, permitted himself one instance in which he interfered, although he could have excused himself on the ground that it was a part of his major policy toward conventional military activities.

Inspired by the picturesque rangers and commandos of World War II, the Army, in 1952, had decided to create an elite corps of its own that it named the Special Forces. Within months, the Army, known for its traditional abhorrence toward elite groups, became disenchanted by the swaggering paratroops with their jaunty green berets and fancy boots. It was a regrettable error that the generals began to rectify by stripping these eager young fighters of their special uniforms and gradually integrating them back into regular units. The corps was almost forgotten when Kennedy informed the Joint Chiefs of Staff that the Special Forces would no longer be the stepchildren of the atomic age and that they should be given new duties. These hardened, well-trained experts in the knife, the pistol and the garrote, the President ordered, would teach their violent trade to the fighters for freedom in the jungles of Southeast Asia, Central Africa and other areas where revolt and terror threatened the people. The 1,800 men were brought back from their exile, got 500 new members and awaited orders. The Army was planning to train many more to fight in this manner, especially if they could speak foreign languages. Their job, under Col. F. C. Fitzpatrick, a World War II tank officer, was to train others to fight. "A 12-man team could train about 1,500 guerrillas," he explained. "A few such teams working behind enemy lines could direct enough sabotage and infiltration to tie up two enemy divisions." This was all part of the President's "putting-out-the-local-fire" campaign. The Marine Corps, which was gaining stature under the new Administration, had proved to the President that all its 175,000 already were trained for behind-the-lines service.

Getting proper personnel for these perilous tasks was at first a problem until the Army decided to qualify two-year draftees with the idea that they could be effective on the home front when they returned to civilian life in reserve groups. The Navy, however, claimed it had the biggest problem in getting the right men for the right jobs. It was difficult to find capable men who were willing to live away from their families the best part of a year. Navy Secretary Connally was "surprised to find that the average Navy man on duty gets to see his family about 90 days out of the year.

Some time ago some of them got only 55 days at home. It's no wonder the Navy has a problem of hanging on to its skilled men." The Polaris submarine posed a special problem. Vice Admiral William R. Smedberg 3d pointed out that each missile submarine required two crews of 100 and 12 officers. Allowing for retirement, illness and transfers, Smedberg said he would need nearly 3,000 men under training to maintain the supply. "Already, we have been robbing the rest of the fleet to get enough specialists for the Polaris submarines," he said. "We take them from the destroyers because the skippers are lieutenant commanders or commanders . . . and can't scream as loud as an admiral."

The Navy was, of course, expected to do its best, but Secretary Connally took no chances. He assembled 4,000 Navy and Marine officers and read them a sermon and a critique. In Navy talk he said the service must scrape off its barnacles and must gear for a space-age change. But Roosevelt had said it better: "To change anything in the Navy is like punching a featherbed. You punch it with your right hand and you punch it with your left hand until you are finally exhausted, and then you find the damn bed just as it was before you started punching."

Connally said he and the President would have none of that. A World War II commander and winner of the Bronze Star, he said he was dissatisfied with much that he found. Officers, he charged, were too defensive when new ideas came along, too enamored of their technological feats, too obsessed with costly, complicated craft when simpler, smaller vessels could perform the same task. It was time to put progress above tradition. He urged changes in the selection system so that bright young officers would get faster promotion. Urging increased modernization of the fleet, Connally echoed the Administration's feeling that "we cannot go on hoping that someone is going to wave a magic wand to modernize our aging fleet. Perhaps the answer is in less sophisticated ships—or more ships of exactly similar design."

Then he touched upon a tender area when he disscussed interservice wars and demanded an end to the bickering so often characterized by leaks and background statements. He said the Navy did not want to "forever explain away some utterance made by a well-intentioned but irresponsible officer that went counter to policy. Recognize and accept your responsibility," he said, "by insisting on being quoted by name, rank and billet."

High-ranking officers were still smarting from an order issued by the President that they were to clear all their public utterances with the Administration. Admiral Arleigh A. Burke, Chief of Naval Operations, had been ordered to rewrite a speech completely and the news created a stir, especially among some Republicans. Senator Bridges wanted to know immediately whether the Administration was advocating an era of appeasement.

Salinger issued a statement saying that the Administration would maintain a continuing review of speeches and other efforts to coordinate policy statements. He noted that Eisenhower's regime had a similar policy. In a gentler tone, the President said that leading military figures should not make speeches in conflict with Administration policy.

Generally, Kennedy's relations with his Chiefs of Staff were based on an understanding of the national problem. What he had to overcome, and he could do it only with the help of an enlightened and intelligent military, was a host of hysterical misconceptions that had been built into the public's mind by misleading headlines and the sensational successes of the Soviet space program.

In his defense message, Kennedy conveyed to the Congress a feeling of urgency and a need for haste. He tried to lift the people of the nation from the complacency of despair in which it had wallowed morbidly under the false beliefs that the United States was doomed to be second to the Soviet Union in military power and world prestige. The message had been militantly optimistic and the people began to look to their eager and intense young President with greater hope. They even got a bit of advice from Nikita Khrushchev, who said that, if America agreed to disarm, "if the United States were to agree to peaceful co-existence, this would open up vast possibilities for developing the productive forces and would lead to greater employment and consequently higher living standards for the American people." What he hoped, of course, was that the loss of $42 billion to industry and labor would throw this country into economic chaos.

The reply was a rather scholarly one. The Research Program on Economic Adjustments to Disarmament, under grants from the Carnegie, Reynolds and Ford Foundations, was making just such a study. Emile Benoit, director of the program, said these studies "will help demonstrate to the Russians and to the world that we really mean business on disarmament." Professor Benoit, on leave from Columbia University, said the studies will "also reassure the public that acceptance of disarmament poses no unmanageable economic problem. When one thinks of what these billions of dollars would mean to the nation and to the world if invested in public health, research, education, foreign aid and tax reductions . . ." A truly fascinating thought.

18. The Nation's Business

As the first hundred days ended, there was a growing, if cautious, tendency to see at hand, if not already in hand, a reversal of the downward trend that the economy had been taken for so many months. Unemployment declined somewhat in April, though government experts were quick to note that the decline was purely seasonal. Nonetheless, though a *Wall Street Journal* survey showed that first-quarter corporate profits were substantially below the figures for the comparative period of 1960, the paper's experts saw unmistakable signs of definite improvement for the second quarter of 1961, particularly in such basic industries as steel, automobiles and electrical manufacturing; the influence of the first two, especially, on the economy as a whole was proverbial. The Labor Department's Consumer Price Index had held steady for five months, despite a rise in its services component and a drop in its consumer-goods section.

President Kennedy had promised a second study of the economy in April to determine whether it needed further help from Government. By the middle of the month the study was well under way; some experts professed to have descried the bottom of the recession as of February and a gradual upturn since, though Congress had taken no action on any of the economic measures thus far offered by the Administration. It was this apathy, coupled with the growing crises in Laos and Cuba, that added to the hesitancy of the executive to offer further proposals. According to the government's figures, the gross national product had declined in the first quarter of the year to an annual rate of $499.5 billion but was expected to rise to a rate of $505/510 billion in the next three months. This forecast was based on an anticipated downward trend in inventories rather than any acceleration of output or employment; the rate of unemployment was expected to remain near 7 per cent for at least the rest of the year. Our own great productive capacity, Kennedy said in a television interview broadcast late in April in England, was creating its own unemployment problems, and he predicted that Britain would ultimately face them too.

The 1960 Democratic platform on which Kennedy was elected had proclaimed as its goal an average annual rate of economic growth of 5 per cent. As means to that end it had pledged an end to the policy of tight money and high interest rates, control of inflation through monetary and credit policies, full employment and concrete action to help depressed areas. In his campaign Kennedy had been more specific, promising: "Wherever we can be certain that tax revision, including accelerated depreciation, will encourage the modernization of our capital plant—and not be a disguise for tax avoidance—we should proceed with such revision." He specifically stressed his preference for voluntary import agreements rather than tariff increases, and he called for a "competitive environment" for "efficient" small business. Kennedy denounced any tax increase in the existing circumstances as deflationary. He also called attention, with somewhat less emphasis, to the outflow of gold.

Within a few days of his inauguration, he summoned to a conference Secretary of the Treasury Dillon, Secretary of Labor Goldberg and Chairman Wilbur D. Mills of the House Ways and Means Committee. Their agenda consisted principally of plans to extend unemployment-insurance payments. Three days later, on January 30, Kennedy sketched his first demands on Congress in his State of the Union message, pointing out the danger signs that demanded immediate action:

1. Business bankruptcies were at their highest level since the depression of the 1930's.
2. Farm income had declined 25 per cent in ten years.
3. More than one million of the 5.5 million unemployed had been jobless more than four months, and some 150,000 per month were exhausting their unemployment benefits.
4. Business investment, profits and construction had declined and more than a million unsold new automobiles languished in inventories.

Promising proposals for remedial legislation within the next fortnight, the President pledged unequivocally that the dollar would not be devalued and that no restrictions would be imposed on either foreign trade or the free flow of dollars. Nor would there be any curtailment of American commitments abroad. The message was well received, in spite or perhaps because of its lack of specifics, and the New York Stock Exchange had the broadest trading day in its history as 1301 issues were included, volume exceeded 5 million shares and the average rose as if the buyers of common stocks were anticipating what many were accustomed to view as traditional Democratic inflation.

Within the next few days Kennedy began to move. He did not want to ask for tax reduction as long as it could be avoided; the probability of a deficit was already too great. His opposition to high interest rates was tempered by the fear that a reduction in short-term rates would mean a greater exodus of money for overseas investment; it was essential to avoid further aggravating the balance-of-payments problem. Its primary solution, he believed, lay in strengthening the domestic economy and in increasing our exports.

To this end he asked Congress to act quickly to grant federal funds to the states to extend unemployment-insurance benefits to a maximum of 39 weeks; to provide area-redevelopment loans that would make possible the immediate relief and the long-range improvement of chronically distressed areas; and to broaden the coverage of the minimum-wage law as well as to increase the minimum at once from $1 to $1.15 an hour and in two years to $1.25. At the same time, Kennedy issued a number of executive orders designed to stimulate the economy. He reduced from 5.75 to 5.5 per cent the interest rate on loans insured by the Federal Housing Administration, in order to stimulate residential construction. He released $724 million of federal highway-improvement funds that had originally been intended to be spread over the rest of the fiscal year (that is, through June). He ordered accelerated payment of $258 million in dividends on veterans' insurance policies and a parallel speed-up of Government procurement and construction programs wherever this was practicable and especially in the depressed areas.

All this was followed almost immediately by requests for legislation directly affecting the question of balance of payments. Kennedy had repealed Eisenhower's executive order that would have recalled the families of American service men stationed abroad, but at the same time he drastically slashed their purchases of foreign goods through post exchanges and canteens by ordering these markets to stock American merchandise almost exclusively and by eliminating such benefits as free transport home for European cars purchased abroad by service men. What he now asked of Congress was, first of all, a reduction from $500 to $100 in the customs exemption on foreign goods brought home by American tourists; in addition, he urged an increase in the interest paid to foreign governments on their dollar holdings lest these be converted to gold. At the same time, he called on the Treasury to consider ways in which this country, co-operating with others, could strengthen international monetary institutions, and he asked the Senate to approve American membership in the Organization for Economic Cooperation and Development. Reverting to executive order, Kennedy proposed to continue the regulations compelling nations receiving foreign aid to spend most of the money here and to direct the Commmerce Department to initiate specific steps through its offices abroad to increase our exports. He made it plain that he would call on the more prosperous of our Allies to share the burden of aid to underdeveloped countries. Underlining his earlier opposition to protective tariffs, he ruled against a recommendation by the Tariff Commission for a higher duty on imported twines and cordage. But he approved a higher tariff on bicycles.

Next the President addressed himself—without illusion—to the business community. "It would be premature," he told the National Industrial Conference Board, "to ask your support in the next election, and it would be inaccurate to thank you for it in the past." Kennedy pointed out that the success of industry and business was intertwined with that of the Administration, and he requested a "full-fledged alliance" to resolve the problems of economic growth, plant modernization and price stability. However, he made no specific suggestions of means or methods. Secretary Goldberg reassured the audience that the Government would not try to force predetermined wage settlements and added that the Kennedy Administration did not want to create a new WPA because "that is not the sound way."

The line taken by the President and his Labor Secretary bore a remarkable resemblance to the thinking of the British Conservative Party.

It was Goldberg rather than Kennedy who was stressing the urgency of the domestic economic situation. But it was an urgency that Congress, despite every effort by the Vice President and the Speaker of the House, refused to recognize. Bills drawn to implement Kennedy's proposals were languishing in committee or had not got even so far. Stung by Republican charges that he had exaggerated the situation in order to exploit it for political purposes, the President told a press conference on February 15 that, while the nation waited for legislative action, he was using his executive powers to provide such assistance to the economy as might be afforded by speeding post-office construction and liberalizing the rules for letting defense contracts to small business. But the popular response, except in those areas immediately affected by the recession, was as apathetic as that of Congress. The very nature of the blight, scattered rather than uniform, and the paradox of a record employment side by side with the disturbing percentage of jobless, tended to make the problem too abstract for the popular mind to grasp.

Such action as could be seen was all executive. While ruling out "made work," Secretary of the Interior Udall ordered an increase in reclamation work. The Pentagon acted to put to work the $690 million it had available for procurement and construction. Without publicity, intensive work was under way to draft a tax-incentive plan that, without basically altering the tax structure, would stimulate investment and industrial growth. The Federal Home Loan Bank Board released more than $1 billion in credit to stimulate residential building; this was accomplished by liberalizing the rules governing both borrowing and lending by federal savings and loans associations. Perhaps it was the very slowness of government action in the economic sphere that contributed to the steady rise that, since the election, had surprisingly characterized both the stock and the bond markets. The surprise lay in the fact that both equity and debt markets were rising together, a most unorthodox manifestation in a capitalist economy and one for which no one had a satisfactory explanation. When Kennedy renewed his pleas for legislative speed on his program to aid the economy, the nettled lawmakers declared that they thought they were "moving pretty fast—as fast as is judicious."

By the beginning of March, though Congress had not yet acted on Kennedy's recommendations to halt the outflow of gold, including the bitterly debated proposal to afford special high-interest inducements to other governments holding dollars (by now coupled with an alternative proposal to exempt the income on such holdings from tax), the President could report that what he described to the authors as "the hemorrhage of gold" had been stanched, at least temporarily. Nonetheless he continued to press for the enactment of his proposals, though he seemed privately uncomfortable at the "buy American" implications of some of them, in such flagrant contradiction to his own as well as his party's traditional advocacy of ever freer international trade. "The only other possibilities of stopping the hemorrhage of gold at once," he said, "would be either reductions in foreign aid and military assistance or increases in tariffs, and neither would be admissible." He admitted that what he was proposing was an emergency measure and was not intended to become a basic policy. "But," he added, "whatever is done now, for a long-range restoration of the balance of payments we must have the assistance of other nations in foreign aid and mutual security."

Organized labor was showing its teeth by March. As it became evident that the Administration, in its concern for renewed vigor in the economy, was determined to evolve some kind of tax-incentive program to spur capital growth, the American Federation of Labor and Congress of Industrial Organizations derided the theory that the recession stemmed even in part from a lack of capital for business expansion. The sole problem, labor declared, was a lack of consumer buying power. The AFL-CIO contended that existing tax regulations for business were already over-generous; it demanded (in the event, without much success) that the tax load of corporations, dividend recipients and large incomes be increased in order to finance greater government spending as the antidote to unemployment and a worse slump.

To a degree this thinking was manifest within some sectors of the President's own Council of Economic Advisers. William McChesney Martin Jr., head of the Federal Reserve System, warned that, even when the recession had ended, a significant "hard core" of technological unemployment would remain and that it was not a problem that could be resolved by mere spending. But he was contradicted by the Council's chairman, Dr. Walter W. Heller, who said that such unemployment was "only an insignificant fraction" that would vanish after "proper" taxing, spending and credit policies had produced "an environment of full prosperity." Branding such policies as Heller's likely to "create serious new problems of inflationary character at a time when consumer prices already are at a record high," Martin insisted that the only sound approach to the dissolution of the "hard core" was training or retraining in new skills needed by expanding industries, and a revision of pension and benefit plans to do away with penalties imposed on workers moving to new jobs. While Kennedy himself, in his campaign speeches, had often emphasized the need for retraining as a countermeasure against the problems created by automation, he seemed to adopt Heller's view, at least for the short term, when on March 8 he announced that $660 million more in federal contracts would be let in order to bring about immediate increases in consumer demand.

But to those who demanded a repetition of the intensive governmental spending of the first New Deal, Kennedy was a disappointment; at no time did he mean to let Government replace private enterprise as the dominant factor in the economy. Instead, it appeared, whether the problem was one of economic growth, of employment, of wage-price policy, Kennedy envisaged the government's role as at most that of a fulcrum. Addressing the first meeting of his new Advisory Committee on Labor-Management Policy— composed of seven representatives from each of three groups: organized labor, industry and "the public"—he called on its members to give the nation continuing direction for wage and price movements in the interests of the general welfare, to be governed in their deliberations by the criterion of what would best serve the national purpose.

The end of March was also unmistakably the end of the nine-month recession. A few weeks earlier, Goldberg had said that the normal operation of the laws of economics would play a part in the change of trend, and an equal part would be played by the new Administration. But it had been in office almost 70 days and it had yet to see one of its measures adopted by a cautious Congress. Even the President's executive orders had not yet had time to manifest their effect, except perhaps psychologically, and it was not impossible that to a considerable extent capital had come out of hiding if only in fear of being either driven out or maimed in its lair by some Roosevelt-like act of government. Informed opinion, too, was already anticipating the promised tax bill, and the announcement of a $2.2-billion budget deficit for fiscal 1961 and another half again as large in the following year became less terrifying as the nation remembered how it had survived the unbalanced budgets of the New Deal and the war. In announcing the deficit, Kennedy almost defensively emphasized that it was not of his making but resulted from the effect of the recession on tax revenues, from mistaken estimates by his predecessor and from "urgent" calls of the arms effort.

Aside from increased military expenditures, Kennedy estimated the outgo for fiscal 1962 at $83.5 billion, the revenue at $81.4, and he foresaw the need for a new rise in the limit on the national debt, which now stood at $289 billion. He was separating his military estimate from the rest of the budget for several reasons. First, it was under exhaustive re-examination. Second, he classified it separately because arms needs were "too urgent to be denied by budgetary restrictions." Third, by isolating the military budget he hoped to drive home his point that his non-military proposals would not in themselves throw the budget out of balance. At the same time, interest policies were being further complicated by an increase to 3.75 per cent for government savings bonds and a ten-year extension of their term, while the subsidence of the gold scare and the visible change in the general economic trend were materially altering the abortive effort by the Federal Reserve System to reduce the long-term interest rate; it was no longer necessary or advisable. Soon thereafter, to the outrage of those who had successfully opposed the Eisenhower Administration's effort to achieve the same end by almost the same means, Kennedy quietly but quite legally rendered nugatory the 1918 law setting a ceiling of 4.25 per cent on the interest payable on government securities of more than five years' maturity. This was accomplished without the necessity for legislation by virtue of a letter from Attorney General Robert Kennedy to Secretary Dillon pointing out that there was no legislative bar to the Treasury's selling its securities at a discount that made the total return on the bond at maturity equal to more than its face value plus 4.25 per cent of that amount per year.

It was just 90 days after his inauguration that the Presi-

dent submitted his long-discussed tax plan to Congress and
to the attacks of conservatives, liberals and special-interest
groups. As organized labor had feared, the plan called for
substantial help to businesses seeking to expand. The tax
message neither raised nor lowered rates; theoretically, it
would increase revenues by recapturing taxes that were not
collectible, though due, under the existing law. In addition,
it sought very explicitly to plug some of the more gaping
loopholes in the tax structure. His plan, Kennedy emphasized, was only the overture to a "comprehensive" reform of
the tax structure a year later.

Under the President's proposal, $1.7 billion in taxes would
be saved to industrial taxpayers by new allowances for
capital expansion, in the hope that this would lead to greater
economic growth and provide more employment that would
take up at least part of the slack caused by existing unemployment and the dislocations that might result from automation introduced under the new tax law. To counter this
loss of revenue, Kennedy proposed several steps. Dividends
and interests would be subjected to withholding taxes,
exactly like salaries and wages. The existing tax credit for
dividend income would be eliminated. The use of tax havens
abroad by individuals or companies would be nullified by
changes in the law governing foreign residence for individuals and foreign operations for businesses trading in "econom-
ically advanced countries." And the individual tax bonanza
of the Eisenhower years, the expense-account income, would
be blown to bits. Under the President's plan, it would be
impossible to deduct from one's taxable income the sums
spent for entertaining customers, expensive gifts to business
contacts, country-club memberships, excessive travel expenditures and "work-or-play" vacations.

The reactions were immediate, and it was openly predicted that every aspect of the President's tax plan would
face a bitter battle when Congress opened hearings on it in
May. Experienced observers forecast that some parts would

be rejected out of hand before the bill reached the floor, for
all were highly controversial. If labor considered the depreciation provisions over-generous, many business men
branded them niggardly and demanded full depreciation
allowances and heavier write-offs for the year in which the
expenditures were made; they sneered at the 10 per cent
credit for businesses investing up to $5000 in new plant
and equipment and at the more complicated formulae for
those investing 50 to 100 per cent of their present depreciation allowances. They protested the proviso that in no case
could the tax credit exceed 30 per cent of a single year's tax
bill, and the exclusion of equipment with a life of less than
six years from the credit category. Tax experts cited the
existing confusion in determining legitimate depreciation
allowances and the years of wrangling that inevitably preceded an adjudication. Self-appointed Congressional watch-
dogs for the "widows and orphans" receiving dividends and
interest bayed righteously at the inroads on these meager
subsistences. Airlines, which receive direct subsidies and
lucrative mail contracts, howled at the suggestion that they
pay the same tax on jet fuel, hitherto tax-free, that is levied
on gasoline, and that the tax on fares be continued. Every
man and woman with an expense account found himself
personally affronted.

Whatever the reactions of individuals or groups, the
President's tax message seemed to indicate, like his other
proposals in the economic field, that, whatever the words of
his party's platform or of his own campaign speeches, he was
neither Rightist nor Leftist. Fundamentally, his economic
policies differed little from those of the Eisenhower Administration; what difference existed was one of degree
rather than of kind. There was to be no departure from the
pattern so firmly established by Roosevelt's economic revolution, but there was to be no development of it. It was not
only the unenthusiastic reactions of Congress to each of the
President's economic messages that led to this conclusion, it

was also the nature of the proposals. Kennedy did not embrace wholeheartedly the philosophy of the New Deal, nor could he accommodate himself to the tradition of laissez-faire. While he was obviously prepared to grant to government a far greater role in the economy than any Republican would have envisaged for it, one could safely predict that throughout his term he would never advocate or support any serious encroachment by the state on the basic more or less free enterprise that existed when he took office.

As if to corroborate Kennedy's fundamental adherence to traditional economic thinking, the end of his first hundred days brought at least a temporary easing of the balance-of-payments problem. In the first quarter of 1961, the Commerce Department announced, American commercial exports had risen to $4.9 billion, against $4.6 billion for the first quarter of 1960, while imports had substantially declined. Primarily this rise in exports owed nothing to management of any economy, here or abroad: it resulted quite naturally from the growing vigor of the economies of those nations that were buying more of our goods. At the same time, the disclosure struck hard at the entrenched belief that economic trends in the United States must invariably be reflected in foreign economies, for these had been developing consistently in capacity and technique while the United States was wrestling with its recessions of 1958 and 1960. The resulting increase in foreign purchases from us was thus contributing to the resurgence of the American economy while its doctors were still debating their remedies. If the patient continued his convalescence, then, it was less and less likely that the doctor would attempt anything beyond putting him on a regimen that might be expected to be more prophylactic than therapeutic.

19. Up on the Hill

In his relationship with the Congress, Kennedy demonstrated a deep sense of purpose that transcended the urgencies for immediate legislation to support the operation of
his New Frontier program. His messages appeared to convey
a strong desire to create a sound foundation for eight years
in office, and his planning indicated clearly that he looked
upon all defeats or modifications of his proposals as only
temporary. It was evident that he counted heavily on his
personal popularity, new coalitions in the House and the
power of patronage to win his long-range battle.

The President's legislative program began significantly
with a minor defeat in the Senate and a major victory in the
House. Senate Majority Leader Mansfield failed to muster
enough strength to put over a move to limit debate and
thereby end agonizing filibusters, yet Speaker Rayburn was
able to reorganize the House Rules Committee so it would
be unable to bury important legislation. Mansfield was not

expected to control the Senate with the same finesse and firmness that his predecessor, Lyndon Johnson, had, but, with Johnson as President of the Senate, the Democrats enjoyed a sort of twin leadership that proved effective. Unlike Johnson, who had prodded the Senate night and day to leap to his command, Mansfield presented a more relaxed approach when he announced: "I don't see any reason for holding the Senate in long session when there is no prospect of a vote. I think we should meet regularly at noon and quit at night in time to have dinner with our families at a reasonable hour."

Mansfield made clear his position in the Kennedy scheme of legislation. "There are bound to be times when I'll personally disagree with the President," he said. "In such instances, I'll have to accommodate myself as best I can to his position. I believe that the Senate Majority Leader who has in the White House a President of his own party should look upon himself as the President's leader in the Senate." Mansfield was fortunate in having two men with verve and drive to help him. One was Assistant Majority Leader (Whip) Hubert Humphrey and the other was Assistant Whip George Smathers of Florida. Having banished all rancor from the bitter primary campaign, Kennedy had specified that he wanted "my guy Hubert" on his Senate general staff. Smathers, who had been an usher at Kennedy's wedding, was a close personal friend and could be counted upon to understand the President's thinking. But it was Johnson who was going to be the strongest Kennedy influence in the Senate, and Mansfield acknowledged this when he invited the Vice President to take part in the steering and policy committees. "I don't want him left standing outside the door," he said.

On the Republican side, Kennedy had to contend with two sturdy old professionals, Minority Leader Everett Dirksen, a smooth and fruity orator, and policy-chief Styles Bridges, one of the ablest strategists, whose philosophy was

to the right of center in his own party. The measure of Dirksen was best illustrated after a private conference with
Kennedy in the White House. When he emerged from the
executive office, he was immediately surrounded by questioning reporters. He explained that the appointment had
been for 15 minutes, but he remained for an hour. Then he
proceeded to parry questions by telling funny stories, banter-
ing with the women in the group, and generally being
exasperatingly genial until one reporter remarked: "Senator,
you can say less in ten minutes than any man in the Senate."
Dirksen and Bridges, who could be counted on to press any
advantage in the long battle ahead, managed to maintain
some discipline in their party despite the presence of such
liberals as Jacob Javits of New York and Clifford Case of
New Jersey and such ultra-conservatives as Barry Goldwater.

In this they had a strong ally in Charles Halleck of Indiana, House Minority Leader, respected master of tactics,
who faced his chief opponent, Speaker Sam Rayburn, with
a ready-made Dixiecrat coalition that periled the Kennedy
program. But Rayburn, a loyal old party stalwart, opened
the 87th Congress with the avowed intention of wrenching
the House free from the traditional stranglehold of the
Rules Committee, through which most major legislation has
to be cleared before it can be brought to the floor for debate
and voting. During the previous Congress (1959-1960)
Howard W. Smith of Virginia had created a united conservative bloc with the Rules Committee's four Republican
members and William Colmer of Mississippi. When considering legislation he disliked, Smith was able to achieve a
6-6 deadlock that buried the bill in committee. Rayburn
staked his reputation, prestige and power when he devised
the plan to add two more Democrats and one Republican
to the committee; this would give it an 8-7 alignment. After
one of the most exciting roll-calls in the memory of the
House, the final tally was 217 for and 212 against. Although
64 Democrats from the South had voted against Rayburn,

Halleck was unable to keep 22 Republicans, mostly from the big cities in the Northeast, from supporting the move. When the outcome was announced, Smith, 78, declared in his best Broad Run, Va., English: "Well, we done our damnedest best." Rayburn, 79, said: "We won and I'm satisfied."

Some political speculators described it as a dark victory for Rayburn and Kennedy because it was a wrangle between Democrats and Democrats that would have to be fought over again on every major bill. They warned that the Democrats had lost an excellent excuse to stall legislation because they could no longer blame the Rules Committee for holding it up. Kennedy was fully aware of this grave situation and proceeded to send help to Capitol Hill in the form of a smoothly operating liaison team directed by Lawrence O'Brien and his two-man staff, Henry Wilson, specialist for the House, and Michael Manatos, specialist for the Senate.

When O'Brien took the job, he had long talks with Bryce Harlow, his Republican predecessor. He concluded that Eisenhower "didn't know the players on the hill," and as a matter of policy was so shielded by his official family that his relationship with Congress and Congressmen was rigid and formal almost to the point of aloofness. O'Brien's hopes for success were based largely on Kennedy's intimate knowledge of the legislators and the legislative process. It became accepted practice that O'Brien moved into the legislative area only after a Presidential message and the accompanying legislation had been sent to the Capitol. Before that, the strategy was mapped by Sorensen and Feldman in constant conferences with the President. After the President decided what he wanted, Sorensen and/or Feldman, working with other assistant counsels, Lee White and Richard Goodwin, completed the task. "It is our responsibility," Feldman explained, "to be in touch with the department and the Cabinet offices and get drafts from them of the proposed message and and legislation. We then go over the draft and

often have to redo it." Kennedy then discussed the plan
with the appropriate Cabinet officer, Sorensen and Feldman. After the President gave his final approval, O'Brien
informed the House and Senate committee chairman of the
contents and the message was sent to the Capitol, to be
followed shortly by the requested legislation. It was up to
Feldman to write explanatory letters, but the main job of
herding the bills through was left to O'Brien and his assistants. While their task was highly complicated, their objective was simple—to produce a majority vote when the bill
came up.

Despite the careful planning and his increasing popularity, Kennedy's program received only a mild reception
on the Hill. During the first several weeks this seemed to be
the almost unanimous attitude of Congressmen of both
parties, who had been sampling reactions of their own con-
stituents by mail, questionnaires and personal contacts.
Somehow, they were inclined to the theory that Kennedy's
personal stature did not translate into voter support for his
programs. The general feeling was expressed by Representative Thomas B. Curtis, a middle-of-the-road Republican
from a suburban St. Louis district, who said Kennedy's
popularity was "like that of a movie actor—not related to
legislation." Senator William Proxmire, Wisconsin Democrat and an early Kennedy supporter, found reaction to his
program "was a little amorphous." Senator John A. Carroll,
Colorado Democrat, found that "everywhere I went in
Colorado there was great warmth and friendship for the
President, but I can't say that the small business men really
go for the minimum wage, and I think that the Federal aid-
to-education program is one where there's considerable
division." Representative Peter F. Mack Jr., an Illinois
Democrat, said he found "great support for Kennedy, the
individual, but many people don't approve of some of the
programs he's been sponsoring." Widespread backing was
found for the proposed medical care tied to Social Security,

but the general public apathy caused considerable concern in the White House until a curious political phenomenon casually appeared on the Hill.

Hitherto the misnomer, *coalition,* had indicated a voting alignment of Southern Democrats and Northern Republicans. It is believed to have functioned for the first time in 1937 in the court-packing fight waged by Roosevelt when a Democratic-controlled Congress won help from the Republicans and defeated proposed legislative restrictions on the Supreme Court. After that the Southern Democrats and Northern Republicans found other issues which they could decide voting in harmony. Under Truman, the Taft-Hartley Act was one of the biggest coalition victories. As a Senator, Kennedy had been a victim of such a coalition in August, 1960, when it defeated bills on housing and medical care. It was embarrassing for Kennedy, the candidate, because the Democratic Convention had written them into its platform, and he had hoped to get them passed before the actual campaign got under way. There really was no coalition leader and the alignment worked only at the convenience of the Republicans, although deals were frequently made when one faction promised to vote "right" on one issue in return for a similar favor on another issue. Civil rights was one of the more regular victims of this arrangement.

The phenomenon that now appeared on the Hill was the counter-coalition, a leaderless and loose alliance of liberal Republicans with the Democrats that began by giving the House reorganization victory to Rayburn, then set up the $394 million program to help the nation's depressed areas, and then gave Kennedy his biggest victory by passing the $1.25 minimum wage legislation. Representative John V. Lindsay, New York Republican, described the new group as a "coalition by accident, motivated by our common interest in liberal legislation. We have no leader, no consultation with the Democrats . . ." Lindsay said he was considering organizing a Republican study group along the lines of a Democratic study group, consisting of 100 liberals who would have their own research staff, their own whip system and their own leader—Representative Holifield of California.

The minimum wage law was the biggest single legislative victory scored by the Administration. The Senate passed it, 64-28, and the House, which had rejected it twice before, approved it, 230-196. The measure provided that 24 million workers already covered by the minimum wage law would get an increase from $1 an hour to $1.15 by Labor Day, 1961, and to $1.25 by September, 1963. For 3.6 million newly covered retail, service and construction workers, the law provided a $1 bottom by autumn with step-by-step increases to $1.15 by September, 1964, and to $1.25 by September, 1965. Retail workers qualified if they worked for establishments doing more than $1 million in annual business and importing more than $250,000 in goods for resale across state lines.

The Administration gave a thorough example on how to apply pressures in its fight for the passage of the minimum wage bill. Every strength and weakness, loyalty and self-interest were utilized to assure success. O'Brien began with group breakfasts for Congressmen every day, pleading that they "go along just this once." He promised that "if the voters at home complain, we'll leave you alone on our other bills." The biggest pressure was put upon the Southern Democrats. Rayburn made the rounds of the delegations recalling old obligations, making new promises and reminding all that the Democratic President's prestige was at stake, besides, 73 new Federal judgeships would soon be ready for distribution among the faithful. The fear of the anti-labor label was paraded before the reluctant and, as the Southern wing began to buckle, six Republicans from New Jersey and five from Massachusetts went along. The six Jerseyans acted in order not to embarrass former Labor Secretary

James Mitchell, who was running for the governorship, and the five from Massachusetts voted *yes* to help lift Southern wages closer to their own and so reduce the exodus of New England industry to the South. Kennedy also made compromises. The bill's coverage excluded 140,000 laundry workers, a chilling example of political expediency recalling a statement Kennedy made in Buffalo during his campaign: "As long as the average wage for laundry women in the five largest cities is 65 cents an hour for a 48-hour week . . . there is a need for our party." The laundry workers were omitted, along with the 15,000 cotton-gin-workers, so that the bill could gain the votes of Southerners. The South has many small laundries that would have been "hurt" by so high a minimum wage. One newspaperman remarked as he examined the compromises in the bill: "We've got the people who make $25 a day safely covered, but we left out the people who are making $25 a week." Doris Fleeson, who generally supported the Democratic philosophy, called the bill "an ignoble monument to political expediency which sacrificed workers in greatest need to an effort to pick up conservative Democratic votes. The end product is not one that President Kennedy can sign with anything but personal humiliation and gravest misgivings. It will force him to swallow many brave and compassionate words of his campaign, and, what is worse, to defend the indefensible." There were others, however, who understood Kennedy's position that some bill was better than none, and that he probably had nearly eight years left to make up for the bill's sins of omission. In his book, *Profiles in Courage*, Kennedy recalled that when he entered Congress he was told: "The way to get along . . . is to go along. Going along means more than just good fellowship—it includes the use of compromise, the sense of things possible. We should not be too hasty in condemning all compromise as bad morals."

The minimum-wage law victory brightened the Administration's must-legislation chances considerably. By the end of 100 days the Congress had passed and Kennedy had signed bills providing emergency unemployment compensation; feed grain price supports; a Sugar Act extension; and continuation of the President's power to reorganize the executive branch. The Senate had ratified a treaty authorizing the United States to participate with 19 non-Communist nations in the Organization for Economic Cooperation and Development. The House had approved a bill providing emergency help for children of the unemployed and was considering proposals to liberalize the Social Security by lowering the retirement age and broadening the area of eligibility. In committee in both houses were bills providing for Federal aid to public schools; Federal aid for colleges; liberalization of the Housing Act and foreign aid. These were merely the main points in an all-embracing legislative program covered in messages.

Both Houses approved a conference version of a bill empowering the President to appoint 73 new Federal judges to reduce the backlog of court cases. This presented the Administration with a major source of patronage. It also placed the principal responsibility for recommending these nominees on Attorney General Kennedy, who would be asked to fill these jobs as rapidly as possible. The Attorney General admitted it would not be easy to find so many highly qualified men who could satisfy bar associations, Senators and their local political leaders.

The pressures on Congressmen are constant and fierce and come from all directions—the home front, lobbies, organizations, the President, newspapers, religious bodies, and last, but sometimes not least, their own consciences. When Kennedy was a Senator, he quoted John Morley's observation that politics "is a field where action is one long second best, and where the choice constantly lies between two blunders." Congress is constantly engaged in the fine art of conciliating, balancing and interpreting the forces and factions of public opinion, and occasionally it resorts to hiding behind a delightful parliamentary device whereby it can put across a piece of legislation in which the entire body makes a decision, but no single member can be held responsible for the action—and that is the voice vote.

It was by such a vote that the House passed a $9.8 billion bill to provide for a Federal highway program during the next 11 years. This would enable the country to build an interstate network of highways 41,000 miles long to be completed in the early 1970's. Naturally, the country needs roads and there seemed to be no reason to hide behind a voice vote. But closer examination showed that the House members had resisted intense pressure from the oil and trucking lobbies by voting to finance the project with a continuation of the four-cent-per-gallon tax on gasoline and diesel fuel and to increase taxes on trucks, tires and inner tubes. Considering that the American Petroleum Institute of New York spent $63,416 during the final three months of 1960 in lobbying, it was easy to understand why individual Representatives did not wish to be exposed to its wrath. Among the other big spenders for that quarter were: the American Farm Bureau Federation, $25,644; AFL-CIO, $33,354; American Legion, $23,408, and the Farmer's Educational and Cooperative Union of America, $19,426. The Federal lobbying law required that all those registering file financial statements every three months with the clerk of the House. About 1,000 filed, but there was no way of ascertaining whether all lobbyists actually registered. These figures demonstrated one area of organized and skillful pressure exerted on members of Congress.

The President, who learned his legislative lessons as a member of both Houses, fully appreciated the pressures and the conflicts, the agonizing soul-searching and the ultimate necessity for the realistic attitude when he wrote that "their consciences may direct them from time to time to take a more rigid stand for principle—but their intellects tell them that a fair or poor bill is better than no bill at all, and that only through the give and take of compromise will any bill receive the successive approval of the Senate, the House, the President and the nation."

20. Politics and Patronage

It is a fixed rule in American politics that, the moment a man is elected President for the first time, he begins to run for his second term. This is a twofold task. The new President must win the approval of the electorate, making him subject to the whims and caprices of fortune, and he must build a personal political machine that will be enthusiastic and disciplined toward the single purpose of electing him again. In the matter of personal popularity, Kennedy scored well in the early days of his Administration and managed to maintain the sympathy of the people despite setbacks at home and abroad. As for his political machine, his great power lay in the single word, patronage, an ancient and accepted instrument of political strength which helps persuade reluctant legislators and brings faltering party bosses into line. It is axiomatic that a machine politician who has obtained a handsome appointment for himself or managed to place an influential constituent in an important govern-

ment job is likely to find his loyalty reinforced by self-interest.

When Kennedy assumed office there were some 8,000
jobs available. At the highest level there were about 100
positions in the cabinet, sub-Cabinet and other policy-making areas ranging in pay from $17,500 to $25,000 a year.
Then came the federal judgeships, ambassadorships and
memberships on commissions and regulatory agencies. At
the Cabinet and sub-Cabinet level, Kennedy's appointments were almost non-political with the debatable exceptions of Ribicoff and the President's brother, Robert.
Below that level, politics was present but not obvious.

The heavy concentration of job-seekers was outside
Washington, and Kennedy moved resolutely to make up
for the patronage starvation of his party during the eight
Eisenhower years. There were 73 new judgeships; 91 regional United States attorneyships, each with at least a
dozen assistantships; about 100 marshal vacancies and a
plethora of other positions such as collector of customs,
bank examiner, officers of the Farm & Home Administration, some 12,500 postmasterships, and hundreds of obscure
little appointments that form the very foundations of the
clubhouse system.

Kennedy understood the agonizing problems of the practical politician, who is also the head of the Government, in
finding men and women competent to sustain the Administration and also politically pure of heart, two qualities that
are not always found together. He had won his own seat in
the House of Representatives from the outrageously gerry-
mandered 11th Massachusetts District, which included
Harvard and the worst slums of Boston. He knew what it
was to be called a carpetbagger by the East Boston street-
corner politicians, who openly promised to deliver their
blocks for a consideration. As he faced the patronage problem he might have looked with awe or professional curiosity upon his predecessors. Hoover, the great engineer, kept

aloof from the clubhouse level; Roosevelt had Louis Howe to do his dirty work; Truman was himself nurtured in the clubhouse; and Eisenhower, who had no background in politics except for the normal intra-Army intrigues, was sheltered from the sordid realities because he was a national hero and because the professional politicians in the Republican Party preferred it that way.

While Kennedy concerned himself mainly with the top-level appointments, the patronage operation was placed in the competent hands of John M. Bailey, chairman of the Democratic National Committee, and Lawrence F. O'Brien, special assistant to the President for personnel and Congressional liaison. A strong-minded Massachusetts politician who helped run Kennedy's two successful campaigns for the Senate, O'Brien cheerfully assumed the back-breaking job of sifting, studying and evaluating the 20,000 applications. He had Bailey employ a large staff of assistants who worked on nothing but patronage. Each application had to contain endorsements to show the candidate's fitness and political reliability. While there was no arbitrary rule about it, proof that an applicant was for Kennedy before the Los Angeles convention was considered helpful.

The most painful and sometimes virtually insoluble complication encountered by O'Brien and Bailey arose when nominations and endorsements for the same position came from conflicting factions within the party. A good example was Ohio, where party leadership was splintered among a Democratic governor, the two Democratic Senators and the state Democratic chairman. New York's two regular Democrats, State Chairman Michael Prendergast and city boss Carmine DeSapio, got a clear snub from Kennedy in a number of appointments. Kennedy indicated to lesser party officials "it was time for a change," and that he favored the leadership of Mrs. Roosevelt, former Governor Herbert Lehman and Thomas K. Finletter, who was Air Force Secretary under Truman.

The Administration's official sense of humor came to light with the appointment of Professor William Cary of the Columbia Law School as chairman of the Securities and Exchange Commission. A White House aide telephoned Charles Buckley, Democratic boss of The Bronx, to get political clearance for Cary. Buckley, who had been the first and most powerful Kennedy booster in New York State, said he had never heard of Cary, but went along with the gesture. "Well, tell me," he asked, "is he a good professor? Do his students like him? Does he write books?" After being assured on all his questions, he gave his approval. The White House caller later explained that "this was part of the President's program to raise the intellectual level of the party. Every local boss must clear at least one professor."

Since it was physically impossible for O'Brien and Bailey to examine candidates at the point of origin, Kennedy devised for them a master measure in which control of patronage was given into the hands of those New Frontiersmen who he believed could build for him an organization of dedicated men and women who would be ready for the battle of 1964. In an admirable survey, *Newsweek* found these to be leaders "who earned the President's faith and trust by hard performance": Mayor Richard Daley of Chicago, whose powerful machine gave Illinois to Kennedy; Governor John Patterson of Alabama, who came out early and strongly for Kennedy when other Southern leaders were supporting Lyndon Johnson, and Edward J. Day of California, who was named Postmaster General.

Another strong Southerner was Governor Terry Sanford of North Carolina, who gave official endorsement to Kennedy at a most critical time before Los Angeles. Sanford, who said he wanted to put North Carolina into the "mainstream of America" and who conducted a vigorous administration, was given full control of patronage. In Pennsylvania, Representative William J. Green, whose Philadelphia organization gave Kennedy a 330,000-vote majority, had pressed ahead of Governor David L. Lawrence in patronage favor and had become the clearing agency for all Federal jobs. Governor Lawrence was relegated to a lesser level because he was late getting on to the Kennedy bandwagon.

Senator Harry Byrd tacitly acknowledged his waning power in Virginia when he graciously found that William C. Battle, a Charlottesville lawyer, was acceptable to him as liaison man with the White House. Battle, a close friend of the President, managed the campaign in Virginia and became the leading influence in patronage. While there seemed to be no obvious conflict in Oregon, where Senator Wayne Morse remained a potent factor in major appointments, Representative Edith Green, who was Kennedy's campaign manager in the state, controlled all other jobs. Her first big reward was a position with the Federal Power Commission for Howard Morgan, a close friend and a former public utilities commissioner in Oregon.

California presented a special problem because the Democratic hierarchy failed miserably to deliver the state in spite of encouragingly heavy party registration. However, the Administration was being more than cooperative, having appointed, in addition to the Postmaster General, 13 party regulars, including Mrs. Elizabeth Smith as United States Treasurer.

The President's genuine and objective desire to improve the status of the Negro in the United States did not in any manner conflict with the practical realization that the Negro vote was one of the most potent in his election. It is not often that a single political asset can be made to perform double duty. Kennedy told his Committee on Equal Employment Opportunity that he was "determined to permanently remove from Government employment and from work performed for the Government every trace of discrimination." Vice President Johnson echoed: "We mean business." Then the Administration sent a score of recruiting agents throughout the country, but mainly in the South, to enlist the services of capable young Negro men and women. There was a flurry of hirings of Negro assistants in top-level agencies; but Edward J. McVeigh, personnel director of the Labor Department, reported after a tour of 18 Negro colleges in the South that he found the students skeptical: they had heard "these fairy tales before." McVeigh managed to convince them so well that he had to send to Washington for more application blanks.

There was no denying that Negroes were impressed with the swift reaction to Kennedy's directive. With Weaver in the Federal Housing Authority, Dollie Lowther Robinson in the Women's Bureau of the Labor Department and Christopher C. Scott as Deputy Assistant Postmaster General, it remained for the Treasury Department to make one of the most provident catches of all. Samuel Z. Westerfield, 41, dean of the Atlanta University School of Business, was named assistant director of the Treasury's debt-analysis staff at $15,200. Westerfield, who was graduated from Harvard University in 1939 and got his master's and doctorate at Harvard in 1950 and 1951, declared: "We are taking a big step toward implementing our democratic principles."

But the problem, which is Jim Crow Washington itself, went deeper than this. It was best illustrated in 1949 by Dr. Ralph J. Bunche of the United Nations when he turned down a Truman offer to become Assistant Secretary of State. "It is well known that there is Jim Crow in Washington," he said. "No Negro finds Jim Crow congenial. I am a Negro." This tragic condition reaches down to the unspectacular rank-and-file civil servant who happens to be a Negro. Promotions are slow even for those who are willing to sweep floors, run errands and sift mail, remaining at Grade 4, about $4,000 a year. One veteran asked in a letter: "Why is it that you never see a Negro above the basement level in a Government building?" The problem that every

President has faced since the days of Theodore Roosevelt was to continue to plague Kennedy: How to get Jim Crow out of Washington?

Kennedy faced another annoying problem that called for long-range planning, appeals to courts, and education of the urban electorate. This was the ogre of the political gerrymander, by which voting power was distributed unfairly between cities and farm land. One of the most disturbing examples of such inequity was in Connecticut, where Hartford, with a population of 162,178, had two seats in the Lower House of the Legislature, and the town of Colebrook, population 791, also had two seats. In Maryland, a state senator from the Eastern Shore represented 15,317 and a senator from Baltimore County represented 490,000. In New Jersey, about 15 per cent of the voters chose a majority of the State Senate. The Representative from California's 28th District (San Diego) represented more than 1 million persons while the Representative from Michigan's 12th in the Upper Peninsula represented 175,000. The Tennessee Constitution provided that districts should be based on population and should be redrawn every ten years. They had last been changed in 1901. In 1961 one member of the Lower House spoke for 4,000 persons and another spoke for 75,000. Since World War II only 17 states had made even minor changes in their Congressional districts. Louisiana had made no adjustments since 1912 and Colorado since 1921.

Kennedy, who described these inequalities as "notorious," encouraged nationwide campaigns to force redistricting. In Tennessee, Maryland, Michigan and Georgia, law suits were begun to force positive action. Hopefully, the Tennessee case went to the Supreme Court, which agreed to consider it. A victory for redistricting would be of great value to the President, whose traditional strength remained in the cities.

As the 100 days waned and Nixon began his announced crusade of "constructive criticism," a new phenomenon began to appear on college campuses and in discussion circles of the intelligent young. Whereas, in the past, the educated youth of the nation had a tendency to idealize to the left of center, a condition tolerantly accepted by their elders as normal rebellion, a survey by the Scripps-Howard newspapers reported a "rumbling groundswell abroad in the land today among students in American colleges. The apathy of the 1950's has faded, and a new serious attitude has taken hold of the undergraduate." The attitude, the series concluded, was toward political conservatism.

The heroes of this movement were Barry Goldwater, Nelson Rockefeller and Richard Nixon, in that order, and subject to the changes engendered by the whim of youth. The series quoted Michael Uhlmann, president of Yale's Calliopean Society, which was founded by William Buckley: "Senator Goldwater is bringing out a conservatism long latent in college. Here is a man suddenly saying the things we believe in. We're on the offensive now." Bruce Chapman, a Harvard senior and publisher of a new magazine, *Advance*, said: "We're moderate. We try to avoid Goldwater primitivism, and we're unhappy with the welfare state. I predict a movement led by Nelson Rockefeller or someone to preserve free enterprise and traditional principles and avoiding the bureaucratic centralization of New Deal liberalism." Myron Belkind, former editor of the Ohio State College daily, *The Lantern*, said: "When I was editor, students used to ask me why the paper printed only the liberal view. The fact is this is all I was getting. Now the conservatives are writing letters to the editors, too." The most speculative appraisal was made by Dean W. H. Masterson at Rice University, who said: "Conservatism is fashionable today and it is saying clearly what it means. Whether it is stronger, I don't know." Charles Lucey, who wrote the series for Scripps-Howard, said that numerous campus observers had made the following analysis:

"The great liberal battles that began with Franklin

Roosevelt are written today in legislation. President Kennedy's New Frontiers have excited college youth but most of his goals are not new. They are extensions. There isn't that great emotional drive for the liberal view as in F.D.R.'s day. So the liberal causes have paled a bit; the liberals themselves may often seem bored. Hence, on the American college campus, a clearly sharper voice for conservatives. Nobody can say how far it will go—or what it means in terms of the political and economic shape of United States leadership ten or 15 years from today." Kennedy, himself somewhat of a conservative in his youth, by the standards of the time, might have been able to understand this genteel revolt from the "starry-eyed" liberalism of the New Deal and the Fair Deal, and the Democratic leaders might well hope that he could deal with it.

If the Republicans were waiting until after the 100 days for an opportunity to assault the Administration, they did not have to. Interior Secretary Udall supplied the ammunition with an old-fashioned political blunder in the sale of $100-a-plate tickets to a Democratic fund-raising dinner. Although he said he solicited only one member of the gas and oil lobby, "an old friend," it was hard to erase the impression that his intention was to reach the members of the gas and oil industry generally. Political "insiders"—a euphemism for rumor-spreaders—predicted that he would be one of the first to leave the Cabinet. Commerce Secretary Hodges was also nominated for an early departure. For a few days, the Cuban affair evoked predictions of wholesale resignations. Sorensen, Meyer Feldman, Richard Goodwin, Lee White and other members of the official family, including Salinger, were written off as on the way out. But the President calmly went about his labors, taking the responsibility for all actions, good or bad, and pondering the political paradox of patronage that, for every friend he made, he would make nine enemies.

The best news in the District of Columbia, to the office

holders, the office seekers and the thousands of residents not connected with the Government, was the passage of the 23d Amendment, giving them the right to vote. Historians had noted that the authors of the Constitution and the early Congresses had merely neglected to consider voting rights for the District. In 1846, one-third of the District's land area, now Arlington County, was ceded back to Virginia. Finally, after 161 years, the 780,000 Washingtonians (54 per cent Negro) would be permitted to vote for the Presidency and Vice Presidency only. They did not get the right to be represented in the Congress, and the municipal government would still be administered by a commission.

21. Far to the Right

Every Administration had consciously tried to ignore the irritating existence of those small but intensely vocal extremist groups—Right or Left—that tend to embarrass people in high places and confuse basic issues. Harding, Coolidge and Hoover had the Ku Klux Klan, Roosevelt had the American Communists, Father Coughlin and the America Firsters, and Kennedy had the John Birch Society, which was founded in 1958 and burgeoned during the first 100 days. It first came into general public prominence when Senators complained that they were receiving an impressive amount of evidently inspired mail calling for the impeachment of Chief Justice Warren.

Admittedly behind the letter writers was the John Birch Society under the uncompromising leadership of Robert W. H. Welch Jr., a retired Boston fudge manufacturer, who claimed chapters in 34 states and announced a membership goal of 100,000 and a fund-raising goal of $1 million. The society had definite attractions for a fringe of the American public that subscribed eagerly to the master plan, which would abolish the Federal income tax, end foreign aid, halt desegregation, oppose the United Nations and the North Atlantic Treaty Organization, and fight the fluoridation of water. Welch had set the tone by calling Eisenhower a "card-carrying Communist," Truman "definitely pink" and Edward R. Murrow a "confirmed Communist." He charged that "creeping Socialism and Communist dupes have hopelessly subverted the White House, the State Department, the labor movement, the churches, the schools, the Ivy League and the Supreme Court."

The public's first reaction toward the Birchers was one of ridicule and scorn. Requests for an investigation by the Department of Justice were casually brushed aside by Attorney General Kennedy, who described the group as "ridiculous." Senator Eastland said there was nothing subversive about the Birchers and saw no reason for an inquiry. A member of the House Un-American Activities Committee said the Birchers' bark was worse than their bite. Senator Goldwater was impressed by the people in the Birch group. "They are the kind we need in politics," he said. With support of this kind, the scorn vanished swiftly and was replaced by concern. The Birch Society's council members, regarded as the elite in ultra-Right-wing circles, made an impressive list. Among them were Clarence Manion, former dean of the Notre Dame University Law School; Cola G. Parker, a former leader of the National Association of Manufacturers, and Brigadier General Bonner Fellers, who was a member of the Defenders of the American Constitution, Inc.

It might have been possible for the President to continue ignoring the Birchers but for the incident of Major General Edwin Walker, the commander of the 24th Infantry Division in West Germany. "Ted" Walker was the dramatic, romantic type of soldier so beloved of scenario writers. During World War II he often led his troops on bloody night raids against German units in Italy. He won even greater combat honors during the Korean war. As an officer who never questioned an order, he commanded the troops of the 101st Airborne Division during the Little Rock school crisis so fairly and effectively that he earned the secret admiration of the segregationists. In his German command, he maintained a strong discipline requiring officers and men to do daily calisthenics garnished with frequent one-mile runs. There was grumbling, but no disobedience, and Walker might have been happy but for the one irritant in his area, the *Overseas Weekly*, an independent American-owned newspaper that had won an enthusiastic and large readership among U.S. troops after printing a number of well-documented stories about officers abusing their rank. One day the *Overseas Weekly* ran a story that Major General Walker was attempting to indoctrinate his soldiers with Birch Society principles. Walker issued a denial and gave a statement to reporters that said in part: "We have Communists and we have the *Overseas Weekly*. Neither one is one of God's blessings to the American people or their soldier sons overseas. Immoral, unscrupulous, corrupt and destructive are terms which could be applied to either."

The press in the United States ran the story prominently, and President Kennedy called upon the Pentagon for some explanation. Meanwhile, Representative Frank Kowalski, a Connecticut Democrat and a graduate of West Point, demanded an investigation, saying: "If Walker has done nothing wrong, he should be vindicated. If not, he should be given the works." The Army recalled Walker from his command for an inquiry, and later "punished" him with a mild rebuke.

At his next press conference, Kennedy was asked: "Your order to investigate General Walker suggests that you look askance at the teachings of the John Birch Society. Can you tell us how you feel about that organization?"

The President replied: ". . . Well, I don't think that

their judgments are based on accurate information of the
kinds of challenges that we face. I think we face an extremely serious and intensified struggle with the Communists. But I am not sure that the John Birch Society is
wrestling with the real problems which are created by
Laos, by Vietnam, by internal subversion, by the desperate
life lived by so many people in this hemisphere and in other
places which the Communists exploit . . . How we fight
that kind of problem, which is going to be with us all
through this decade, seems to me to be one of the great
problems of the United States. And I would hope all those
who are concerned about the advance of Communism
would face that problem and not concern themselves with
the loyalty of President Eisenhower, President Truman,
Mrs. Roosevelt or myself or someone else."

Kennedy told the reporters that he had ordered the action
on Walker. "When I saw the stories . . . I called Secretary
McNamara and asked him to investigate. Secretary Mc-
Namara then, I believe, suspended General Walker." Kennedy stressed that McNamara had not acted "merely because he felt that General Walker was teaching—talking
against the Communists."

The President has indicated his general abhorrence for
such extreme groups as the White Citizens' Council, George
Lincoln Rockwell's American Nazi Party, the Anti-Tax
Foundation for Economic Education and the American
Renaissance Party, whose heroes were Castro, Hitler and
Nasser. At the other end of the spectrum from White
Citizens' Councils was the rejuvenated group known as the
Black Muslims, which preached black superiority and
supremacy and rejected the white man's Christianity. It
was a highly disciplined, militant group, claiming 100,000
members among America's almost 19 million Negroes. The
Muslims' special appeal was mainly to the young and the
poor, who made up more than 80 per cent of the group.

How these organizations, together or apart, would in-

fluence the next election remained in the realm of speculation. Kennedy believed that extremes in politics were dangerous at either end. He took no action against any of them,
but he indicated his displeasure in a subtle but clear manner. He declined an invitation to address the annual meeting of the U.S. Chamber of Commerce because he regarded
it as one of the most potent forces lobbying against his programs. It was also possible that the refusal was based on the
dubious compliment given Kennedy by Arthur H. Motley,
publisher of *Parade* and president of the Chamber, who
called him an able politician, "the ablest in the White
House since Roosevelt and maybe smarter than F.D.R."
Motley expressed doubt that Kennedy held Socialist views
and continued: "I don't think he believes what Schlesinger
and Galbraith and those other jerks from Harvard tell him."
And when the Continental Congress of the Daughters of
the American Revolution made its traditional request for
a "special, members-only" tour of the White House it was
refused—for the first time since 1890.

22. Reaching the People

There was a time in this country when the President spoke publicly only to the people and to the Congress, leaving the press to report, interpret and comment without any manner of direct contact. There were only rare exceptions to this until Theodore Roosevelt lowered the barrier slightly by giving exclusive interviews to correspondents of favored newspapers. Subsequently editors became suspicious of his generosity because Roosevelt frequently used these "exclusives" as trial balloons and, when the public reaction proved unfavorable, he would deny that the interview had taken place and soundly denounce the correspondent, the editor and the newspaper. Wilson was the first to invite reporters to an official press conference in his office. On March 15, 1913, he faced 100 reporters (he had modestly expected only 25) and answered questions politely and cautiously. He did not permit discussion. He continued these sessions irregularly, showing his annoyance with some persistent questioners and acting like a pedantic schoolmaster lecturing a group of inquisitive urchins. When World War I began, he stopped the press conferences altogether. Harding set up a system in which written questions were submitted in advance. He selected those he would answer, prohibited direct quotation, discarded all embarrassing questions and allowed no informal talk. Coolidge half-heartedly continued the sessions, which he, intentionally or naturally, made short, unproductive and dull. Hoover's press meetings were dry, unsatisfactory, and as the Depression became more acute, grew tense and bitter.

The pattern for the modern press conference was set by Franklin Roosevelt, who "enjoyed" the most hostile press any President ever had. He allowed, even encouraged, banter, chit-chat and a kind of informal intimacy the reporters had never experienced. He answered questions, advised, lectured, joked and informed, calling many correspondents by their first names, and was able without giving offense to parry inquiries that were awkward or to which he did not wish to reply directly. These "gab fests" became so legendary that on many occasions anti-Roosevelt publishers asked to be invited and came away completely charmed by the man, and, trying to justify their position, blamed all the New Deal excesses on "those brain trusters." Truman followed Roosevelt's program, but without his grace and agility, supplying instead peppery commentaries that could not be printed. Eisenhower, under the clever guidance of James Hagerty, broke precedent by allowing direct quotations but reserving the right to edit the transcript. Then, in 1955, Eisenhower opened the conference to photographers for the first time—television, newsreels and stills. It was a historic advance in pictorial journalism, but again the White House properly reserved the right to black out any exchange that could be misinterpreted. It is to the credit of Eisenhower and Hagerty that few scenes were edited despite the "fluffs" and ear-wrenching grammar.

Roosevelt discovered radio as an excellent way to bypass

the press attacks on him, his Administration, his wife, his
children and his dog. The "Fireside Chat" was his most
effective weapon against the printed word. Kennedy, who
enjoyed a better press than any of his Democratic predecessors, found the medium of television a powerful supplement
in the task of rallying public opinion toward his long-range
eight-year program. In this projection he was not unduly
optimistic, considering a statement made by Nixon shortly
after the end of the 100 days that "the odds favored President Kennedy's re-election in 1964 barring some major
catastrophe."

During the campaign, Kennedy's forceful, energetic personality on television had won to his cause many doubters
and reluctant voters. Therefore it was natural that his first
television press conference should draw an enviably large
audience. One week after he took office, Kennedy stood
on the rostrum in the spacious auditorium of the new State
Department Building facing 418 news men, a record attend-
ance. He set the pattern by opening with a statement—the
most startling ever made at a press conference. He announced: "Captains Freeman B. Olmstead and John R.
McKone, members of the crew of the U.S.A.F. RB-47 aircraft who have been detained by Soviet authorities since
July 1, 1960, have been released by the Soviet Government
and are now en route to the United States." When the
excitement had subsided, he continued with discussions of
other plans, speaking quietly, incisively and clearly. Then
he answered 31 questions in 38 minutes, impressing the
reporters and his television audience with his knowledge of
all matters that came up for discussion. He used his right
arm in a waving motion as if to put punctuation and emphasis to his replies. The news men were visibly impressed and
the viewers at home were enthralled and enchanted with a
President who seemed to know all the answers. And the
intellectuals were delighted with a President who understood syntax and spoke in sentences.

As the news conferences on television continued, always beginning with announcements and statements from the President, the veteran reporters examined this new method and found several flaws. Aside from the fact that the conference lacked the give-and-take atmosphere of Roosevelt's and Truman's sessions, there was a growing resentment that the announcements shrank the time left for questions in the traditional 30 minutes. Since it was impolite to break into a discussion while millions watched, reporters suffered the unhappy feeling that Kennedy was using the haphazard method of selecting his questioners to play favorites. The President was not at fault alone. Criticism was leveled at reporters who used the television scanners in the interest of publicizing themselves and asking trivial and unanswerable questions; for example: "Would you welcome a visit from Mr. Khrushchev in the next few weeks or months?" "Do you propose to spark from the White House the one-man movement started by a Republican relative of yours in Oklahoma to restore the sound dollar?" (The Republican was no relative). "Have you determined whether any in the State Department helped to advance the Communist foothold in Cuba, and if so will you take steps to remove them from office?" The President managed to answer these and many other silly questions with poise and patience. And he impressed his listeners with his exact knowledge of a molasses shipment from Cuba and several other matters that appeared as if the questioner had specifically copied some obscure figures for the sake of demonstrating his erudition.

Nevertheless, the televised press conference served Kennedy well. Arthur Krock wrote in *The Times*:

In this revitalized atmosphere of government by a Chief Executive who has an intelligent and tireless interest in its over-all and detailed functioning, the White House news conferences themselves have become even more the instrument of the President. The questions grow fewer because Mr. Kennedy has em-

ployed them more as a platform to make important announcements of acts and policies. Through the projection of television,
live or canned, this expansion of the President's role has well
served the dual purpose of informing the United States and the
world on vital and timely matters and providing him with a
better forum than has been built on that foundation before. And
that is one of the most effective means of transmitting to the
furthest reaches of the planet an impression of new vitality
in Washington.

Kennedy's intense desire to arouse the people from their
apathy of the "Easy Fifties" and to cast a brighter light in
broad areas of ignorance showed some gratifying results.
While the public-opinion polls indicated his popularity
was growing in a rather casual way, other statistics were
even more heartening. The White House switchboard was
60 per cent busier than it was before Kennedy took office;
mail arrived at the rate of 30,000 letters a week, and the
same general attitude of awakening was reflected in the
phone calls and mail received by Cabinet members. Yet
there was the grave concern that the vibrant New Frontier
might wear out its welcome with the easily distracted mass
of television viewers who could retreat to their cowboy or
gangster violence and just say: "Let Jack do it."

The President repeatedly told the people that the world
looked to the United States for leadership despite Communist propaganda; that our leadership depended largely
upon an informed electorate, and that no Administration
could succeed if the country did not understand. He was
openly disturbed by reports that only three in ten voters
were aware of the major problems in foreign affairs and that
two in ten could be considered reasonably well informed.
In defense of this state of affairs it was noted that never
before in the history of this nation had its foreign affairs
been so perplexing, so varied and so complicated. The
tones and shadings became increasingly confusing. The
ordinary citizen could not understand why tiny Laos, so

far away, was important. He had been conditioned by the films and television to understand the difference between the good guy and the bad guy. He felt secure in the single knowledge that Communism was the bad guy, Uncle Sam was the good guy. As for the rest, it was up to the man who was President.

In striving for the greater dissemination of information, Kennedy indicated that what we do not know is certain to hurt us. These words were to come back later in a different light when he addressed the American Newpaper Publishers' Association in New York. He began gently by asking the publishers to reconsider the meaning of freedom of the press. Then he outlined the "distinct" advantages that a closed totalitarian society held over an open society. "Its preparations," he said of the closed society, "are concealed, not published. Its mistakes are buried, not headlined . . . No expenditure is questioned, no rumor is printed, no secret is revealed. It conducts the cold war, in short, with a wartime discipline no democracy could ever hope—or wish —to match."

The President went on to show that every democracy recognized the necessary restraints of national security— "and the question remains whether those restraints need to be more strictly observed if we are to oppose this kind of attack as well as outright invasion." He declared that this nation's foes had openly boasted of acquiring through American newspapers information they would otherwise hire agents to acquire through theft, bribery or espionage. "Details of this nation's covert preparations," he said, "to counter the enemy's covert operations have been available to every newspaper reader, friend and foe alike." He pointed out that the size, strength, the location and nature of our forces and weapons, and our plans and strategy for their use, had all been pinpointed in the press and other news media to a degree sufficient to satisfy any foreign power; and that, in at least one case, the publication of details concerning a secret mechanism by which satellites were followed required its alteration at the expense of considerable time and money.

"The newspapers which printed these stories," he said, "were loyal, patriotic, responsible and well-meaning. Had we been engaged in open warfare, they undoubtedly would not have published such items. But in the absence of open warfare, they recognized only the tests of journalism and not the tests of national security. And my question . . . is whether additional tests should not now be adopted. That question is for you alone to answer.

"I have no intention of establishing a new Office of War Information to govern the flow of news. I am not suggesting any new forms of censorship or new types of security classifications. I have no easy answer to the dilemma I have posed, and I would not seek to impose it if I had one. But I am asking the members of the newspaper profession and the industry in this country to re-examine their own responsibilities—to consider the degree and the nature of the present danger—and to heed the duty of self restraint which that danger imposes upon us all.

"Every newspaper now asks itself, with respect to every story: 'Is it news?' All I suggest is that you add the question: 'Is it in the interest of national security?' And I hope that every group in America—unions and business men and public officials at every level—will ask the same question of their endeavors, and subject their actions to this same exacting test.

"And should the press of America consider and recommend the voluntary assumption of specific new steps or machinery, I can assure you that we will cooperate wholeheartedly with those recommendations."

The President made clear to the publishers that he had no desire to stifle controversy or criticism, and that his Administration intended to be candid about its errors. He quoted an old adage that "an error does not become a mistake until you refuse to correct it." He quoted Solon, the Athenian law maker, who said that it was a crime for a citizen to shrink from controversy. The publishers listened politely and even laughed when he said he had not come to "deliver the usual assault on the so-called one-party press. On the contrary, in recent months I have rarely heard any complaints about political bias except from a few Republicans."

The reaction was as expected from a press traditionally suspicious of any move to control it—even benevolently.

"There is no need for further restrictive machinery," said the *New York Herald Tribune*. "In days of peril especially, the country needs more facts, not fewer. In the long run, competent, thorough and aggressive news reporting is the uncompromising servant of the national interest—even though it may be momentarily embarrassing to the Government."

The *Portland Oregonian* made the point that what is needed "far more is discipline among government officials, both civilian and military; first, to keep the people properly informed; second, to guard legitimate secrets from leaks, lies, misinterpretation and inter-agency sabotage."

The *Newark Evening News* asked who was to define the national interest. "The press believes the public's right to know is a fundamental of democratic government. But where does this right collide with national security? If Mr. Kennedy . . . can tell us, he will not find the press uncooperative."

The *Louisville Courier-Journal* said the President "did not and probably could not spell out what he meant . . . for self-restraint, like virtue, is a matter that lends itself to individual interpretation."

The *Nashville Tennessean* said: "There is not an ethical newspaper publisher or editor . . . who is not ready to recognize that any war, cold or hot, presents new problems and responsibilities . . . Rights of the free press are not

going to be tampered with, but patriotic cooperation . . .
can be taken for granted."

If Kennedy intended to enter into debate with the editorial writers, he did not get the immediate opportunity because at this time the Cuban adventure exploded all over
the front pages, keeping him and his press secretary fully
occupied. Salinger himself was nursing wounds suffered at
a panel session of the American Society of Newspaper
Editors where Peter Lisagor, Washington bureau chief of
the Chicago *Daily News,* had finally openly voiced the
complaint that reporters were "little more than props for
the TV press conference." Lisagor and others said it would
"be nice to know when the Irish temper behind the Harvard façade had been excited. This could be accomplished
by sitting a little closer to the President." The normally
good-humored Salinger replied rather testily that "people
who long for the good old days of F.D.R. are unrealistic.
Television is here to stay." It was only natural that Salinger
should be subject to comparison with his predecessor.
White House correspondents felt that Salinger had not yet
achieved "the polish and sure-footedness of Hagerty;" that
he properly spoke less for Kennedy than Hagerty did for
Eisenhower; that he often ignored telephone calls; that he
was frequently late in holding his twice-a-day press brief-
ings and that he was often not certain of his information.
But all agreed that "Plucky Pierre," as he was sometimes
called behind his ample back, did a prodigious amount of
work, was willing to admit errors and definitely made no
attempt to create a wall around the President. Salinger's
own appraisal of his work so far was: "I think the people
are getting a closer view of the President than they've ever
had—and that's just what we want."

The closer view evidently favored Kennedy, as private
and public polls showed an ever-increasing popularity and,
what was even more encouraging, a genuine sympathy for
his burdens of office. He made it a practice on some quiet

weekend afternoons, rare though they were, to walk into the press room, which is really a large anteroom to the executive offices, and have a casual chat with reporters. Such visits were generally not mentioned and definitely were not to be construed as any form of press conference, briefing or background session. Shortly after the Cuban mishap, someone remarked that the Gallup Poll indicated that his popularity had reached a new peak. "My God," he exclaimed, "it's as bad as Eisenhower. The worse I do, the more popular I get."

23. Overalls and Wages

The Administration moved boldly, swiftly and dramatically to demonstrate its power and prestige (and eagerness) in the settlement of labor disputes. The setting was New York Harbor, where a strike of 660 railroad tugboat workers not only had tied up the city's river traffic but had also come close to throttling its railroad services. The strike had come after a year of negotiations between Eastern railroads and three unions over the size of the crews on 47 diesel tugboats that haul coal and food to Manhattan from the New Jersey railheads. There was no quarrel over the wages of the tugboat men, whose earnings ranged from $440 to $674 a month. What the unions wanted, their leader, Paul Haul of the Seafarers, said, was a contract guaranteeing that crews would consist of five men. Management sought to maintain the right to cut the crews, but offered to freeze the size for one year, thereafter promising to give 120 days' notice before making any reductions and submit any disputes to binding arbitration.

When the tugboat men struck, many members of the bigger railroad brotherhoods refused to cross their picket lines. This astonished management because in the past the big unions had not always been sympathetic with the tuggers. But the brotherhoods felt that to submit to management this time would set a precedent affecting all the old featherbedding practices, such as the one in which diesel engines, under union contract, still carried firemen. The railroads contended that this and other featherbedding schemes cost them $500 million a year.

The pickets managed to shut down the New York Central Railroad and the New Haven Railroad, forcing hundreds of thousands of commuters to seek other ways of getting to work. While New York was only a few days from starvation, a snowstorm struck the area, making trucking almost impossible. Mayor Wagner sought desperately to find a solution, and even Governor Rockefeller tried and made no tangible progress.

Arthur Goldberg had not yet been sworn in as Secretary of Labor when he started action toward a solution. Even Kennedy was not aware that Goldberg had offered his services to Rockefeller and Wagner. Goldberg acted on his own initiative because it had been reported to him that, if the strike continued, all freight moving into the metropolitan area of New York would be halted. A few hours after he was sworn in, he flew to New York and negotiated with the unions and management for 14 hours. The brand-new Secretary of Labor came armed with a powerful weapon. He told both sides that President Kennedy felt strongly that a strike settlement was required in the national interest. A long truce was agreed upon when management and the unions accepted a plan to delay the decision as to which side had the right to fix the size of work crews, pending a recommendation from an Eisenhower-appointed commission on railroad work rules headed by former Secretary of Labor Mitchell. The idea was not new, but Goldberg promised to arrange that the Mitchell commission would consider the tugboat problem separately.

This was a sensational victory that gave the Administration a good start with enthusiastic headlines, an applauding populace, satisfied commuters and happy housewives who had been depleting their freezers. Praise for Goldberg came from the strikers, management, Rockefeller and Wagner, as well as the two men who had borne the major weight of the negotiations, Robert O. Boyd and T. E. Schoonover of the National Mediation Board.

Goldberg, 52, the second oldest member of the Cabinet (Hodges was 62), scored another triumph for the Administration when a month later he was instrumental in settling the most paralyzing airlines strike in the nation's history. It began when 3,500 flight engineers resisted a government order that would absorb them into the larger, 16,000-member pilots' union. For more than 16 hours, Goldberg had met continuously with all the factions involved, not seeking a permanent solution, but trying to arrive at a modus vivendi which would result in a truce and get the commercial planes into the air once again. When Kennedy announced the settlement the following afternoon, the Secretary stood quietly at the President's side. Kennedy gave due credit to Goldberg, who, he said, "had acted on my behalf."

The airline strike pointed up the economic disruption that could be caused by a jurisdictional dispute. It lasted only six days, but it cost the carriers and their 85,000 workers about $40 million in revenue, maintenance costs and wages. More than 500,000 travelers were thrown into turmoil and confusion. Vacation resorts lost staggering sums —Florida $3 million a day and the Carribean area an equal amount. These were only the measurable, statistical losses. The anguish, frustration and dismay of the passengers who never got off the ground was incalculable except in ill will toward both sides.

More than any other Cabinet member, Goldberg acted

as a direct extension of the President himself. The number of unemployed was approaching 5 million, and there seemed no easy road toward any reduction. Business leaders as well as the unions were gravely concerned. The President sent Goldberg on an inspection trip through five states that were representative of unemployment areas generally. When Goldberg returned, the Labor Department issued a salvo of statistics that brought into focus what the people in the country had only dimly perceived.

The report showed that more than half the nation's 150 major industrial areas qualified as depressed. Unemployment was becoming more chronic with 7.7 per cent of the country's 3 million workers listed as jobless. The number made idle for 15 weeks or more rose from 1 million in December to 1.3 million in January. More than half this number had been jobless for more than six months. Negroes, the young just starting their careers in industry, and the unskilled were the hardest hit. The so-called war babies outnumbered the jobs available for them, one out of three of the unemployed being 24 years or under. Unemployment among married men increased from 4.3 per cent in January to 6.1 in February. Industrial employment was down 900,000 from the year before; one out of eight laborers was out of work; mining jobs were at an all-time low; auto, steel and machinery industries were dangerously below their employment peaks of 1955-1957. In Pittsburgh and Detroit, almost 12 per cent were out of work. Illinois was hurt by the slowdown in the manufacture of farm machinery; Maryland and California by the decline in airplane construction; North Carolina and Massachusetts by the poor market in textiles, and Pennsylvania by the slump in metals, coal and oil. Texas wept over its biggest unemployment problem in 20 years.

Relocation of workers as a solution to regional unemployment was found unworkable. Aside from lack of opportunity in other areas, the Labor Department gave as more pertinent reasons family ties, home ownership, educational facilities, pension and benefit rights and, above all, inertia. The workers living in small towns who moved into the nearby big cities failed to get jobs and simply added to the relief and unemployment rolls. Fortunately for the jobless as well as the nation, there were economic cushions that prevented hysteria. Unemployment insurance from the states was supplanted by a Federal emergency unemployment compensation bill passed quickly by both Houses and signed by the President. In addition, there were bank savings, veterans' pensions, railroad retirement payments and social security payments. The President asked for $394 million in loans and grants to areas of chronic depression and labor surplus and Congress passed a bill giving him essentially what he asked. It was admittedly stopgap, but it was of some help.

There was a seeming paradox in the record number of unemployed and the record number of employed. The coming of age of World War II babies was pouring a million new workers into the market every year and larger numbers were expected. Technology and automation were reducing drastically the demand for labor. The Department cited one example: in 1948 it took 21 men to produce a ton of steel; in 1961 it took 12.

Projections made by statisticians and economists showed the President that, if there were no depression and the country's business developed as expected, the number of jobless would remain constant at about six per cent of the labor force. While there was a divergence of views as to what was a safe figure, most economists agreed that anything greater than six per cent would be dangerous. Kennedy announced a goal of four per cent.

Based on the trends during the 1950's and carried into the 1960's, the composition of the labor force also was expected to remain constant. Workers under 25 and over 45 were the most likely to lose their jobs first. By 1970, the under-25 group was expected to increase by 46 per cent and the over-45 group by 20 per cent. This over-all projection was modified to indicate that these figures might not hold true in highly skilled fields. Education was regarded as the key factor in professional, technical and managerial jobs, where the age level was not so important. The projection indicated that the number of unskilled workers would not change by 1970; the number of farm workers would decrease sharply and employment opportunities would increase faster in the service industries than in production.

With these figures as a base, the Administration began its long battle for a minimum wage bill that would go up to $1.25 an hour and embrace many more workers. With Kennedy and his legislative team behind him, Goldberg worked valiantly to win all the original provisions, but quietly settled for what was finally passed. A breakdown from labor and management points of view showed that the bill, among other benefits, would have a tremendous pump-priming effect upon the economy.

The annual payroll costs of the entire series of rises were estimated officially at $836 million for workers already covered and $700 million for new groups. Millions of workers received pay rises as an indirect result of these changes. These were the higher-paid employes, who would get rises at the same time lower-bracket employes were raised to the new federal minimum in their companies.

Rules for determining what firms were covered by wage-hour regulations were written into the new law. Coverage in industries newly brought under the act was based on their volume of business. It became possible to include a store operating only inside one state, whereas formerly all retail stores were exempt.

These changes were viewed as the most drastic revisions made in the Wage-Hour Act since its passage in 1938. Congress had boosted the minimum wage several times but never before had it broadened the coverage to new groups of workers. More than 2 million of the workers getting coverage were in the retail service fields. Of this group, 584,000 earned less than $1 an hour. They included employees of department stores, grocery stores, apparel stores, furniture and appliance stores and the larger repair firms.

About 30 per cent of the wage earners in retail trade were covered. But only about three per cent of the retail stores of the country were under the Act—since smaller stores still were to be exempt. Labor Department experts estimated that 19,600 firms with a total of 58,000 individual stores were being brought under the Act. This left some 1.7 million stores uncovered. The retail stores were those that had $1 million or more in annual sales volume, excluding excise taxes, and that brought at least $250,000 worth of goods across state lines. Chain stores and single-store firms were affected. However, small stores having less than $250,000 in annual sales were not covered, even if they were part of a chain that aggregated $1 million a year in sales.

Some service establishments also were included if they met the $1 million test and brought at least $250,000 worth of goods across a state line.

There were many exceptions in the service field. Congress specified that, regardless of money-volume tests, certain types of business were not being brought under the law. These included automobile dealers, hotels, motels, restaurants, motion-picture theaters, hospitals, nursing homes, and schools for handicapped or gifted children. Others exempt included amusement or recreational facilities operating seasonally.

More than 2 million workers in the retail and service fields were covered by the law for the first time under the minimum-wage and overtime provisions.

In addition, 86,000 employees of gas stations were given

minimum-wage guarantees. A gas station was included if it had $250,000 or more a year in sales, excluding excise taxes.

Firms in construction with an annual business of at least $350,000 were covered by the wage and overtime clauses—bringing 1 million employees under the Act. Suburban and intercity transit lines doing a million-dollar business came under the rule. About 93,000 employees were affected. About 100,000 seamen also were put under the minimum-wage provision, although not under the hours guarantee. All the seamen received at least $1 an hour, but some 10,000 would get rises when the minimum reached $1.25 an hour.

Employees of processing firms operating in interstate commerce got minimum-wage protection but not overtime protection. Of 33,000 affected, 10,000 had been getting less than $1 an hour. About 30,000 telephone operators got new wage and hour protection, resulting in pay increases for about 5,000. The law applied to operators working for independent companies with 750 or more telephones. Previously, the law covered the larger telephone exchanges but exempted the small offices, even if part of a large firm.

An additional 100,000 employees came under the rules on wages and hours because they worked for firms that already had some employees covered. These were in jobs that affect interstate commerce. This extension was mainly in wholesale trade, along with some firms in manufacturing, transportation, public-utility and communications with a million-dollar business.

No overtime rate was required during the first two years. In September, 1963, time-and-a-half rates must be paid after 44 hours a week. In September, 1964, the overtime was to start at 42 hours and in 1965 it would start at 40 hours. The Labor Department estimated that about 460,000 of the newly covered employees in the retail field were then working more than 44 hours a week; about 576,000 were working more than 42 hours and 715,000 worked more than 40 hours.

Even with the broader coverage, more than 16 million employees were still excluded from wage-hour protection. These embraced such groups as 5 million in small retail businesses; 2 million in agriculture, 1.5 million in restaurants, 1 million in non-profit organizations and education, and 2.4 million domestic workers. The arbitrary distinctions that were to cause confusion in the administration of the law were the result of a gerrymandering that sought to appease an almost infinite number of conflicting pressure groups.

Goldberg was gratified that there was no major criticism from the union leaders with whom he had worked as a labor lawyer. From the time he took office, he had been subjected to some praise and some mild criticism. Labor and management observers who lauded his actions in the tugboat and airline strikes cited the flaw in both achievements—that Goldberg settled strikes but failed to settle the central issues. Others said that, like his chief, Goldberg was willing to compromise for the best possible results and wait for better things.

The most controversial single expressions of Goldberg's policy, and his most important, was his creation of the President's Labor-Management Advisory Committee, consisting of seven representatives from business, seven from labor and five from the public, the chairmanship alternating between the Secretary of Labor and the Secretary of Commerce. Goldberg was the first chairman. In proposing the committee to Kennedy, Goldberg had envisioned it as a last-ditch referee in national strikes, a solid wall that would stop labor-management disputes from creating a national crisis. But Kennedy tempered this by giving the committee the prestige and power of Government sponsorship, but stopping short of making it the final arbiter. Goldberg explained Kennedy's position by pointing out that the President did not seek "to foster a compulsory system of wage and price policy." He said it was not the intention of the Government to "get a group of people together and hand them resolutions to be followed to the letter. I don't want anybody in the business or labor community to get the notion that this committee is designed to replace collective-bargaining machinery."

He made this statement with an eye toward the opinions of the nation's labor leaders, who were watching cautiously the course that he was steering. Goldberg had made it plain at the outset that he considered himself "counsel for the public interest, and I am not representing the labor movement in this Administration." At their midwinter meeting in Florida, the members of labor's high command pondered the Goldberg statement with active interest and a tinge of suspicion. George Meany, David Dubinsky, Walter Reuther and David McDonald agreed that Goldberg had done a magnificent job in the airline and tugboat strikes. They approved of the Administration's opposition to Section 14B of the Taft-Hartley Act, which permitted states to enact so-called right-to-work laws prohibiting compulsory union membership. Goldberg's position was that management and labor should be free to work out their joint union-security settlements without being hampered by state or regional restrictions. He also opposed proposals to prohibit strikes in public utilities, saying he preferred to encourage labor-management responsibility in this field, with both sides having fair weapons at their disposal.

But Meany, speaking for the high command, warned that the Labor-Management Advisory Committee would be "doomed from the start" if its public members tried to "throw their weight to one side or the other." Meany, Reuther and Dubinsky were among the labor members of the committee. The labor leaders also deplored the President's advocacy of tax incentives to business and, instead, urged large-scale tax reforms that would benefit workers, including a temporary reduction in personal income taxes and an increase in the "grossly inadequate" social security retirement benefits. The general attitude of the union leaders was that Goldberg's "heart was in the right place," and everything he had done so far showed his good intentions.

Goldberg and Secretary of Agriculture Freeman gave Kennedy a demonstration of good intentions and the Cabinet team spirit in their quest for a solution to the cruel problem of migrant labor. During the Eisenhower Administration a public quarrel developed between Secretary of Labor Mitchell, who sought to tighten regulations and improve standards in the migrant labor field, and Secretary of Agriculture Benson, who vigorously opposed him. Goldberg supported proposals made by Senator Harrison A. Williams, New Jersey Democrat and chairman of the Senate Migrant Labor Subcommittee, and Freeman declared that he was sympathetic with the idea. Williams' plans to ease the lot of the 500,000 migrant workers and their families included per capita grants of $300,000 to the states to operate some 60 summer schools for migrant workers' children; appropriation of $250,000 to promote interstate planning, development of educational materials, and the transmission of school records for these children; Federal aid of $2 million a year to make up for local school taxes that migrant workers could not pay; outlays of $25,000 a year for practical education for adult migrant workers on such matters as sanitation, diet, family budgets and personal health.

In the housing field, Williams urged Federally insured loans to growers and grower associations to build homes for migrants. Farmers had complained that they could not get private financing for these projects. Children of migrant workers were to be the major beneficiaries of the Goldberg-supported proposals. These included $250,000 for day-care centers and $3 million for the Public Health Service to enlarge its work with farm laborers. To regulate "crew leaders" —men who act as labor contractors supplying harvesters—

a registration requirement was suggested to remove abuses. There were only eight states that had some form of control over these men. Conspicuously absent from the proposals were a minimum wage for the workers and a ban on child labor in the fields. Both these faced such concerted opposition from the farm bloc that any insistence upon their adoption might endanger the entire program. The Administration, once again, indicated it would settle for the best possible bill and strive for a better one in the next seven years.

The President might well have wondered how much public pressure he could apply on Congress for better labor legislation in the years to come. Surely there was no economic crisis, nor an unemployment problem of the magnitude faced by Roosevelt in his first hundred days, when the people were hungry and so were the labor leaders. The question the President might have asked was whether the labor leaders, lolling in luxury at the Americana Hotel in Bal Harbour, near Miami Beach, could inspire in their members and the public at large the sense of urgency that would make itself felt in Congress. As *Newsweek* reported, "Meany and Dubinsky were playing gin rummy, Reuther walked through a jam-packed lobby, McDonald puffed on a pipe and studied the Atlantic Ocean." Was any one of them thinking of the workers left out of the minimum wage bill, or the migrant workers, or the millions without work?

If Kennedy or the labor leaders could not impress the nation with the immediate problem, they were aware that the country was moving toward a long-range crisis created by an inflation that had begun with Roosevelt and was continuing unabated. The irresistible upward spiral of price and wage boosts showed no signs of leveling off. It seemed that all negotiations between industry and labor began with this assumption.

Business refused to recognize the advantage of cutting prices as a result of increased productivity because it calculated on a constant rise in wages. Labor, assuming a continuous increase in prices, sought more wages. What Kennedy proposed was that, if both sides could discard these false philosophies, higher productivity could be translated into lower prices and this into increased real wages.

Professor Henry Wallich of Yale, former economic adviser to Eisenhower, urged labor to restrict its wage increases to the level of national productive gains of about two per cent a year. Federal Reserve Chairman Martin warned that the "wage-price process has got to be faced squarely by both labor and management, and they have got to pass on some of their productivity gains to the consumer in lower prices." Walt Rostow, economist of the Massachusetts Institute of Technology and a high-ranking adviser to Kennedy, favored a wage-price treaty in automobiles and other key industries whereby labor "would accept the continuation of existing money-wage contracts and the industries concerned would undertake to pass along in lower prices the productivity increases achieved within the time period of the contract." Industry, he suggested, would retain enough of the income for reasonable profits and plowbacks for new technology and expansion. Walter Reuther, who had shown the way by tying wages to the cost-of-living index of the Labor Department, indicated labor's long-range position by framing his demands in general terms of an annual wage and a shorter work week without a reduction in pay.

Kennedy hoped that management and labor would strive for a foundation of real wages—the actual purchasing power of workers' earnings—instead of an ephemeral dollar total that vibrated the economy and encouraged inflation. He was sitting solidly in the center between big business and big labor, but he was encouraged by the emergence of a new understanding by both that they were inexorably tied together with the nation's welfare and stability.

24. The Welfare of the Nation

In the steady evolution from the simple country school-house to the massive, complex university system, Americans have always been conscious of the value of education. In the early years this interest manifested itself in a primitive desire to attain at least a minimum of literacy, higher learning being reserved for an elite few. After World War II, when the Government provided every willing ex-soldier with a free education and when commerce, industry and the professions raised their educational requirements, the need for more and better schools became so apparent that the entire country grew intensely preoccupied with the progress of its young from grade school to college. Another motivation was the cold-war rivalry with the Soviet Union, whose educational system was reported to be burgeoning enviably beyond America's. The people as well as the educators were looking toward the Administration for a bigger and more generous school-aid program than had ever been proposed.

In his Federal-aid-to-education message, Kennedy requested $3,327.5 million over the next five years for undergraduate scholarships and for the construction of college classrooms and dormitories. There seemed to be no question that Congress would grant this with only minor modifications. Then Kennedy asked for $2,298 million for public-school development in three-year grants to states, with the choice that the money could be used for building and/or teachers' salaries. Religious schools were specifically omitted.

The omission was not unexpected. During his campaign, Kennedy had clearly stated his uncompromising philosophy of the separation of church and state. He had left no room for argument or doubt that Federal aid to parochial schools would be unconstitutional, and he appeared to be prepared for the denunciation of his church and the bitter domestic controversy that was to follow.

When the contents of the education message had been carefully analyzed, the 13 members of the administrative board of the National Catholic Welfare Conference, which includes more than 200 cardinals, archbishops and bishops who guide church policies in the United States, authorized Archbishop Karl J. Alter of Cincinnati to announce that the church would oppose the bill unless it was amended to include long-term, low-interest loans to all the nation's private schools, including the 12,000 run by Catholic groups.

Although the Catholic position was foreseen, it still was a reversal of an early stand. Six years before, the hierarchy had generally regarded Federal assistance to private education as the first step toward Government control. In 1949, Cardinal Spellman of New York said: "We do not ask nor can we expect public funds to pay for the construction of parochial school buildings." In 1955, Cardinal (then Archbishop) Cushing of Boston declared that "we are not looking for any Federal or Government aid to build our schools." Kennedy himself, as a Representative, had supported some kinds of Federal aid for parochial schools, but he changed his position before he became a Senator.

Kennedy as President had spoken frankly, taken his fixed position and transferred the major portion of the controversy to the more politically sensitive and vulnerable Congress, especially the House, where many members had to account for their actions to large Catholic constituencies. Representatives, liberal or conservative, Protestant or Catholic, were wondering how they could save the bill and not appear hostile to the church. To add to their dilemma, Cardinal Ritter of St. Louis said he was "personally opposed to Federal aid of any kind; but, if such aid is voted, then all the children should share in that benefit." Cardinal Spellman declared it was "not for me to say whether there should be any Federal aid to education, but, if Congress approved it, it would be unfair and discriminatory if Catholics did not share the benefits." The most reasonable approach was made by Monsignor Frederick G. Hochwalt, educational director of the National Catholic Welfare Conference: "If an intellectual and scientific breakthrough is to be realized," he said, "who can tell whence will come the leadership of the nation—from the public schools or from their partners in education, the private schools?"

Militant opposition to the Catholic stand came from Protestant and Jewish clergymen in testimony before Congressional committees, even though many had denominational schools of their own. In essence they asked for a "bigger and thicker" wall between church and state.

A group of 19, headed by retired Methodist Bishop G. Bromley Oxnam, retired Episcopal Bishop Henry Knox Sherrill and the Reverend Dr. Eugene Carson Blake, of the United Presbyterian Church in the United States, signed an opinion that it would "be most unfortunate for a major church to press its own interests in a way that would threaten the strengthening of our basic educational system." Dr. Robert E. Van Deusen of the National Lutheran Council told the House that a "religious group with its own high-school system should provide the necessary financial support, thus insuring its own continuing autonomy and freedom." The Association of Reform Rabbis of New York declared: "We uphold the President's definite stand against the extension of any portion of Federal aid to parochial schools."

Editorialists, with a few exceptions, managed to tread tenderly on the religious issue, but the Catholic position was clearly summed up by the Reverend Francis P. Canavan, S.J., writing in the Jesuit weekly, *America:* "The demand now made by Catholic and other parents for some relief from the burden of supporting both their own and the public schools is a request for the rethinking of a policy, not for a revision of the Constitution." The Protestant *Christian Century* said: "The Roman Catholic hierarchy has drawn the line on which the battle for Federal aid to education will be fought, and has dared the Congress to step over it. The challenge should be accepted. If they have their way, Federal funds will be used for religious purposes, despite the Constitution, or there will be no Federal funds for public education."

The likelihood that the school-aid controversy would eventually come before the Supreme Court caused Kennedy and the opposing Catholics to examine decisions that had historically attempted to decide the claims of two strong and conflicting principles. One was the Jeffersonian "wall of separation between church and state," and the other was the modern philosophy that the "right of all children to an education entitled any and all students to Government assistance on an equal basis."

In 1930, the Supreme Court upheld a Louisiana statute providing for the distribution of non-religious textbooks by the state to children of public and private schools alike. In 1947, in a more potent decision, the Court approved a New Jersey law permitting free bus service for parochial-school children—but made a clear distinction between service to students and service to schools. Justice Hugo Black, writing for the majority, stated that "no tax in any amount can be levied to support any religious activities of institutions." This was regarded by many as the crux of Kennedy's position. In two other decisions, the court created some confusion. In 1948 it ruled against the Illinois practice of permitting religious education in public-school buildings during the school day. But in 1952 a six-man majority ruled in favor of a New York program that released public-school children for religious instruction outside city or state property.

In that ruling, Justice William O. Douglas, writing for the majority, declared that the First Amendment "obviously cannot mean that there must be a complete separation of church and state. Otherwise the state and religion would be aliens to each other—hostile, suspicious and even unfriendly. Prayers in legislative halls; appeals to the Almighty in the messages of the Chief Executive; the proclamation of making Thanksgiving a holiday; 'so help me God' oaths in our courtrooms—these and all other references to the Almighty that run through our laws, our public rituals, our ceremonies would be flouting the First Amendment. When the state cooperates in religious instruction, it follows the best of our traditions."

In spite of the support given Kennedy by such influential groups as the National Council of Churches and the American Jewish Congress, legislators began to whisper compromise. Majority Leader John McCormack, a Massachusetts Democrat and an old friend of Kennedy, came out for parochial-school loans. He noted that 12 Catholic members of the Senate and the 87 Catholic members of the House were under tremendous pressure of conscience, even though a good deal of their mail was obviously inspired. Senator Eugene McCarthy, a Minnesota Catholic, who also favored the loan compromise, reported that many of the

letters he had received had accidentally included printed
instructions on how they should be written. But this was a
further indication of the high-pressure position the Catholic
Church had taken.

The President, fully aware that the bill, as it stood, had
little chance for success, might have been secretly pleased
with the talk of the loans. He said the idea "raises a serious
constitutional question which, after reading the cases and
giving it a good deal of thought, in my opinion would be
unconstitutional." He declined to predict, however,
whether he would veto an education bill with the loan
rider attached to it. He suggested that Congress should
pass the Administration's school bill as presented and consider private school loans in separate legislation—if at all.

Having somewhat eased the tension and having been
heartened by predictions that Congress was eager to arrive at a solution that would please the President and appease the Catholic bishops, Kennedy faced another entrenched interest in his proposals for a national health
program. This time the uncompromising enemy, with a
long record of successes against "Governmental meddling,"
was the American Medical Association. After long conferences with Secretary of Health, Education and Welfare
Ribicoff, the Administration created a set of proposals that
generally met the approval of voters but found a seemingly
insurmountable barrier in the American Medical Association.

In its continuing war against the Administration's health
plan for the aged, the American Medical Association was
expected to win every battle except the last one. Although
precedent favors the AMA, which in its 114 years has never
lost a major fight over legislation affecting the scientific,
economic or social aspects of the practice of medicine, time
and the increasing number of men and women over 65 assure a victory for Kennedy's program. Of the 14.2 million
citizens over 65, about 11 million on social security would

get these major benefits from the Kennedy plan: 90 days of hospitalization for any single spell of sickness; 120 days of care in a nursing home after discharge from a hospital. When the President offered the program he said it would be financed by increased social security payments of $1.5 billion a year.

As soon as the bill (HR 4222) was introduced by Representative Cecil D. King, California Democrat, the AMA's president, Dr. E. Vincent Askey, a Los Angeles surgeon, denounced it, charging that it would "place the free practice of medicine in a strait jacket." The AMA's powerful lobby, which had spent $72,635 in 1960, began its work on members of Congress while the home office in Chicago issued a flood of literature warning doctors with a red-inked poster called "Socialized Medicine and You" that "your freedom is at stake." The doctors were urged to display the poster prominently in their waiting rooms. Advertisements were placed in 29 leading newspapers praising the Kerr-Mills law passed by the previous Congress, which provides 120 days of hospitalization but required that the aged who apply prove economic need. The advertisement denounced the Kennedy "compulsory health program" and urged all to "write your Senators and Congressmen to reject socialized medicine." Forty FM radio stations across the nation carried spot "messages" urging defeat of the bill. The general theme was expressed by one housewife who told her radio audience by way of a taped commercial: "I can't stand the thought of socialized medicine."

Kennedy assigned Ribicoff to lead the fight for the bill. Charging that the AMA was using "scare tactics by claiming that the bill would limit a patient's choice of his doctor," Ribicoff explained that Kennedy's proposal "would do nothing of the kind." Dr. Askey immediately challenged Ribicoff to a "national debate" on the bill to give the public the opportunity to decide how deeply involved the family physician would be, actually and potentially, in govern-

ment medicine. When Ribicoff promptly accepted, Dr.
Askey backed out, offering a substitute.

The immediate problem faced by the Administration
was whether it could pry the bill out of the House Ways
and Means Committee, where only nine out of 25 members favor the measure. Kennedy told the press conference
that "it is possible that someone might offer the bill in the
Senate as an amendment . . . it is very possible that you
could get a vote in the Senate this year. The House is a
different problem." Despite his chief's cautious statement,
Ribicoff remained strongly optimistic, and with good reason. He pointed to the ever-growing number of men and
women over 65 (the estimate for 1970 is more than 20
million) whose influence in an election should outweigh
the 179,000 AMA members. And he was cheered by the
privately expressed opinions of many physicians that some
form of Federal health insurance seems inevitable and
necessary. For the long battle against the AMA, Ribicoff
depends largely upon Professor Wilbur J. Cohen, 48, Assistant HEW Secretary for Legislative Matters. Professor
Cohen, a New Dealer with 22 years' experience in Washington, was one of the architects of the Social Security Act
and has been a close advisor to all Presidents since. It was
Professor Cohen who discovered an impressive number of
dissenters among the younger members of the AMA and
who reported privately that members of Congress had been
receiving heavy mail favoring Kennedy's proposal—and
that the letters were not only from the elderly but from
groups that were at least ten to 15 years from the retirement
age. As the 100 days came to a close and HR 4222 (67
pages of double-spaced typing) lay uneasily in the files of
the Ways and Means Committee, Ribicoff and Cohen
echoed the President's sentiment: "I don't think the AMA
will get its way."

Ribicoff managed to keep busy between battles with the
AMA. His department, playing an increasingly important

and direct part in the everyday lives of the citizens, concerned itself with infant care, youth fitness and all the physical ailments that beset the population. Every month, the department paid out $575 million in old-age and widows' benefits and $200 million more to the needy. It provided millions of vaccinations for children; its research grants went out into the nation's laboratories probing the secrets of cancer, heart disease, neurological illness and many others. HEW scientists were busy spot-testing antibiotics that were sold in American drug stores and kept control of the chemicals that went into the artificial colors that brightened Florida oranges. HEW crews checked incoming ships and airplanes for plagues and radiation. The department cared for lepers in Louisiana and in Hawaii; trained adults for new vocations; supervised Federal credit unions; printed and distributed books in Braille; operated the country's only college for the deaf and the only general university for Negroes in Washington.

Ribicoff was eagerly pressing for Kennedy's welfare increases that provided food for the needy; retirement at 62 with benefits somewhat reduced in order to ease the unemployment situation; increased benefits for older widows; new definitions for disability, and a broader insurance base. Congress was listening respectfully to the able arguments presented by Kennedy and Ribicoff, who said that some 5 million citizens would benefit by approval of these requests.

The Administration took the broadest approach in welfare, seeking to embrace all the facets of a good and full life for its citizens. It presented a vast housing program designed to revitalize cities, provide more middle-income and low-income dwellings while fighting the recession.

Citing the need for "improving our pattern of community development and providing for the housing needs of all segments of our population," Kennedy outlined these proposals with a view toward the nation's economic growth: a four-year commitment to urban renewal at a cost of $2.5

billion; no down payment and 40-year mortgages for families with moderate incomes; long-term loans for rental and cooperative housing; subsidies for private rehabilitation of slums; liberalized authority for the Federal Housing Administration to insure home improvement loans; grants and loans for local purchases of "open space" for parks, playgrounds and other facilities; construction of 100,000 new public housing units, half of them for the aged, and additional aid for metropolitan area planning, community facilities and the development of cheaper home-building techniques.

The Administration even had a kind thought for the commuter. "Nothing is more dramatically apparent," Kennedy said in his housing message, "than the inadequacy of transportation in our larger urban areas. The solution cannot be found only in the construction of additional urban highways—vital as that job is. Other means for mass transportation which use less space and equipment must be improved and expanded. Perhaps even more important, planning for transportation and land use must go hand in hand as two inseparable aspects of the same process."

It was estimated that the proposals would require the expenditure of close to $800 million, excluding loans. This was $90 million more than Eisenhower had estimated. The projected cost, Kennedy indicated, would be higher, since by the end of the decade a building rate of more than 2 million new homes a year would be required to keep up with the normal population increase.

Congress heard these proposals attentively and proceeded to approach them cautiously with a general tendency toward a favorable response. Kennedy had emphasized the importance of his housing program by announcing his intention to establish a new Cabinet post of Housing and Urban Affairs to oversee the program. It was noted that the Administration's proposals were based on recommendations made by Dr. Robert C. Weaver, head of the Housing and

Home Finance Agency, a near-Cabinet-level post. It was expected that the agency would form the core of the new department and that Weaver would become the first Negro to hold a Cabinet post.

In his housing program, Kennedy felt that the New Frontier was carrying out its pledges of a dynamic future for the nation. It was a good method to provide for big business and big labor and the biggest segment in the nation—the ordinary voter.

25. The Land Is Too Good

Before the President prepared his message and legislation on agriculture, he surveyed the perennial farm problem, concluded that it was inescapably interrelated with the economic health of the city and directed his long-range planning toward assuring the farmer of an income comparable with that of the rest of the nation.

Under the prevailing agricultural programs farm production was rising at a faster rate than the ordinary markets could absorb. This meant that, with no change in the programs, the United States would continue to accumulate surpluses and the cost of Federal price supports, storage and disposal would be between $2 billion and $4 billion. The overproduction of grain was the crux of the surplus dilemma. During the fiscal year the nation had added 400 million bushels of grain to the carryover and the rate was expected to be constant. Corn and feed grains were getting price supports but had no restrictions on production. There was a better balance between production and markets in other major commodities.

Kennedy realized the danger of finding the grain surplus unmanageable. Unless it was brought under control, it would spill rapidly into the livestock industries, resulting in increased production of meat, dairy products and poultry and sharply lowering prices and net incomes. The livestock industries were in good balance with demand because of the Government's policy of withholding a considerable amount of grain from the open market.

The growth of population was expected to increase the domestic food consumption, but not spectacularly. By 1965, there would be more heavy-eating teen-agers, a Department of Agriculture announcement said, but they would be offset by the lighter-eating group of over-65's, whose number would also increase. If consumer income continued to rise at the same rate as in the Fifties, per capita disposable income in 1965 would be 10 to 15 per cent higher than in 1959. However, this increased income would have only a minute effect on the per capita demand for food. A diet-conscious America, while excellent for the health and silhouette of the nation, was not considered as the most promising market for the farmer's goods.

There was little hope for expansion of the export market, and, while the President sought actively to encourage the use of surplus food in hungry countries, there was little hope that even this could be used as a solution to the surplus problem. Distribution of free food under a stamp plan to people in depressed areas in the United States, while helpful, made no great inroads in the overfilled granary. Kennedy had to face the unpleasant prospect that, if the prevailing farm program remained unchanged, he could expect a further decline in the net income of commercial farmers in the next five years. Gross income was expected to increase as the result of larger volume at about the same level of prices, but costs of production would undoubtedly continue to rise.

The number of commercial farms (devoted exclusively to agricultural products) was not expected to change within the next five years although a steady decline in the non-commercial farms (where the head of the family has additional means of support) was expected to continue. The number of farms with gross sales above $2,500 remained steady, and the decline was noted mainly in farms of low productivity and low income. The speed of the decline was connected directly with employment in industry. The general desire and trend toward work in the cities had eliminated many marginal farms from the market. Income to farm families from non-agricultural sources was about one third of the total. The danger to these farm workers, therefore, came from overproduction on the land and lack of production in the factories.

A Kennedy task-force report suggested that "the most practical way to deal with the grain surplus was to undertake a greatly expanded land retirement program. This land would be removed from production of any crop for market, or for livestock feed or for pasture. Participation in the land-retirement program at some minimum level should be a condition for receiving price supports or other benefits from farm programs. Land retired from cotton, wheat and other crops with acreage allotments should be placed in the conservation reserve. An effort should be made to retire a considerable amount of land that has been planted to feed-grains. An effort should be made to curtail Government programs that are tending to increase production of farm products. We believe it would be unwise to raise price supports for wheat and corn under present circumstances. Land reclamation and other programs increasing land cultivation should be curtailed."

The report noted that cotton and rice were also in surplus

but the maladjustment of supply and demand was not too serious. It suggested that the general level of dairy price supports should not be changed because accumulation at the prevailing support level should not be excessive.

When the President finally sent his farm message to Congress, it contained suggestions for self-help putting the burden of the solution on the farmers themselves. The message suggested that growers of each important farm commodity elect from their ranks the members of an advisory committee, and that these committees, in consultation with Secretary of Agriculture Freeman, draft whatever production and marketing controls they saw necessary for their own crop. The program would then have to be approved by the farmers themselves, and, if two thirds of the farmers agreed, the program would become effective unless either the House or the Senate disapproved it within 60 days. The farmers would then be under production and marketing controls, but these would be of their own making.

The effect of the proposal was to lift the drafting of farm legislation from the Congress and place it in the hands of the farmers. When Representative William R. Poage, Texas Democrat, made a similar proposal the year before, one colleague said it was like letting smugglers write the customs regulations. At that time the House buried it deep.

Secretary Freeman pleaded that "all the farmer is asking for is equality of economic opportunity. As it now stands, the consumer does have a good bargain in food prices measured against income. I am confident that this is not a program that will cost more. It will cost less." There was considerable praise for the program and some sharp dissent. Senator Dirksen called it a "do-it-yourself kit for every farm commodity . . . in which the executive branch could completely divest itself of all responsibility." Senator George Aiken, Vermont Republican, asked: "If farm groups can write their own tickets, why not let labor or industrial groups do the same thing?" The conservative American

Farm Bureau Federation, with a membership of 1.6 million families, predicted threats of regimentation, inefficient production, lower incomes and higher taxes. The National Farmers' Union and the National Grange approved the President's plan as realistic and comprehensive.

The President reminded Congress that farming spent more than $40 billion a year for goods and services, that it employed more people than the steel, automobile, utility and transportation industries combined, and that, unless we had a progressive and prosperous agriculture, the alternative was a weakened nation. Congress agreed to this but remained cool to the proposals. The coolness could be traced partly to Secretary Freeman's first major official act, when he increased cotton subsidies. Charles Shuman, president of the Farm Bureau Federation, attacked this "rash move" on the grounds that exports had been reducing the cotton surplus and that the decision would "reverse these favorable trends" by pricing United States cotton out of some overseas markets. Commerce Secretary Hodges tried hard to maintain a façade of Cabinet loyalty, but could not restrain himself from complaining that Freeman's generosity had made it more difficult for United States cotton-textile mills to compete against imports from abroad. There seemed to be no pat answer to the situation. Even the President admitted that "we cannot expect to solve the farm problem in a day or in a year, or perhaps even in this Administration."

No amount of pessimism would make the Administration falter in its long-range projection to strengthen the agricultural community, Kennedy indicated. In addition, he spoke emphatically for the preservation of natural resources. He appealed for an effort to retain an America of "open spaces, fresh water and green country where wildlife and natural beauty cannot be despoiled." In an address before the National Wildlife Federation, he pointed out that the two Presidents who had shown the greatest interest in conservation had been the two Roosevelts, both from New York, proving that the cause of conservation was not a regional or a Western problem. He recalled the lines from Robert Frost's poem read at the Inauguration: "The land was ours before we were the land's."

26. The Courts and the Agencies

In the decade preceding Kennedy's inauguration the dockets of the Federal Courts had become so clogged that important private and public litigation was often delayed as much as four years. In 1954 Eisenhower had won Congressional approval of a modest increase in the judiciary, but his subsequent attempts to obtain a discretionary law authorizing the President to augment the judgeships in the District and Circuit Courts as needs dictated were blocked by a Democratic-controlled Congress fearful lest he appoint too many Republicans. In February of 1961 Kennedy sent his brother, the Attorney General, to ask Congress to create 50 new judgeships in the District Courts and nine in the Circuit Courts.

The move by the President and the Attorney General was based on the findings of a long and intensive study conducted by the Judicial Conference of the United States, composed of the Chief Justice of the United States, the chief judges of the Circuit Courts, the chief judge of the Court of Claims and one district judge from each of the eleven Circuits. It was the Conference that had established the number of new judgeships that the Administration asked; subsequently the Conference raised its own estimate of the minimum need to 69 new jurists. In addition, the President was to be called upon to fill some 20 vacancies arising from deaths and retirements: hence Kennedy would appoint, according to the American Bar Association, more judges than any other President had done. This highly conservative organization believed that the need was even greater than stated by Kennedy's proposal, but it urged the President to distribute his appointments evenly between the parties.

The Democrats in Congress complained at once that the plan to make the biggest increases in the heavily populated areas, such as New York State and Western Pennsylvania, where the courts were most heavily bogged down, was unfair and discriminatory because the increases were not evenly distributed. Judgeships, after all, were prime patronage tools, and Attorney General Kennedy was expected to face his first major test in his handling of the political attacks on the judgeship plan. Considerable promise was seen in his objective approach in the first instance, for there was nothing political in his reasoning. He cited a 20 per cent increase in the population in the preceding decade, outstripped by an increase of more than 30 per cent in the business of the Federal Courts. During the same period the number of district judges was raised by 11 per cent and the Circuit Court personnel was increased by eight per cent.

Congressional reaction, however, was somewhat lacking in such admirable objectivity. Despite the closely documented and reasoned report of the Judicial Conference, Republicans and some conservative Democrats protested that the need had been exaggerated. Other Republicans immediately raised the cry of "pork barrel" and almost, though not quite, insinuated that the Administration was seeking to Democratize the judiciary. Nonetheless, action was relatively quick and both Houses tacked a few more judgeships on to the original requests before enacting the legislation, which a substantial number of Republicans ultimately supported.

It was passed before the end of April, but no judicial appointments were made immediately in the concentration of attention on the kaleidoscope of international crises. The actual work of selection of candidates was expected to devolve on Deputy Attorney General Byron White, and he was counted on to honor the President's campaign pledges to put more Negroes on the federal bench. It was also believed likely that, to stem some of the harsh criticism of the Administration's attitude toward women, a handful of woman lawyers would also be elevated.

One subject that was certain to occupy more of the Federal Courts' attention was violations of the anti-trust laws. In 1960 the General Electric Co., the Allis-Chalmers Manufacturing Co., the Federal Pacific Electric Co., the ITE Circuit Breaker Co. and the Westinghouse Electric Corp. had pleaded guilty or *nolo contendere* to charges of conspiracy to fix prices and rigging bids on more than $25 million worth of goods sold to federal agencies and the Tennessee Valley Authority over the preceding nine years. A District Court in Philadephia had fined the companies $1.9 million and, almost unprecedentedly, sentenced seven of their executives to 30-day prison terms, which were served. This was the springboard for more vigorous action by the new Administration.

On March 14 the Justice Department and the TVA filed a joint action for damages against the companies that had already faced criminal charges. Two days later the President prepared an executive order designed to prevent recurrences of such incidents by requiring federal agencies to publicize every instance of the submission of identical bids on contracts. While a Senate Judiciary Subcommittee was conducting its own investigation of illegal price-fixing, the Government impaneled a new grand jury in Philadelphia to reopen and broaden the investigation that had resulted in the 1960 prosecution. "Conspiracy to violate the anti-trust laws," a representative of the Anti-Trust Division of the Justice Department told the convention of the American Bar Association, "is economic racketeering which gains no respectability by virtue of the fact that the loot is secured by stealth rather than by force. Those who are apprehended in such acts are, and will be treated as, criminals and will personally be subjected to as severe a punishment as we can persuade the courts to impose."

Neither the Administration's determination to reinforce the judiciary nor its position on monopolies could ground, in even the wildest reactionary, any fear of tampering with the courts. In fact, there was nothing in Kennedy's background or in his philosophy of government to indicate any important discontent in this area. On the related subject of administrative agencies, however, he had already made it clear that he planned vigorous action. But he was moving slowly and deliberately in implementing or tabling the various recommendations presented by the task force on administrative agencies headed by Landis.

Kennedy had been in office almost two months when he sent to the Congress, on April 13, his first message dealing with these quasi-judicial bodies. While he dealt with the agencies in general, he also singled out the Federal Power Commission for immediate action, intimating that emergency measures were required because of its "incredible backlog" of cases. Drafted largely by Landis, the message followed in the main his report to Kennedy in December but omitted such Landis proposals as that for White House supervision of the agencies and coordination of their activities in transport and other fields.

Kennedy stressed the need for greater cooperation between Congress and the President in the discharge of their respective responsibilities toward the operation of the agencies, specifically in coordinating regulatory practices. He pointed out that the growing complexity of our society had caused certain problems, such as mass transportation or the interdependence of industries, to become the concern of not one but several agencies and, consequently, a given activity encouraged by one agency might cause conflict with the prohibitions imposed by another. Within each agency, he called for increased authority and responsibility for its chairman with respect to staff, budget and organization; he proposed that all rather than some agency chairmen be subject to executive appointment (or removal). As a corollary of his emphasis on greater responsibility, he recommended that each agency chairman write his own decisions so that, like a judge, he would bear the responsibility for them. More routine work should be delegated, the President said; much unnecessary toil was being performed at top levels whose attention should be reserved for only the most important issues, though they should retain a discretionary right of review of the work of their individual or panel subordinates. For this Kennedy cited such precedent as the use of the petition for *certiorari* in "clearing up the overburdened docket of the Supreme Court" under the Judiciary Act of 1925. Higher standards for hearing examiners were recommended. At the same time, by executive order, Kennedy established the Administrative Conference of the United States, to undertake a study directed toward a general reform of administrative procedures and render a report by December 31, 1962. Its 50 members were to be drawn principally from the agencies themselves, with a leavening of judges, lawyers and scholars in the field.

With respect to the Federal Power Commission, which had pending some 4000 petitions for rate increases by independent natural-gas producers and pipelines, Kennedy proposed that its membership be increased at once from five to seven. In addition, he asked for legislation entirely exempting from FPC jurisdiction a number of smaller producers of natural gas whose interstate activities accounted for only 10 per cent of the total flow. Somewhat more complicated exemption was proposed for pipeline construction. "The formulation of these standards," Kennedy told Congress, "will require creative imagination, but the alternative is to defend bureaucracy for bureaucracy's sake."

On the whole, the message made few specific recommendations and left to Congress the problem of working out techniques to realize the President's goals of better personnel and greater efficiency for the six major agencies that, regulating huge sections of the economy, had long been considered the prisoners of the industries they were supposed to govern: the Civil Aeronautics Board, the Federal Communications Commission, the FPC, the Federal Trade Commission, the Interstate Commerce Commission and the Securities and Exchange Commission. In one instance, the FCC, the new chairman appointed by Kennedy, Newton Minow, had already indicated that he conceived the President's goal to be a greater and more positive role for these regulatory groups. Minow had begun, as soon as he took office, to insist that broadcasters live up to the terms of their franchises in terms of programming; he had cracked down on the flagrant bartering of television licenses; he had not hesitated to fine broadcasters who violated FCC rules; and he had indicated that the Commission would step in to prevent excessive commercialization.

Minow's agency and the SEC were the next agencies to be chosen by Kennedy for reorganization. On April 27 he asked Congress to act to increase their efficiency and make them more flexible, under plans that would take effect automatically within sixty days unless disapproved by a majority of either chamber. Preliminary surveys indicated that opposition would be minimal.

The President's proposals offered, in fact, more than

greater efficiency and flexibility: they afforded in addition somewhat greater safeguards to the rights of industries under the two groups' jurisdiction. Procedurally, the plans for the FCC and the SEC followed the general lines laid down in Kennedy's earlier message on agencies in general. In each body the chairman would be authorized to delegate final decisions in both rule-making and quasi-judicial proceedings to panels of commissioners, an individual commissioner or a staff member. This would obviate the ridiculous situation cited by Minow when he said: "We [the full commission] sit here worrying whether a shrimp boat's radio license should be revoked." Decisions would be reviewed by the full commission at its discretion unless a losing party requested such action. In that case, the petitioner could obtain his review by a vote of one less than a majority of the full commission. In the case of the FCC, Kennedy also specifically abolished the review staff that had always written the Commission's opinions.

For neither agency did the President request the wide staff and budget powers mentioned in his original message: observers attributed this omission in part to the existing authority of the FCC and SEC chairmen and in part to a two-fold fear: that other members of the commissions might resent such a formal augmentation of the powers of their chairmen and that Congress might view such a proposal as a subtle technique for strengthening Presidential power over the agencies.

That further suggestions would come from the White House to improve the rest of the administrative agencies was obvious; but it was to be doubted whether there would be any drastic proposals before the Administrative Conference completed its study. Yet it was clear that Kennedy was keenly sensitive to the phenomenal growth in the importance of such bodies since Roosevelt had introduced them to American government and that he would rely on them increasingly to function as socio-economic gyroscopes.

27. The Rights of Man

"As a moral leader, the next President must play his role in interpreting the great moral issues which are involved in our crusade for human rights. He must exert the great moral and educational force of his office to . . . support the right of every American to stand up for his rights, even if on occasion he must sit down for them. For only the President, not the Senate and not the House and not the Supreme Court, in a real sense only the President can create the understanding and tolerance necessary as the spokesman for all the American people, as the symbol of the moral imperative upon which any free society is based."

—John F. Kennedy, September 9, 1960

The announcement by the President-elect that he had requested J. Edgar Hoover to remain as director of the Federal Bureau of Investigation combined with the pre-inaugural dickering over the promised Senate fight against the filibuster to arouse a certain pessimism, even before Kennedy took office, as to the future progress of civil liberties and civil rights during his putative eight years in office. His aloofness from the McCarran controversy, his long reluctance to take a stand against McCarthy were gloomily recalled to memory; those who had read his *Profiles in Courage* went back to his apparent endorsement of compromise even on basic principles.

A large and sinister part of Kennedy's inheritance from the Eisenhower and Truman Administrations was a great mass of legislation, executive orders, departmental regulations and emotional prejudice concentrated on the maintenance of "security"—officially in the Government and its contractors and by extension in the whole society. The House un-American Activities Committee and the Senate Internal Security Subcommittee still flourished; the Federal Courts had on their dockets a backlog of prosecutions against individuals who had defied these groups. The Democratic platform of 1960 had affirmed the party's support for freedom and civil liberties as "vital to our national strength"; it had promised revisions of Congressional investigative and hearing procedures, protection for the common-law rights of those accused (including the right to confront their accusers and to know the evidence against them), the abolition of the naive loyalty oath in non-sensitive areas, the protection of the right of travel, and opposition to treaties that discriminated among Americans on grounds of race or religion. These pledges were made public on July 13, 1960. The subject has never been mentioned again.

The men appointed by Kennedy had to undergo the same humiliating and basically useless security checks that had been applied to their predecessors. They filled out FBI questionnaires in quintuplicate. Their friends and relatives were asked whether they drank and how much, how they preferred their sexual pleasures, what they read, what their interests had been in their college days, what hours they kept, who were their friends, what were their hobbies. Within ten days of Kennedy's inauguration, the Defense Department (without the authorization of the new Secretary) had bought 30 prints of *Operation Abolition*, a film made by the un-American Activities Committee, in order to use them to show new recruits the techniques of Communism. The purchase had been made despite an adverse recommendation by the department's counsel, who said the film was distorted. Nonetheless, the Defense Department, vigorously abetted by Hoover, was urging the State Department to duplicate the purchase. This was the film that purported to tell the truth about the San Francisco student demonstrations against the committee's hearings (and in spite of which the one student brought to trial on charges made by the committee was uncompromisingly acquitted late in April).

It was not only the retention of Hoover, a man who, Torquemada-like, sought to force a whole government to embrace his bigotries, that worried genuine liberals (that is, those who recognized the right of others to hold opinions they found untenable for themselves). There was also the President's backing down from his initial effort to humanize the nation's immigration policy by appointing as head of the Immigration and Naturalization Service a Pittsburgh lawyer, Thomas Cooley, who had amassed years of experience in defending the victims of an increasingly narrow interpretation of the relevant laws. But Chairman Francis P. Walter of the House un-American Activities Committee, co-author of the bitterly controversial McCarran-Walter Act that virtually closed the country's borders to non-conforming aliens, was closely linked to the incumbent commissioner, Joseph M. Swing, whose thinking was dominated by the phobia of Communism that Walter shared; and Walter told the President that he would not tolerate the appointment of Cooley. The reason was simple: Cooley, dean of the Law School of the University of Pittsburgh, had sharply criticized the McCarran-Walter Act and opposed Walter's pending bill to limit judicial review of deportation orders to a single litigation. Kennedy yielded at once. He distressed thoughtful observers again when he reappointed Harry J. Anslinger as Federal Narcotics Commissioner, for Anslinger had made his reputation, despite the growth of narcotics addiction and the increase in medical and psychiatric understanding of the problem as one of medicine and sociology, by his uncompromising insistence on treating every addict as nothing but a criminal, ignoring both the human and the social implications of the expanding problem.

The Administration had been in office almost a month before it evidenced in the field of civil liberties any trace of the liberalism it professed. In mid-February the Justice Department ordered a review of the eleven-year Post Office policy of seizing so-called subversive mail entering the United States from abroad, except for material sent first-class. For the first eight years of this regime the Post Office did not even notify the addressees that their mail had been confiscated; in 1958 it modified its rules in a manner that was at best questionable. The addressee would be advised that the Post Office had confiscated "foreign mail addressed to you consisting of certain publications which contain foreign political propaganda" that, while "ordinarily treated as non-mailable," would be delivered "when it has been ordered, [or] subscribed to or is desired, and is not for dissemination." The Post Office was acting on a 1940 ruling by Attorney General Robert Jackson, holding that the Foreign Agents' Registration Act of 1938 applied to such agents outside this country and hence mail sent by them could be stopped unless they had registered here under the Act. Suits had been brought to obtain a judicial decision on Jackson's ruling but the Government had prevented their going to trial by delivering the seized mail in each case; and lawyers of probity had denounced the "distasteful picture of government officials, charged with acting unlawfully, continuing the challenged conduct and at the same time bending every effort to keep the issue from being decided in an orderly way by the courts."

Within a month the recipients of the perilous publications reported that their mail was no longer being held up, even for customs inspection. The Justice Department had won the support of the Treasury (which controls customs) and the State Department, as well as the Post Office Department; all four ministries had urged the President to order the end of the interception of mail. The first reason given for the recommendation was that the seizures served no useful intelligence purposes; only secondarily did the official explanation touch on the crucial issue of the legal right of the Government to take such action in direct infringement of Constitutional rights. A few days later Walter demanded legislation that would reinstitute the policy. And on the same day, almost unnoticed, the House passed another Walter bill to bar employment in the merchant marine or on the docks for anyone who refused to answer his committee's questions on so-called subversive activities. The platform on which Kennedy was elected stated: "We shall provide a full and fair hearing, including confrontation of the accuser, to any person whose public or private employment or reputation is jeopardized by a loyalty or security proceeding."

But Kennedy and his Attorney General had no comment on this bill. Nor did they plan any move to revise the McCarthy-inspired security legislation adopted during Truman's and Eisenhower's Administrations despite pre-election condemnation of such quasi-totalitarian measures. The new Administration argued that fanatic enforcement of the restrictive rules had ebbed and that inequities could be prevented—or, if they occurred, redressed—by a sensitive and intelligent application of the rules. To attempt either by legislation or by executive order to eliminate the source of such inequities, the Administration argued, would serve only to arouse a cyclone of right-wing reaction. Among many observers there was also the suspicion of an unspoken fear in the Administration that such action might jeopardize its legislative support in other areas where it must count on the backing of members of Congress of many divergent views. Apparently it did not take into account the very real danger that this kind of temporizing merely left the way open for some less enlightened Administration to revive the witch-hunts with the sanctification of statute and prior Presidential instruction. Thus civil liberties, instead of being guaranteed by law, were to be left to the mercy of men.

Politically the decision to make no decision may have been practical. Senator James Eastland of Mississippi was the powerful chairman of his chamber's Internal Security Subcommittee and commanded considerable support among other Democratic Senators, particularly those from the South; it was obvious, if not admirable, why the Administration feared to antagonize him. Even in April he went unrebuked when he declared that the Supreme Court had handed down more pro-Communist decisions "than any judicial tribunal outside the Iron Curtain." By that time the John Birch Society had attained considerable notoriety and Eastland was making impressive noises about the possibility of his committee's having to investigate potential subversiveness in an organization whose views and aims were hardly different from his own; but no one expected him to make an affirmative decision. What troubled those who believed in civil liberties and in the Democratic Party's and President Kennedy's concern for their preservation was a more fundamental problem: would Kennedy permit the witch-hunts to go on, whether on the Right or on the Left? was Eastland to become the shame of Kennedy's Administration as McCarthy had been the blot on Eisenhower's?

The specter of Eastland also dogged the only slightly less delicate question of civil rights. The issue of civil liberties for highly unpopular political fractions or eccentric individuals might attract only a few partisans to the defense; it was too abstract to strike with any depth into the mass mind. But rights for 18.8 million Negroes—more than 10 per cent of the total population—were a concrete question that was a part of everyone's daily experience and little detached consideration of the problems might be expected. Kennedy had reiterated, during his campaign, his party's pledges to work unremittingly toward the elimination of second-class citizenship for any racial or religious minority; but perhaps the biggest individual opponent he would have to confront would be this same Eastland, heir to the rigid segregationist tradition of Bilbo and Rankin, and a formidable power to be taken into account in any effort to ease the procedural path for civil-rights legislation.

But Kennedy was allowed no such respite on civil rights as he had enjoyed in the field of individual liberties. Within nine days of his inauguration he was called on publicly by the Southern Regional Council, a bi-racial group, to put into effect a broad program of demands that the Council had served on him before he took office. The Council pointed out that quite constitutionally the President could accomplish a great deal by executive order (as Kennedy himself had emphasized in a press conference on October 1, 1960). In sum, the Council was really repeating many of Kennedy's own campaign-speech ideas when it requested:

1. "Purely personal action" by the President to show his support of the principle of equality.
2. The appointment of a staff adviser on race relations to interpret problems and programs to the country, assist in framing and administering executive orders and provide liaison between the Federal Civil Rights Commission and the Justice Department.
3. The creation of a new watchdog agency to replace existing executive committees on discrimination in Government employment and contracts.

4. The deliberate selection of competent Negroes for appointive jobs, specifically in the South.
5. The acceleration of desegregation in the schools.
6. More vigorous enforcement of laws protecting personal security and voting rights.
7. Insistence on non-discrimination in Federal expenditures for health programs, school aid and recreation facilities.
8. "A final, decisive effort" to end segregation in public transport.

In his State of the Union message the next day, the President mentioned the whole problem only once, as a "sore spot on the American scene." Almost immediately he was subjected to new pressure from Representative Adam Clayton Powell, a Negro who was the new chairman of the House Labor and Education Committee. Specifically, Powell insisted that his own proposal to bar Federal aid to schools that practiced segregation be implemented by an immediate executive order—a principle that had already been endorsed by Eisenhower's Attorney General and Eisenhower's Civil Rights Commission with respect to publicly aided higher institutions.

The President was also subjected to questioning on an existing case of school segregation. For months two public schools in New Orleans had been boycotted after a Federal Court ordered them integrated. In this early February press conference Kennedy went as far as to say he would use the moral authority of the Presidency when he "thought it is most useful and most effective," but he was obviously taking every precaution to avoid jeopardizing Southern Congressional support for other phases of his program. Meanwhile, he implied, he had already taken the New Orleans situation under study. In principle, he repeated, he stood for complete desegregation.

Kennedy's position was unenviable. He was acutely aware of a substantial debt to Negro voters; he was equally uncomfortably sensible of his vulnerability to Republican attack, particularly since, as a candidate, he had frequently taunted Eisenhower for refusing to exercise the Presidential power to implement integration in schools and public housing. But Kennedy dared not imperil his legislative backing in a Congress already sharply divided; hence he relied on executive action where inaction could not be avoided. It was generally accepted that Housing Administrator Weaver was only the first of many Negroes who would be appointed to policy-making jobs; and it was expected that Kennedy would order the Justice Department to become more active in enforcing voting rights. In mid-February the Attorney General took a bold step in a Federal action in the New Orleans school crisis that had been initiated during the Eisenhower Administration.

Shelby M. Jackson, Louisiana's superintendent of public education, had already been made the defendant in a Federal civil-contempt action, based on his defiance of the old Supreme Court orders on desegregation. On February 16 the Government revised and broadened its complaint in order to compel Jackson to release $350,000 in Federal school aid that he had been withholding during the controversy. A week later, while the action was awaiting trial, Representative Wellborn Jack of Louisiana offered a rabble-rousing tirade on the House floor in which he accused the Administration of secretly seeking a compromise of the issue to preserve its legislative majority; Jack sneered at the possibility that Jackson and other school officials might be jailed for contempt if they did not obey. "I say the President . . . won't have the guts to do it," Jack ranted.

He was wrong. There had been no effort at a face- or vote-saving compromise; the court found the desegregation activities unconstitutional and Jackson and his fellow-intransigents capitulated. Representative Jack had no further comment.

The racial issue was also affecting the employment situation. Secretary Goldberg had pointed out in February that, though the unemployment rate for the population as a whole was 7 per cent, it was 13.8 per cent for the Negro labor force. From one side, the Republicans were scolding Kennedy for having done nothing on civil rights and were proposing to offer their own legislation; from the other side, the National Association for the Advancement of Colored People was making the same reproach: no legislative proposals, no executive action. It was March 6 before the President took his first step in the field by creating a committee to fight racial discrimination in hiring for Government work and by vesting it with enforcement powers. The move was not devoid of courage, for, in addition to compelling employers to submit, it empowered the new Committee on Equal Employment Opportunities to move against those powerful labor unions that still barred Negroes from membership and otherwise discriminated against them. The committee was ordered to investigate, on its own or through the Labor Department or the appropriate Government contracting agency, any violation of equality of employment rights, and to enforce its rulings through publicity, civil and criminal actions by the Justice Department, termination of contracts and refusal of new ones as long as the violations persisted. To preclude any connivance by the military establishment, the largest single contractor, the Secretaries of the Army, Navy and Air Force were made members of the committee, whose nominal head was Vice President Johnson but whose working executive was Goldberg. With this action Kennedy went far beyond the lip-service of the Eisenhower Administration, which had created two similar committees but studiedly avoided arming them with any enforcement power at all.

Kennedy believed that at the moment the most effective aid he could give the Negro was economic. His backers argued that a formal civil-rights legislative program that would alienate Congressional support from basic economic measures benefiting the whole nation could only harm the Negro. Hence he preferred to concentrate on employment, not only in government contracts but also in government itself, and early in March an intensive recruiting drive was launched in Negro colleges among students ready to graduate. As a kind of teaching by example he was also committed to the selection of qualified Negroes for important high positions; yet at the same time he was capable of choosing their outstanding enemies, as in the pre-inaugural effort to make Vandiver Secretary of the Army and, in March, the selection of Charles Meriwether, the right-hand man of Alabama's outstanding white-supremacist and anti-Semite, John Crommelin, as a director of the Export-Import Bank. While liberals were attacking Kennedy for this singularly unfortunate choice, the President was being assailed by Senators Russell and Talmadge of Georgia for planning to appoint to the Civil Rights Commission the Rev. Benjamin E. Mays, president of a Negro college in Atlanta, whom Talmadge, using the standard segregationist mud-slinging device, denounced as having been "identified or associated with at least four different Communist-front organizations" —a charge exploded by *The Atlanta Constitution*.

A more trivial but all the more ironic civil-rights problem arose out of the imminent celebration of the centennial of the Civil War. One of New Jersey's representatives to the centennial commission, about to meet in Charleston, S. C., was denied equal housing with the other delegates because her skin was the wrong color. New Jersey withdrew from the meeting and was followed, as a matter of principle, by New York and Illinois. The President remonstrated sharply to Major General Ulysses S. Grant 3d, chairman of the commission and grandson of the Civil War victor. Apparently uninformed of the famous pledge of his ancestor, "We'll fight it out along this line if it takes all summer," the current General Grant had already bowed meekly to the Rebels and had no intention of changing his views. The commission of which he was the head refused to accede to the President's request that it eliminate the segregation. Kennedy noted tartly that the commission was a Government body using Federal funds and hence should observe Government policies on racial equality. It took the President of the United States more than a week to win a limited victory; the commission finally agreed to move its sessions to the integrated United States Naval Station in Charleston. To prove he meant what he said, Kennedy turned to the Washington Redskins, a professional football team, and warned it unsubtly that, if it continued to refuse to hire Negro players, it could not contract for the use of the new District of Columbia stadium.

Though he might not wish to challenge the segregationists in Congress directly, the President was moving steadily forward in his determination to make civil rights a reality. Heartened by the court victory in Alabama in which, in an action instituted during the Eisenhower Administration, the Government succeeded in invalidating the gerrymandering that had illegally deprived the Negroes of Tuskegee of the right to vote, the Justice Department moved in Tennessee to appeal a District Court ruling that denied the Government's application for an injunction to compel white landlords to renew the leases of Negro farmers. The leases had been terminated as a reprisal for the Negroes' having attempted to register and vote.

Implementing his recent ban on discrimination on hiring for employment on federal contracts, Kennedy ordered immediate action on a complaint by the NAACP that the Lockheed Aircraft Corp., fulfilling a billion-dollar jet contract at its plant in Marietta, Ga., was barring Negroes. Postmaster General Day went farther and ordered his department to include non-discrimination clauses in all property leases it signed. The Justice Department launched three new legal actions: one in Dallas County, Ala., and another in Shreveport, La., to enforce voting rights for

Negroes and the third in Prince Edward County, Va., to compel the reopening of public schools closed two years earlier in an effort to prevent integration. There could no longer be any doubt of the Administration's seriousness on the subject, even if its efforts were to be marred by such local stupidities as the barring of Negroes from a Democratic Party function in Columbia, S. C., at which Secretary of Commerce Hodges was to be the guest of honor late in April. Kennedy took his first step in the middle of that month to raise the issue of civil rights in Congress when he announced that he would seek legislation to renew the life of the Civil Rights Commission, scheduled to be dissolved in September of 1961. At the same time he appointed two new members: Deans Erwin N. Griswold of the Harvard Law School and Spottswood W. Robinson 3d of the Howard University Law School. Though Robinson was a Negro, neither the appointment nor the proposal to prolong the commission's life was expected to stir real opposition in Congress.

It was only by indirection that, at the very end of the hundred days, the issue of civil liberties came to the surface again; and it did so in a most vexing fashion. On April 30 Goldberg told a dinner audience in New York that he was determined to eliminate segregation and prejudice in every aspect of American life, citing specifically a private club in Washington that had refused membership to Negroes and Jewish clubs elsewhere that barred non-Jews. Philosophically, at least, he raised an extremely nice question as between the right of every man, regardless of race or religion, to go where he liked and the parallel right of every other man to choose his associations.

On a more practical and serious level, certain deductions seemed evident from the course the Administration had taken thus far. It was most unlikely that (unless they should be spectacularly threatened, as appeared most improbable) civil rights would receive any real attention; but civil rights would be inexorably strengthened and broadened in a determined, if undramatic, fashion. Barely a week after the end of the hundred days, Congress got a civil-rights bill unaccompanied by a Presidential message; nonetheless its Presidential imprimatur was readily inferred from the fact that the bill came from Senator Joseph S. Clark of Pennsylvania and Representative Emanuel Celler of New York, whom Kennedy had appointed in September of 1960 as a committee of two to implement the party's civil-rights pledges with draft legislation.

The Clark-Celler bill dealt with several aspects of the problem. It would require every school board running a segregated school to adopt an integration plan, file it with the Secretary of Health, Education and Welfare and institute "first-step compliance" before the start of the 1963-4 school year. There were strict provisions for enforcement and each integration plan was required to be described in detail. In addition, the new bill would make the Civil Rights Commission a permanent body, strengthening its fact-finding powers. Judicial and administrative sanctions were requested to be invoked against employers and unions guilty of civil-rights violations in hiring, discharging and promoting workers. Finally, the Attorney General's authority to file civil injunction actions to prevent the denial of voting rights was to be broadened to cover any denial of civil rights based on race, color or religion.

It was reported that, while the Justice Department had been consulted on parts of the program, the bill had not been cleared with either the President or the Attorney General. Many observers feared that Kennedy was timid or reluctant in taking a firm public stand. "Without persistent White House backing," said Senator Kenneth Keating, a New York Republican and a vigorous proponent of cogent civil-rights legislation, "there is little likelihood that the majority party in Congress will move forward." A day later Salinger announced unequivocally that the Clark-

Celler bill had no Presidential approval and that Kennedy believed no civil-rights legislation was necessary for at least a year because the needs of the situation could be met by existing legislation and executive orders.

Within a fortnight of the Administration's repudiation of the Clark-Celler bill, the massed bigots of Alabama put Kennedy's pledges to the test. A bus carrying white and Negro passengers who called themselves Freedom Riders, because they were deliberately challenging the South's defiance of the law, was stopped and burned by a mob that savagely beat all the riders it could reach. Another group of Freedom Riders reached Montgomery on a second bus and defied the local and state statutes requiring segregation in bus terminals. Hundreds of the flower of Southern womanhood and chivalry fell upon them with stones, clubs and fists. Governor Patterson, one of the loudest of Kennedy's backers before the nominating convention, refused to accept the President's telephone calls; when Kennedy sent an aide to convey to the Governor the President's request that law and order and basic rights be maintained, the emissary was injured by the rioters.

The attack in the terminal occurred on a Saturday morning. By midnight Attorney General Kennedy had sent hundreds of United States marshals into the area to reestablish the public order that neither the Governor nor the municipal authorities cared to uphold. The Attorney General and the President elected to employ the marshals, rather than the Regular Army troops sent to Little Rock by Eisenhower, in order to avoid, if possible, any hint of military action. Both Kennedys were aware that the only authorization for the use of the marshals lay in a law enacted shortly after the Civil War, a reminder of the Reconstruction era still virulently hated throughout the South.

While the marshals were arriving through the night and early on Sunday morning, the mob was re-forming for the Sabbath. The Negroes had scheduled a mass meeting in a church, in which the whites besieged them, separated from their quarry only by a line of armed marshals. The infuriated Governor threatened to arrest the first marshal who sought to enforce the law. Screaming and hurling stones, the mob rushed the marshals and Patterson hastily proclaimed what he called "qualified martial law," pressing into service as the mainstays of decency the local National Guardsmen, many of whom, until ordered into uniform to protect the "nigras," had been active members of the mob on which they now fired tear gas.

Patterson emphasized that he was acting to put down disorders provoked by "outside agitators . . . the Federal Government has by its actions encouraged these agitators to come into Alabama to foment disorders." Injunction action was hastily obtained in the Federal Court against the Ku Klux Klan and other leading elements in the rioting. The Freedom Riders—those who were fit to travel and scores of new recruits—announced that they would travel as an integrated group from Montgomery to Jackson, Mississippi; and Washington let both states know that no interference with interstate bus commerce would be tolerated.

The bus was escorted to the state line by Alabama troopers; over the border, it was convoyed by Mississippi patrolmen. There was no disorder. But, when the passengers disembarked and flouted the "White" and "Colored" signs on waiting-rooms and lavatories, they were arrested. Professors who had to return to classes and examinations posted bond for trial later and went back to work; the other criminals refused to pay the rather reasonable fines imposed on them and elected to serve their time in the local jail and work-camps. For weeks afterward more Freedom Riders poured into Jackson, until a hundred or more were in cells and on the roads in convicts' clothes.

The Federal Government did no more. The marshals were withdrawn from Montgomery when order was restored there, and, in the face of Jackson's deliberate violation of

Federal law by arresting passengers in an interstate bus terminal, Washington took no further action. Existing legislation designed to protect civil rights was valueless in Mississippi because no one attempted to enforce it; executive orders to support Congressional enactments and Supreme Court decisions were simply not issued. Observers concerned with the progress of civil rights wondered when and whether the Administration would move to implement the promises that had been so important in its election; the more cynical began to compare Kennedy's "leadership" in civil rights with the apathy for which the President had so rightly, if righteously, attacked Eisenhower.

28. Looking Forward

As the Administration moved with purposeful deliberation into the future, the question was how well Kennedy had kept his campaign promises in the first days of his Administration. The promises were of two kinds: those that could be translated and understood in practical legislation and executive action, and those of a dynamic and aggressive philosophy that would carry the nation, and the free world with it, to greater achievements for the betterment of man.

There was the legislative compromise so necessary in democratic government; there were errors and blunders, and positive accomplishments, in every sphere; but there were also a firmness and a steadfast quality in the young President and the men around him that gave courage and hope and cautious expectation.

Acknowledgments

The authors wish to acknowledge their gratitude to those who were helpful in the preparation of this book: to Mary Sherwin, who suggested the title; and to Sam Blackman of The Associated Press; Peter Dinella, chief librarian, *The New York Post*; Mrs. Jean Dunning, Democratic National Committee, Washington; Mortimer Feuer, Esq.; Sidney Garfield, Columbia Broadcasting System; Stan Opotowsky, author of *The Kennedy Government*; Robert Parrella, the *New York Herald Tribune*; John Pope of St. Martin's Press, Inc.; Michael Reddington, chief librarian, *The News*, New York; Alexander Rylander, National Broadcasting Company; Paul Sann, executive editor, *The New York Post*; Pierre Salinger, Washington; Robert Spivack, Washington; Richard Sherwin, New York; James A. Wechsler, editor, *The New York Post*; Herman Weiller, librarian, *The New York Post*.

Index

DATE DUE

APR 15	FEB 14 '72	13 14 '82
APR 29 64	FEB 28 '72	NO 29 82
JUL 24 '64	MAR 13 '72	
	MAR 29 '72	DE 22 '8
APR 7 '65	FEB 27 '74	MAY 4 '87
APR 12 '65	MAR 13 '74	FEB 12 '89
MAY 12 '65		MAR 29 '89
NOV 22 '66	APR 16 '74	
APR 9 '68	F	
MAY 7 '68	APR 12 '76	
FEB 18 '70	NO 8 '77	
MAR 10 '70	AP 17 '78	
SEP 21 '70	OC 27 '79	
NOV 18 '70	FE 14 '8?	
DEC 2 '70	FE 28 '83	
DEC 9 '70		
DEC 3	MR 14 '83	
FEB 22 7	FEB 27 '87	
MAY 3 71	MAR 20 '87	
F		S.A.